Reinventing
Leadership

SUNY series in Leadership Studies
Barbara Kellerman, editor

Reinventing Leadership

Making the Connection
between Politics and Business

BARBARA KELLERMAN

STATE UNIVERSITY OF
NEW YORK PRESS

Published by
State University of New York Press

© 1999 State University of New York

For information, address the State University of New York Press,
State University Plaza, Albany, NY 12246

Marketing by Fran Keneston
Production by Bernadine Dawes

Library of Congress Cataloging-in Publication Data

Kellerman, Barbara
      Reinventing leadership : making the connection between politics
and business / Barbara Kellerman.
            p.   cm.
      Includes index.
      ISBN 0-7914-4071-0 (alk. paper). — ISBN 0-7914-4072-9 (pbk.
alk. paper)
      1. Leadership. 2. Political leadership. 3. Management.
4. Business and politics. I. Title.
      HD57.7.K448   1999
      658.4'092—dc21   98-45762
                                                                          CIP

1   2   3   4   5   6   7   8   9   10

For Charlie, and Joe, and Jack

CONTENTS

We are shaping the world faster than we can change ourselves, and we are applying to the present the habits of the past.

—WINSTON CHURCHILL

Introduction
Reinventing Leadership

Two 800-pound gorillas. The field of leadership has two 800-pound gorillas that look a lot alike and even sound much the same, but for some peculiar reason—probably our proclivity to compartmentalize what we know into "areas of study," or "disciplines," or "fields of concentration"—the two lugs have never met. One is all about creating change in the public sector, and the other all about creating change in the private one. Walk into a bookstore of any size at all and you will see that the materials on leadership in government are located in one place, while the materials on leadership in business are located somewhere else. The presumption is that leaders in the political domain bear absolutely no relation to leaders in the corporate one.

To be fair, in the past the distinction had some merit. As this book will testify, once upon a time political leaders and business executives were in fact quite different sorts. Moreover, the contexts within which they operated, and which government and business constituted, were also dissimilar. But times change. Now the differences between public sector types and their private sector counterparts are far outweighed by the similarities—which makes the separation between them nothing if not passé.

In the last few years, conceptions of leadership and management have converged. After decades in which definitions of political "leadership" and business "management" were for all practical purposes qualitatively different, the gap started to close. More particularly, during the 1980s it became clear that models of management that had once worked well for American business and industry were less effective than they used to be. And in the quest for what might work, organization theorists, business school professors, and

1

management consultants settled on a set of principles and strategies that sounded remarkably like what had been since the beginning of the Republic the basic principles of democratic political leadership.

Similarly, by the 1990s the drive to scale down government and make it more efficient motivated public sector types to turn to private sector practices. The very notion of reinventing government was lifted from those whose experience in business and industry had obliged them to think lean and be nimble. As a result, for perhaps the first time, political leaders were expected to be, of all things, efficient.

It is difficult to overestimate the degree to which, so far as leadership issues are concerned, politics and business have remained distinct. Until rather recently, the intentions and behaviors that in government were referred to as leadership were referred to in business as management. Being charged with mobilizing others to follow in politics made you a leader; being charged with mobilizing others to follow in business made you a manager. The antecedents of this distinction are not difficult to fathom. Because of the American Revolution, the constitution that followed, and the particulars of the American experience, our political culture has always demanded of our elected officials that they appear to take seriously a few basic principles including freedom, democracy, equality, and participation in government. Clearly, these precepts, which have been described as constituting the American Creed are, to a degree, antileadership.[1] Each implies that one individual is as good as the next, and that no one has the God-given right to rule over, or dictate to, another.

The structures of our political institutions further support this antileadership mentality. The American system of checks and balances ensures that none of the three branches of government has the capacity to thwart the other two. Moreover, the fact that we have state and local governments in addition to the one at the federal level generally precludes any single individual's or institution's gaining too much control. Put another way, while the United States has had to struggle with an array of political problems since its inception, the threat of autocracy has not been one of them.

The importance of the American Creed means that by and large ideology plays a larger role in determining political outcomes than performance. American voters are more interested in whether or not their political leaders do what they want them to do, than in how

well they do it. (In keeping with this principle, it makes no difference to most voters that since the time of Franklin Roosevelt the
size of the federal government has grown exponentially. By 1972,
federal spending on human resources regularly exceeded spending
on national security.)

Business and industry, in contrast, have had a quite different
trajectory. As the United States made the nineteenth-century transition from becoming a society that was largely agrarian to one largely
industrial, the exigencies of work resulted in rigid organizational
structures. Indeed, in the interest of turning a profit, the industrial
workplace shed altogether the niceties of democracy that prevailed
on the outside. Men, and often women and children as well, were
virtually forced into work lives that bore scant resemblance to the
autonomous, if hardscrabble, lives that earlier generations had experienced as farmers, ranchers, and merchants.

Of course, the rise of unions in this country was big labor's
response to abuse and inequity in the workplace. Unions testified to
the fact that for most Americans work outside the home and beyond
the small town was difficult, unrewarding, and unfair. Even the
archetypical image of work for much of the twentieth century, the
assembly line, showed men and women as mere cogs in an all-powerful industrial machine.

The truth was that once Americans began to labor for someone
other than themselves, they had almost no say about what they did,
about the conditions in which they worked, or about how much they
got paid. They were free to quit—and to suffer the economic consequences thereof. But if they stayed, they had, in effect, no control
over how they spent their time.

The notion of the manager rather than the leader grew out of
this circumstance. The word *leadership* implies a contract of some
kind between the leader and the led. Ideally at least, leaders are supposed to do their work on behalf of the led, and they are supposed to
influence rather than coerce.

But for most of this century the notion of influence was quite
irrelevant to the workplace. Employees were told what to do; and
even their immediate superiors were, by and large, individuals who,
like themselves, had little say in how they did their jobs. Only on
high was there a man who might in contemporary parlance be called
a leader, but who was, of course, not required to participate in any

of the interactive behaviors we now associate with the term *leader-ship*. There scarcely was such a thing as leadership in the early stages of industrialization. By most measures the relationship between those in charge and those under them was autocratic rather than democratic.

By midcentury America's blue-collar worker had nevertheless attained a certain status. Labor unions were in their prime, having secured for the average worker fair wages, decent benefits, and a reasonable measure of job security. What unions never really did achieve, however, was what we now call participatory management. Workers were not allowed to negotiate with their managers in any meaningful way, either to determine the specifics of their tasks or to change the way they were being compensated. As before they were being managed rather than led—which means that leadership was not a notion that, even in the later stages of the industrial society, had much application to the workplace.

By the 1950s the blue-collar worker began to be supplanted in the American workplace by the white-collar worker: the man in the grey flannel suit came into his own. Images of rustbelts and smoke-stacks receded, while large organizations housed in tall buildings in big cities became, in effect, corporate America.

On the surface, workers in offices bore scant resemblance to their predecessors in factories. In particular, as the tags "white" and "blue" collar suggested, they looked different. Men who worked in offices were outfitted in suits and ties and they brought to work not metal lunch pails but leather attaché cases. For their part, women, who quickly became indispensable to the operation of the office, dressed up. They wore skirts and blouses or nice dresses, and pretty shoes with transparent stockings. Lipsticks, combs, and compacts were carried in nice handbags, along with the nickels and dimes that enabled them to get to work by no later than nine in the morning and home again by about six at night.

The physical plant also looked different. Modern offices where paper was pushed were nothing like factories where steel was forged or shoes cobbled. Offices were clean and relatively quiet. They were furnished mainly with desks and chairs. And when those who worked in them returned home at the end of the day, they looked and smelled more or less they way they had when they'd left, nine or ten hours earlier.

But for all the superficial differences, the men and women who worked in the service sector during the fifties, sixties, and seventies bore profound resemblances to those who had earlier stoked furnaces and assembled cars. Like the industrial workers who immediately preceded them, office workers in midcentury struck an implicit agreement with their employers: In exchange for decent working conditions, they would do more or less what they were told.

Yet unions never took hold among white-collar workers. Why? For one obvious reason: by and large those who worked in offices felt they were getting a good deal. In comparison with what their parents had experienced, working conditions were good. Salary and benefits, even at the lowest levels, were deemed adequate. And like union members when unions were at their peak, those who worked in telecommunications, or advertising, or financial services, or retailing, or in any other vaguely analogous service sector job, enjoyed a real measure of security.

In the lower ranks, jobs were generally safe so long as performance was deemed adequate. Middle-level managers were virtually guaranteed a position until retirement age, and then a decent pension, while upper-level managers could count on financial rewards far in excess of almost everyone else's in the American workplace.

Thus do the differences between politics and business begin to emerge. In the public sector relations between leaders and led have generally been characterized by a deep sense of equity and by the clear understanding that if voters were dissatisfied they could throw the rascals out. (However, elected officials are not usually defeated at the polls for poor management. Voters have been tolerant of political leaders who are poor managers—even though they have over the years assumed enormously expanded responsibilities including improving education, delivering health care, combating crime, and eliminating racial injustice.) In business and industry, in contrast, gross inequities between management and labor have tended to prevail. In fact, because most workers are located toward the bottom of the organizational pyramid they have no relationship whatsoever with those closer to the top. Even now workers are usually expected to follow orders given by immediate superiors; the failure to fall into line is likely to be costly.

To this day, students of leadership reflect the different traditions. Those who study political leadership in America (historians and political scientists) generally focus less on organizations per se, and more on leaders and voters and on the local, state, and national contexts within which they operate. (Scholars in the field of public administration are the exception to this general rule. But they do not write very much about leadership.) Conversely, since private sector work is housed mainly in large organizations, students of business and industry emphasize the importance of bureaucratic hierarchies. This substantive divide is echoed throughout the field of Leadership Studies. Political scientists and historians typically have no contact whatsoever with faculty in schools of business; and the work they all produce on leadership and management rarely even alludes to the fact that in many ways they cover the same ground. (The shared focus on "great men" is an exception to the rule.) The popular press follows suit. Publications such as *Time* and *Newsweek* stick largely (albeit not exclusively) to politics, while the likes of *Fortune* and *Business Week* cover business and industry.

Until recently, the cleavage was widened by nomenclature. The word *leadership* was used in political discourse because in America there has always been a legal and ideological basis for the assumption that the relationship between citizens and their elected officials is one of influence rather than coercion. Whatever the pitfalls of American politics, and however limited the original cohort of led (no African Americans or women need apply), from the start there was presumed to be an authentic exchange between them and those who would be their leaders.

Contrast this with the historic conception of management in the American workplace. Unlike leaders, managers were not required or even expected to influence. Their job was to command, to control, and, if necessary, to coerce. Further, communication between managers and those who were being managed was in one direction only: from the top down. Finally, it was the organization that set the goal—and in business the only goal that has really mattered is to turn a profit.

But now times have changed. The old rules no longer apply. To create change in the twenty-first century a more eclectic approach will be required. More precisely, 1) politicians will have no choice but to take cues from their corporate counterparts; 2) business executives will have no alternative but to learn lessons from leaders in government; and 3) leaders in both domains will have to reinvent themselves to create something altogether new.

Because of the perceived failure of the liberal model that has dominated American political life since at least the New Deal, those who would manage the public's business are increasingly held accountable. In the old days, say, during the heyday of Lyndon Johnson's Great Society, it was axiomatic that even the most intransigent social problems could be addressed by one or another government program. Now we know better. We know that throwing federal funds at whatever ails us does not necessarily work, and produces a budget deficit that symbolizes nothing so much as political leaders who are grossly inefficient.[2] The result? Voters are demanding of their political leaders that they, like their private-sector counterparts, demonstrate fiscal responsibility and the capacity for good management.

David Osborne and Ted Gaebler's unexpected best seller, *Reinventing Government*, tapped into this sense of unease. Indeed, their argument was based on the proposition that the New Deal mentality that had dominated American political life for so long was now so badly outdated that an entirely new paradigm was called for—one in which government borrowed heavily from ideas and practices in business and industry. While Osborne and Gaebler did not pay more than passing attention to the role of leadership in this transition, they did point out that elected officials able to "piece together a new way of doing government" were often new to public service. "Many are young," they wrote, "many had previous careers, as journalists or business people, or social activists. When they entered government, they could see the anomalies fresh." [3]

Of course, for every political leader who ought to take lessons on how to be a better manager, there is a business executive who ought to learn how to make friends and influence people; how to delegate and decentralize as necessary and appropriate; how to respond nimbly to customer demands; and how to engage employees in collective decision making. In other words, private-sector leaders who would ignore changes in the political culture and global marketplace do so at their peril.

The first premise of this book is that the failure of government has shown earlier models of political leadership to be inadequate. It is no longer enough for our leaders to be democrats, to invite us to participate in public life by the simple act of pulling a lever on Election Day. The anger, alienation, and disenchantment that has characterized the American electorate in recent decades reflects a deep disappointment in our elected officials that is at least in part a consequence of their perceived incompetence and of their reluctance genuinely to collaborate with those whom they would lead. Too often they fail to deliver what they promise. And too often they refuse to explore in depth those social, political, and economic problems that are in fact the most vexing.

The second premise is the private sector analogue: that change has made traditional notions of management irrelevant and that conceptions of democratic leadership as they have long existed in the American polity will to a considerable degree replace them. Put another way, the model of leadership that is increasingly being touted in the private sector as if it were something altogether new, bears a powerful resemblance to leadership in the political sector as it has been preached since 1776.

The third and final premise of the book goes back to our two 800-pound gorillas. It is about the disadvantages of keeping them apart, and about the abundant advantages of bringing them together—about fostering a relationship that will be to the benefit of both. Of course, I am speaking here not only of theory, not only of tearing down the academic divide between public- and private-sector leadership, but also of practice. I am talking about ending once and for all apartheid in America between government and business. (For the sake of simplicity, the nonprofit sector is marginal rather than central to my argument.)

In the twenty-first century it will become increasingly plain that in order to be effective, in order even to have followers, both private- and public-sector leaders will have to create something new. Unable to depend on old repertoires, and in the face of dauntingly rapid change, only those who break with the past will manage to stay out front. Listen to Vaclav Havel on the transition to what some call the postmodern. "There are good reasons for suggesting that the modern age has ended. . . . It is as if something were crumbling, decaying and exhausting itself, while something else, still indistinct, were arising from the rubble. . . . We are in a phase when one age is succeeding another."[4]

In fact, the term postmodern—or, for that matter, postindustrial, postinformation, postimperial, post-Marxist, poststructuralist, post-Cold War, post-Gutenberg—does not really convey the message I want to send. By definition, such labels smack of the past. As Eric Hobsbawm has observed, "Like funerals, these prefixes [take] official recognition of death without implying any consensus or indeed certainty about the nature of life after death."[5] Moreover, the notion of a posthumous world seems somehow to preclude changing this one. And so, while on the one hand this book is about leadership for an age that manifestly postdates the one we are in now, it also sends a different message: that leadership for the new millennium will be no more, and no less, than a creative amalgam of what came before.

Part I of the book is about the divergence, about recent decades—the 1950s to the 1980s—during which conceptions of leadership and management in government and business were dramatically different. Part II of the book is about the convergence, about the shift, if you will, to a new and different time in which the historical divide between political and corporate America no longer makes sense. And Part III is about fusion, about repairing fault lines that continue to bedevil us, and about how leaders, and leadership educators, might actually do what they are supposed to do—lead the way.

The inevitable outcome of what I like to conceive of as a Darwinian process is the reinvented leader: the man or woman whose capacity to create change will confirm that what works in one domain is nearly identical to what works in the other. What will be equally clear is that the sooner we smash walls that still separate, the better.

AND A METHODOLOGICAL NOTE . . .

Throughout the book I try to avoid getting caught in the usual leadership traps. Let me at this point address three in particular.

The first entirely predictable snare can simply be tagged "definitions." So far as I am concerned, too many leadership scholars are waylaid by endless hothouse arguments about precisely how certain terms should be defined. The upside of my decision to steer clear of these debates is, I would argue, a victory for common sense. Most readers have a pretty clear understanding of what is meant by terms such as leadership and management.

The downside is that my colleagues in the field—other academics in Leadership Studies—might find my use of these admittedly key terms to be less precise and consistent than they would ideally like them to be. So to appease this constituency of my peers, I now provide the following definitions which I generally, albeit not slavishly, adhere to.

• Leadership is the effort by leaders—who may hold, but do not necessarily hold, formal positions of authority—to engage followers in the joint pursuit of mutually agreed-on goals. These goals represent significant, rather than merely incremental, change.

• Management is the effort by managers—who always hold a position of authority at some level—to get the trains to run on time. While it may, or may not, involve an element of coercion, management does not, in and of itself, involve significant change.

The second methodological sticking point pertains to sample. Once I decided to look at the public and private sectors in tandem, the question became: on precisely which parts of these sectors will I train my lens? For example, in my exploration of public-sector leadership, I could have decided to focus on some of the thousands of municipal and county governments across the land or, perhaps, on some of the hundreds of thousands of public school districts. Similarly, in my investigation of the private sector, I could have decided to stay with small to medium-sized businesses that employ say, 100 to 100,000 workers—or even with some of the countless Ma and Pa operations that provide work for so many Americans.

I chose instead to think big. I chose in this first effort to tie leadership in government to leadership in business to focus on big government and big business. This is not because I quarrel with the proposition that it would be instructive to make comparisons at different levels. In fact, I agree with the former mayor of Missoula, Montana, Daniel Kemmis, who has argued persuasively that we have too much of a tendency to view our politics in terms of the presidency and the national government.

Still, when most of us think government we think Washington, and when most of us think business we think *Fortune* 500. For good reason. We assume, quite reasonably, that, if only because of size and scope of influence, what big government and big business do matters more. More people are still affected by what happens in Washington than by what happens in Missoula—however innovative politics in Missoula might be. Moreover, I assume absolutely that if change in America is to take place on a large rather than small scale, big institutions, in both the private and public sectors, will have to become involved. And so I chose to equate the obvious: the public sector with the federal government and the private sector with major corporations.

Finally, since leadership and even management are activities associated with relationships of one or another kind, I faced the question of exactly which relationships to explore. Clearly, if they are to be successful, both public- and private-sector leaders must effectively engage multiple constituencies. Political leaders must win over a range of players including the media, interest groups, their own bureaucracies and personal staffs and, if they are elected officials, the voters to whom they are ultimately accountable. Similarly, business leaders must bring along a cast of characters that includes customers, stockholders, board members, and, of course, those employed by the organizations they lead.

How, then, to avoid comparing apples and oranges? This is a case where parallels can mislead. The president of the United States or, for that matter, his state and local analogues, does not have the same relationships to employees of the federal government as the president of IBM has to employees of IBM. In fact, one might go so far as to argue that the president of the United States has no more of a relationship to a middle-level manager at the Department of Housing and Urban Development than he does to a middle-level manager at IBM. Above all, political leaders must bring on board citizens who make it possible first for them to gain a position of influence, and then to create change. This truism holds whether the political leader is elected or appointed to a formal political role, or whether instead he or she has informal power. (Incidentally, *power* is another term that sends leadership theorists "round the bend.") Martin Luther King, to take an obvious example, was never elected or appointed to anything.

Business leaders, in turn, are centered in the organizations they head. Of course, they typically have a product to sell, and in this sense they must at the end of the day persuade those who would be customers to buy their wares. But, measured by how CEOs and upper-level corporate types spend their time, and with whom they personally engage, it is those affiliated with the organization who count: employees, stockholders, and the boards to whom business leaders ultimately report.

The literatures on public- and private-sector leadership reflect these obvious patterns. The former is primarily about the relationship between political leaders—usually elected officials—and their most obvious constituency: the American people. The latter is primarily about the relationships between corporate leaders and their employees and, to a lesser extent, their stockholders and boards. My decision, therefore, to compare in a general way top elected officials with top corporate leaders does not imply that I consider the analog perfect, or that I consider the differences I am choosing to avoid unimportant. I am simply taking a first crack at closing the divide between leadership in the public and private sectors, and I am doing so in a way that focuses on those men and women who are the most visible, the most obviously accountable, and arguably the most influential. Moreover, I happen to believe that if the traditional and unproductive standoff in America between government and business is to end, elected officials (as opposed to, for example, senior-level leaders of public bureaucracies) and their corporate counterparts are those who must lead the way.

I do not doubt the work that follows is vulnerable to the usual methodological debates. At the same time I trust that whatever issues arise, they will not obscure the persuasive powers of both common sense and the big picture.

Part I

STANDING APART

1

The 1950s and 1960s
Different Worlds

In the 1950s and early 1960s the literatures on leadership in the public sector and management in the private sector could hardly have been more different. Whereas the first was increasingly permeated with what might be labeled the three *P*s—pluralism, participation, and persuasion—the second was still replete with images of coercion and control. This chapter will explore the ideas underlying these differences, and how they actually shaped the practice of creating change in government and business.

POLITICAL LEADERSHIP

The ideas
The 1950s were the Eisenhower years. It was a time when law and order still prevailed, when those in authority—at home, in church, in school—were paid due deference, and when leaders in government could count on a certain amount of homage paid them simply by virtue of the office they held.

Above all, it was still a time when leaders in the public sector were held in generally high esteem, and when politics—especially at the national level—was by and large considered an honorable profession. The great historian Henry Steele Commager once pointed out that in eighteenth-century America the opportunities for leadership and distinction were almost wholly in the public arena. While two centuries later the private sector had obviously caught up, the 1950s were arguably the last full decade in which this great tradition of public service was meaningful to most Americans.

Similarly, it was the end of an era in which political leaders were,

15

as a matter of course, held to a high standard of excellence. The fall 1961 issue of the *Journal of the American Academy of Arts and Sciences* was dedicated to the subject of leadership. Its subtitle: "Excellence and Leadership in a Democracy." The assumptions were that men (yes, men) became political leaders in the first place because of the outstanding qualities they demonstrated well before assuming leadership roles, and that they would as a matter of personal pride strive for superior performance in every aspect. As one contributor put it, "The thesis of this essay is that the kind of excellence most explicitly recognized in the United States is leadership, and that the reward of recognition is, by and large, more leadership."[1]

The widespread assumption during this period that leadership and excellence were generally equated was the more remarkable for the antileadership mentality that had since the beginning of the Republic been part of the national culture. So far as leadership was concerned, three beliefs comprised the American Creed: 1) antagonism toward governmental authority; 2) ambivalence toward constituted leaders; and 3) uncertainty about what constitutes effective and proper management in public life.

Maybe it was because the 1950s were a time of peace and prosperity. Or maybe it was because of the nature of the man with whom the decade became synonymous—Dwight Eisenhower. The indicators, in any case, were clear. By an overwhelming majority, Americans believed in their government, and trusted their leaders to act wisely and well in the national interest.

By the early 1960s there was another reason to celebrate the quality of political leadership in America. According to the conventional (albeit scarcely undisputed) wisdom, power was now shared. Perhaps the most influential ode to what came to be known as pluralism was Robert Dahl's book, *Who Governs?* Researched in the mid-1950s and published in 1961, *Who Governs?* provided the "scientific" basis for the belief that power in America was now being shared. Dahl claimed that whereas in the past power was distributed among only a relatively small number of people ("patricians"), by about 1955 it was held by a range of men including bureaucrats, experts, and politicians. "Within a century a political system dominated by one cohesive set of leaders had given way to a system dominated by many different sets of leaders. . . . It was, in short, a pluralist system."[2]

Dahl's book also confirmed that most Americans believed in what he called the democratic creed. "The common view seems to be that our system is not only democratic but is perhaps the most perfect expression of democracy that exists anywhere."[3]

In the early 1960s scholars went another step further. Americans were now being urged to take advantage of a political system that was more open, flexible, and responsive than it had been before. For example, in 1963, Pulitzer Prize-winning historian James Mac-Gregor Burns published *The Deadlock of Democracy*, in which he argued that the American people lacked "popular control of the policy-making process. Our splintered parties set up barriers between the people and their national government."[4]

Note the subtle distinction between the pluralism that Dahl touted and the popular control Burns espoused. Demonstrating that power is distributed among a few key groups is one thing. Arguing that citizens should aggressively participate in political decision making is quite another. But how was this political engagement to come about? Replied Burns: "The national parties must build grass-roots memberships. Colonels, lieutenants, and sergeants are not enough; the parties need the same foundation that every other big, politically active organization . . . already has: an extensive card-carrying, dues-paying membership."[5]

The first manifestations of what we might call an evolution from pluralism to participation were the Civil Rights and women's movements. The modern Civil Rights movement may be said to have started when Rosa Parks refused to surrender her seat on a Montgomery, Alabama, bus to a white man. The year was 1955, and Martin Luther King took up the cause.

The basis of King's power was of course not money or position, but rather his extraordinary ability to mobilize ordinary people on behalf of what he believed to be right and true. The Montgomery bus boycott catapulted King to national prominence and demonstrated to the black community its strength in numbers—if those numbers were effectively marshalled and mobilized. Put another way, it revealed how in this country at that time grass roots activity could compel significant political change.

Less than a decade after Rosa Parks refused to move, Betty Friedan published what turned out to be the revolutionary tract of the modern women's movement—*The Feminine Mystique*. On the surface, everything was fine. Women in television commercials beamed at glistening glasses and shiny floors. In fact, however, suburban wives and mothers were feeling increasingly bored, restless, and trapped in the confines of their grassy suburban enclaves. Insisted Friedan, "We can no longer ignore that voice within women that says, 'I want something more than my husband and my children and my home.'"[6]

However, Friedan did not at that time imagine a political movement. Rather she called on women as individuals to take responsibility for their own lives. "A girl should not expect special privilege because of her sex, but neither should she adjust to prejudice and discrimination. . . . Not until a great many women move out of the fringes into the mainstream will society itself provide the arrangements for their new life plan."[7] Meanwhile, Friedan became politically active; in 1966 she became the first president of the National Organization for Women (NOW).

Like the Civil Rights movement, which had Malcolm X as counterpoint to Dr. King, the women's movement was marked by a schism between moderates and radicals. The radicals were the focus of press attention—at the 1968 Miss America gala they protested that the contest created "an image that oppresses women in every area"—but it was the moderates who drew in the numbers. By the end of the sixties women of all ages, races, and classes considered themselves part of what by then had become an authentic political movement.

No discussion of how the late fifties and early sixties gave new meaning to political participation in America would be complete without reference to the student movement that began at the University of California's Berkeley campus. What began as a demand for the ultimate in free speech became a national phenomenon. The student movement and the energy it derived from its escalating opposition to the war in Vietnam changed everything fast. Indeed, protests against the war in Southeast Asia eventually led to a precipitous decline of authority in many areas of public life, and ushered in what might fairly be called a new age of leadership in America.

The old rules that had governed the relationship between leaders and led no longer applied. College campuses, only recently models of civility and decorum, became hotbeds of dissent. The police, only recently symbols of law and order, became fascists and pigs. And by the late 1960s politicians nationwide found themselves running for cover. Even the president, Lyndon Johnson, found that the times and the war and the protests from below made it impossible for him to continue as the nation's chief executive.

We come now to the third "p" (after pluralism and participation) that characterized political leadership in America during the 1950s and 1960s: persuasion. As we shall see, even during the decade in which the old models of authority were still in place, the 1950s, the public sector was replete with ideas and behaviors that had virtually nothing to do with coercion and control and everything to do with persuasion and influence. In other words, even during a time in which the old order still held, elected officials realized that in order to lead they would have to rely on their own personal capacity to persuade others that it was in their best interest to go along.

Perhaps the literature on politics at the highest levels of government is the most revealing. Even presidents and senators, we were repeatedly told, could only do so much. Clinton Rossiter's classic text from the period was *The American Presidency*. Rossiter devoted as long a chapter to the "limits" of the presidency as he did to the "powers" of the presidency. "A genuinely indecent performance by the President will arouse fierce opposition . . . and even a questionable course of action . . . will move Congressmen, administrators, lobbyists, and politicians to unite in opposition." [8]

Senators, we were told, faced similar constraints on their ability to lead. As Donald Matthews wrote in *U.S. Senators and Their World*, "Even the limited goals [senators] set for themselves are very difficult to achieve. They have no control over the raw material they are expected to unify." [9]

What to do? How to get others to go along? How could leaders lead—even presidents and senators—when they had so few sources of power and authority? The conclusion was clear. By 1960 the evidence pointed to the importance of personality, in particular the leader's ability to get others to go where he wanted them to go. Matthews continued: "The party leader's principal weapon is his own persuasiveness. A major share of his time is devoted to lobbying—flattering, cajoling, appealing to the senators' sense of party loyalty, arguing the merits of legislative measures." [10] In other words, even though party loyalty was still a powerful resource for keeping others in line, if it failed, the only other option was to persuade.

Presidential scholars made a similar discovery. Rossiter's focus on presidential constraints notwithstanding, until Richard Neustadt's seminal book, *Presidential Leadership,* was published in 1960, we had only a weak understanding of the degree to which presidents relied on influence. Of course the trappings of position have always counted for something. We are not now nor have we ever been immune to the seductive appeal of the Oval Office. Nevertheless, after a long tradition in which the chief executive was considered "a kind of magnificent lion," Neustadt's analysis was as original as it was pointed. "The essence of a President's persuasive task," he wrote, "is to induce [others] to believe that what he wants of them is what their own appraisal of their own responsibilities requires them to do in their interest, not his."[11]

The progression from the demure pluralism of the 1950s to the strident participation of the 1960s had a considerable impact on our thinking about leadership in the public sector. What became clear was that political leaders simply did not have available to them the resources of their private-sector counterparts. Business executives could reward, and punish, their followers, particularly employees. Political leaders could do the same only infrequently—or not at all (for example, vis-à-vis voters). Compelled to function in an environment in which the ideology was ardently egalitarian, and in which the system was designed to check and balance at every turn, America's political leaders had to persuade to progress.

Ironically, the shift to a time when political leadership was even more difficult than it had been before coincided with a president's promise to bestow on voters the moon and the stars— and butter. Lyndon Johnson's Great Society was, after Franklin Roosevelt's New Deal, the most ambitious program of social reform in the nation's history. The Great Society offered something to everyone: health care, educational assistance, tax rebates, a higher minimum wage, farm subsidies, vocational training, housing for the homeless, poverty grants.

But in spite of his big dreams, by the time Johnson left office the balance Neustadt had described roughly a decade earlier had given way. The importance of presidential authority declined; as a consequence presidential persuasion became that much more important and that much more difficult. Like their less elevated counterparts, presidents unable to persuade others to go along were, so far as their capacity to create change was concerned, dead in the water.

The reality

To belong to the so-called "Eisenhower Generation" has always been considered something of a mixed blessing. On the one hand the fifties are seen as a time during which individual feelings and impulses were repressed in favor of conformity imposed by family, school, church, and government. On the other hand, the post-World War II era provided many Americans with a strong sense of confidence and security.

In the 1950s, the United States was the world's most powerful, rich, and envied country with many opportunities (especially for white males) for success and happiness. Moreover in retrospect at least, the temper of the time was almost carefree. To be sure, there were worries about a nuclear attack by the Soviet Union. But children walked to their neighborhood schools free of the fear of being mugged or shot, and when they ate supper both Mommy and Daddy were usually at table.

The man who presided over these apparently tranquil times capitalized on two conflicting impulses in the American people. Despite his long and illustrious career in the military, Dwight David Eisenhower governed with a loose rein. By freely delegating important assignments to others, by adopting what Fred Greenstein has referred to as the "hidden hand" (indirect, sometimes covert) style of leadership,[12] and by drawing freely and deliberately on a million-dollar grin that served as leveller between the president and the people, Eisenhower shed the military leadership style he had spent a previous lifetime mastering.

But "Ike," as he was affectionately known, also responded to the people's need for a leader who can provide direction and security. He kept his promise by extricating the United States from the Korean War, and proceeded then to preside over a time in America which, for all its limitations, is now generally conceded to have been one of the most peaceable and productive in American history.

Greenstein has written of Eisenhower that "by obscuring his steady involvement in political machinations while publicizing his ecumenical appeal to all Americans and his congenial outward manner, [he] escaped a catch-22 built into the presidency."[13] In other words, Eisenhower conveyed the impression of a man in charge—without giving offense.

As it happened, the times supported the man. In particular, the fifties were the last decade during which there was a sense that the old order (the Eastern establishment) still had control. Dahl's aforementioned treatise notwithstanding, while in mid-century America the upper class was not as important as it once was, it still mattered. Moreover it was widely believed that "there are a variety of foundations, associations, committees, and institutes within which members of the upper class participate if they wish to be active in determining policy."[14]

Whatever the deficits of this circumstance, it did also send a benevolent message: the United States was stable and well run, and important decisions about domestic and foreign policy were being made by the best and brightest.

Moreover, top political leaders were still held in high esteem. They were not generally demeaned, nor were their secrets revealed. In particular, the press operated under rules of conduct that forbade unseemly attacks on character.

Again, Dwight Eisenhower was particularly well placed to benefit from all this gentility. In 1955 *Time* described Ike as "crisp and cheerful" despite the "muggy heat." He "adroitly" fielded questions about a possible second term and quipped with such dexterity that his audience of newsmen "roared." The president of the United States, it was reported, "gave fresh meaning to the nation's foreign policy."[15]

But Eisenhower was by no means the only one who benefited from the midcentury proclivity to give leaders the benefit of the doubt. When Oklahoma Democrat Carl Albert became majority leader in the House, *Time* described him as follows: "He deplores the sort of backroom bloodletting that has sometimes spattered the records of quick-drawing majority leaders of the past. . . . On the other hand, Albert is tough enough to demand votes when the outcome is crucial."[16]

The presidency of John F. Kennedy seemed to signal no more than a changing of the guard. Kennedy was young, a Democratic, and Catholic—and in these important ways a departure from past patterns. But he had been a member of Congress for years, belonged to a rich and well-connected Massachusetts family, and promised as chief executive to continue most of the important domestic and foreign policies developed by his predecessors.

Because Kennedy's relationship with the press was so good, and because reporters did not in those days chase stories about private proclivities for sex and drugs, his image remained untarnished. To be sure, there was the usual carping about policies and procedures. But there was at the same time an unending appreciation of this attractive, witty, and charming man, and his glamorous, young, and terrifically photogenic family. In other words, Kennedy was president during a time when political leaders were still respected authority figures who, despite their need to mobilize political support in order to effect change, nevertheless profited from a mindset that gave leaders in high places the benefit of the doubt.

It should be noted that the Kennedy presidency has not, in fact, been considered very successful by the experts. In a 1982 nationwide survey of American historians, Kennedy ranked only thirteenth in presidential performance; and in a similar poll conducted in 1995, he dropped to eighteenth.[17] Still, mixed reviews notwithstanding, the Kennedy assassination fueled the Kennedy myth. Whatever the verities of Kennedy's performance in the White House, during his lifetime his personal qualities won friends and influenced people. And since his death, despite unsavory revelations about his private life, his standing among the American people (as opposed to American historians) has remained high.

While it is impossible to pinpoint changes in the Zeitgeist, with regard to leadership in America it is not too much to say that the period between Kennedy's assassination in November 1963 and Lyndon Johnson's withdrawal from public life in March 1968 constituted a turning point. In less than five years the United States metamorphosed from a country in which everything seemed possible to one riddled with dissension and self-doubt. As a consequence, the capacity of our political leaders to get others to go along was severely compromised.

It has often been said of the American presidency that it is an office far less powerful than is generally imagined. I would argue, moreover, that when the nation's chief executive suffers a setback, the impact is felt well beyond Washington. I am proposing, in other words, that the undermining of the presidency of Lyndon Johnson led over time to a weakening of leaders more generally. What happens in the White House is infectious. Leaders in other places—in both government and business—become vulnerable to whatever ails the nation's highest elected official.

The trajectory of Lyndon Johnson's tenure as president is poignant precisely because it was so sharp. What began as an administration full of promise ended in a withdrawal from public life that was as humiliating as it was significant. Never before in American history had a president fallen so far so fast. And never before in American history had a president decided not to run for a second term because of the domestic strife his mere presence in the Oval Office seemed to trigger.

In the beginning, LBJ could do no wrong. He helped a shattered nation recover from the trauma of Kennedy's death, and promised a period in which the Democratic agenda would become law. Moreover he delivered. In fact, he was so effective a leader that his domestic record will be forever hard to match. Johnson's intimate knowledge of the Congress, particularly the Senate, and his overwhelmingly powerful personal style—he harangued, threatened, promised, wheedled, and cajoled—combined to forge a leader who in the domestic arena was as effective as any the United States has ever known. His promise and performance were confirmed in the 1964 presidential election. "It was," Johnson later recalled, "a night I shall never forget. Millions upon millions of people, each marking my name on their ballot, each one wanting me as their President."[18]

What turned everything around was of course the war in Vietnam—"Lyndon Johnson's war." The escalation of American involvement in Southeast Asia undermined the president's ability to govern and was virtually solely responsible for the steep, swift decline in his popularity. (Between 1964 and 1968 his support in the polls plunged thirty-six points.)

But numbers don't adequately convey what happened in America during Lyndon Johnson's tenure in office. The real story was the growing distrust of Americans in government—and in those who would lead it. What had been up to then a modicum of respect bestowed on those in high positions of political authority eroded with remarkable alacrity.

The peace movement began small and slow, but in quick order teach-ins and marches were followed by sit-ins and lie-ins which, in turn, were followed by the burning of flags and draft cards, the bombings of buildings, and desertions from the army. By early 1968 the country was in turmoil and sharply divided. What began as street protests by the young and restless grew into something much more powerful: a sweeping national movement in which the original rebels were joined by the liberal establishment—including members of Congress, the press, and opinion makers all across America.

Lyndon Johnson's credibility as president was under attack from all sides. Even key members of his own administration began to desert the sinking ship. Moreover, what had started as a national debate over differences in policy escalated into ugly quarrels over fact and fiction. During the last years of his presidency LBJ suffered from a growing "credibility gap." The American people's increasing reluctance to believe that what their president was telling them was the whole truth and nothing but gradually undermined his capacity to govern. Doris Kearns reconstructs the moment: "Sometimes it seemed as if Johnson himself did not believe what he was saying, as if all the surmises were a bizarre recreation, a way to relax. But at other times Johnson's voice carried so much conviction that his words produced an almost hypnotic effect."[19]

By mid-1967 the handwriting was on the wall. Johnson had lost control of the war abroad and of the war at home as well. As McGeorge Bundy, one of Johnson's (and Kennedy's) closest aides put it, "What has happened is that a great many people—even very determined and loyal people—have begun to think that Vietnam really is a bottomless pit."[20]

The president had sunk far in just a few years, and his opportunity to achieve greatness was lost. But if for LBJ Vietnam was in the end a personal tragedy, for the nation it was a rude awakening. Not only were the policies of its most important political decision makers apparently wrong-headed and costly, they were embedded in a tissue of lies that made it difficult if not impossible for many citizens to remain true believers.

What happened during the mid-1960s, one of the most important five-year periods in American history, is that the president of the United States was stripped of his protective cover. The war in Vietnam had done its handiwork and television had changed the national dynamic. Vietnam became the first "living room war" and TV covered the chaos both at home and abroad. By early 1968 the twin demons of turbulence and technology had done the job. Lyndon Johnson, the quintessential American pol, was pushed from his perch. So far as leadership in America was concerned, the president's fall from grace was merely the harbinger of far greater changes to come.

BUSINESS MANAGEMENT

The ideas

Throughout most of the 1950s and 1960s, business and industry were wed to a model of governance in which leadership was a component of management rather than the other way around. Put another way, the question of how those at the top could get those further down to accomplish their tasks was only one of many managerial tasks—and not an especially important one at that.

Moreover motivation was not an issue. Because employees toed the line through the exercise of "supervision" and "control," the question of how actually to motivate them to go along was irrelevant. Management simply consisted of planning, organizing, and controlling.

Consider the matter of how managers used their time. One 1955 study showed they spent more hours with subordinates than with superiors or peers; more time on planning than on any other administrative function; and more time checking up on others than on any other single task.

Two other studies conducted during this period suggest the similarities in how all executives allocated their work. Typically the day was divided as follows: supervision (39 percent of the time); planning (18 percent); investigation (8 percent); coordination (6 percent); negotiation (5 percent); evaluation (4 percent); and miscellaneous (7 percent).[21]

The use of time was determined, of course, largely by where employees stood on the organizational ladder. First-line supervisors spent most of their day on employee supervision, employee contact and communication, union-management relations, manpower coordination and administration, work organization, planning and preparation, manufacturing process supervision, and manufacturing process administration. The nature of their jobs was, in any case, predetermined. As William H. Whyte Jr. observed, the primary function of those at the lower levels of the organizational hierarchy was to perceive their task accurately and conform to it.[22]

In contrast, higher-level managers did more long-range thinking and planning, more coordinating of other organizational units, and more work on external relations. Yet even they were not exempt from the ideology that pervaded business and industry in the aftermath of the Depression and World War II. The modus operandi for those both high and low on the organizational ladder was to behave well, work hard, and keep the corporate ship on a steady course. The reward for good behavior was clear: the American dream.

Nowhere was this model of conformity more vividly described than in William H. Whyte Jr.'s classic, *The Organization Man*. Published in 1956 to widespread attention and acclaim, the book made clear that during the Eisenhower era the private sector valued convention over autonomy. Throughout the organization, individual expression was discouraged and propriety rewarded. Men in grey flannel suits in one organization looked like the men in grey flannel suits in other organizations, and their fantasies were ostensibly the same: settled lives circumscribed by white picket fences. Here is Whyte's description of what he called a litany increasingly standard: "Be loyal to the company and the company will be loyal to you. After all, if you do a good job for the organization, it is only good sense for the organization to be good to you, because that will be best for everybody."[23]

Arguably, there was one major departure from the culture of conformity that pervaded the literature on business management during this period: Philip Selznick's slender volume titled, tellingly, *Leadership in Administration*. Selznick was one of the first to distinguish between leadership and management. In particular, he charged top executives with personal responsibility for the welfare of the organization. It is the institutional leader who is "primarily an expert in the promotion and protection of values."[24]

Selznick's leader transcends his specialization and sees the institution whole. He brings to his task "a blend of commitment, understanding, and determination." Moreover, unlike his flannel-clad contemporaries, he is self-aware. He understands his own strengths and weaknesses and also those of the organization for which he is responsible. Still, Selznick's corporate leader does not interact with subordinates. In other words, the leader described in *Leadership in Administration* does not engage followers, influence them, or bother to motivate them to follow his lead. In fact, Selznick makes a clear distinction between the less-important "interpersonal leader" and the more-important "institutional leader." The interpersonal leader is charged with "smoothing the path of human interaction, easing communication, evoking personal devotion, and allaying anxiety." However, the interpersonal leader has "relatively little to do with content; he is more concerned with persons than policies."[25]

Now, of course, Selznick's book seems somehow quaint. Today no leader of a major American enterprise would admit to turning over the interpersonal aspects of his job to someone else, and no leader would admit to a domain confined to policy. In fact, it is the fashion at the end of the millennium to say that persons are as important as policies and that, indeed, good policy can only emerge from good—that is caring—interpersonal relations.

In 1960, there was another break with the past. In *The Human Side of Enterprise* Douglas McGregor gave us Theory X and Theory Y. Theory X was, in effect, the traditional model of direction and control, and it was based on three key assumptions. First, average people have an inherent dislike of work and will avoid it if they can. Second, because of this dislike, most people must be coerced, controlled, and directed in their work. And third, the average person prefers to be directed, wants to avoid responsibility, has relatively little ambition, and wants security more than anything else.[26]

McGregor's argument for a new approach was based less on a moral imperative than on self-interest. Put simply, McGregor maintained that once workers were motivated by more than the need to subsist, the old model of management did not work very well. In other words, it was in the organization's best interest to adopt new policies and practices—those of Theory Y.

Theory Y elevated all employees to a new level, bestowing on them the capacity for self-direction, self-control, responsibility, imagination, ingenuity, and creativity. As a consequence, it was assumed that whatever organizational problems did occur were not the fault of those lower down but rather of those higher up the organizational ladder. "If employees are lazy, indifferent, unwilling to take responsibility, intransigent, uncreative, uncooperative, Theory

Y implies that the causes lie in management's methods of organization and control."[27]

Needless to say, McGregor's model of leadership is quite different from (and far more contemporary than) Selznick's. For McGregor relationships are absolutely central to the manager's task. "Perhaps it is clear by now that the all-important climate of the superior-subordinate relationship is determined not by policy and procedure, nor by the personal style of the superior, but by the subtle and frequently quite unconscious manifestations of his underlying conception of management and his assumptions about people in general."[28]

But for all of McGregor's later influence, his ideas took time to take hold. By and large the 1950s and even the 1960s were characterized by only a weak conception that people matter to management. Consider this issue of the *Harvard Business Review* (HBR), published late during the period January/February 1967. The contents:

— How Much Should a Corporation Earn?
— The Case of the Latent Lobby
— Operations Research in Marketing
— Capitalists and Managers in Communist China
— Marketing Ethics and the Consumer
— Regional Management Overseas
— The Effective Decision
— Computers: No Impact on Divisional Control
— Put People on Your Balance Sheet
— The Johnson Treatment
— Corporate Disclosure/Insider Trading
— Zip Code—New Tool for Marketers
— Using Credit for Profit Making
— Checkers or Choice in Manpower Management[29]

Only late in the decade (September/October 1969), did the HBR carry a major article in which employee interests were front and center.[30] To be sure, once again the justification for the focus on worker satisfaction was that it was good business. That is, there was growing evidence that in both good times and bad the ability of management, unions, and employees to get along contributed to organizational efficiency and success.

But something else was at work here: an ideology that was starting to infuse the organizational culture and that made employee participation and satisfaction a value unto itself. The article referred to above described what was then known as the Scanlon Plan. The Scanlon Plan was first tried in 1947, in a machine tool company. And in fact McGregor talked about it (largely admiringly) in his 1960 book. In particular, McGregor extolled the Plan for providing for every member of the organization the opportunity "to contribute his brains and ingenuity as well as his physical effort to the improvement of organizational effectiveness."[31]

But it was not until years later that the principle of collaboration began to be appreciated for what it did for employees—rather than merely for how it helped the business. Put another way, the Scanlon Plan and those that in one or another way emulated it addressed the changing notions of how, for various reasons, work should be managed and organizations directed.

But this was collaboration between labor and management only up to a point. In the end, the HBR article makes perfectly clear who was in charge and at whose discretion the Scanlon Plan was being initiated. "In applying a Scanlon Plan, a company in essence says to its employees, 'Look, we can run the company [and] we can run it well. But we think we can run it much better if you will help us. We're willing to listen.'"[32]

To compare the 1950s and 1960s literatures on leadership in politics and management in business is to be struck by the dramatic differences between them. Whereas the former talks of pluralism, participation, and persuasion, the latter is largely stuck in the language of control. In general, public-sector followers were imagined as equals and private-sector followers as subordinates. Only toward the end of this period did any of the work on management in business and industry reflect even dimly the ferment that had by then become endemic to American politics.

The reality

In August 1955 the president of the Reed Roller Bit company of Houston, Texas, told *Fortune* magazine that he could not "accept the idea" that the Executive Committee of his corporation could make a major mistake. His thinking was typical. In 1955, "a surprising number of executives believed that the outcome of their decision was a certainty."[33]

The business executive was still seen as a remote and elevated figure whose control was exercised from on high. The separation between those at the highest levels of management and those further down was complete. In no way did their personal or professional lives intersect; in no way was it considered the executive's responsibility to communicate with subordinates; and in no way was he required to demonstrate the interpersonal skills that came to be important later on. Business management was, in other words, still management by fiat.

Captains of business and industry were not like you and me. At work they were "typically decisive, and somewhat aloof, and generally regarded by employees with a certain awe." What transpired outside the office was even more mysterious; so magazines like *Fortune* gave us the scoop. In July 1955 readers were told that executives "do have common characteristics" and that there is a "kind of composite way of executive life." The successful American executive "gets up—about 7:00 A.M.—eats a large breakfast, and rushes to the office by train or auto. It is not unusual for him, after working from 9:00 A.M. until 6:00 P.M. in his office, to hurry and eat dinner, and crawl into bed with a briefcase full of homework. He is constantly pressed for time, and a great deal of the time he spends in his office is extraneous to his business. He gets himself involved in all kinds of community activities either because he wants to or because he figures he has to for the sake of public relations."[34]

Needless to say, the executive's wife figured prominently in the arrangement. As a 1956 article in HBR made clear, the wife's role was no less than critical to her husband's professional success. "The least [the wife] must do is see that the activities of the household do not interfere with [her husband's] work. She must be prepared to take on the major task of rearing the children. She must not demand too much of her husband's time or interest. Because of his single-minded concentration on the job, even his sexual activity is relegated to a secondary place."[35]

Our curiosity about corporate America's high command was satisfied by profiles in newspapers and magazines that accentuated the positive and eliminated the negative. This was not a time for letting it all hang out, or a period to satisfy those with prurient interests, or an era in which tabloid journalism was mainstream.

As a consequence, every top executive of every major organization was portrayed as somehow special—colorful, clever, and, of course, terrifically effective. The following descriptions are from 1955 and 1956 editions of *Fortune:*

W. L. Lyons Brown, the chairman of Brown-Forman, was "forty-nine, a huge, voluble, impetuous Kentuckian with a strong bent for selling and an impatience with detail." The president of the company was his brother: "G. Garvin, forty-three, a cooler and more cautious man." This control of the company by the family did not of course "mean that executives who do not happen to be Browns are treated as second-class citizens. The Brown brothers have close social ties with most of the other company officers. They believe, in fact, in mixing business with pleasure whenever possible. Much of this mixing is done at the lunch hour. . . . The Browns and their lieutenants gather shortly after noon each day to whet their appetites with shop talk and bourbon. Each August a dozen or so home-office executives spend two stag weeks at a lodge [on a Canadian island]. The agenda includes poker, fishing, drinking, [and] beard growing. . . . On the last day, all liquor remaining on the premises . . . is dumped into a huge pitcher and nobody may leave until the pitcher has been emptied."[36]

As a young man, Roger Blough, the new chairman of U.S. Steel, took a job as a lawyer with White and Case, "where he worked longer, harder, and more effectively than most young Wall Street law clerks." Now, even though he was top dog at one of the nation's leading companies, Blough's "modest, careful demeanor" tended to mask his "important talents." Blough, it was said, had a "capacious mind, abundantly stocked with sharply differentiated facts. . . . He is not one to be put off by appearances or to take nonsense from anyone. He knows what is going on in the world, and he has a sharp tongue. . . . Probably no man has more intimate knowledge of [U.S. Steel's] strengths and weaknesses, or a clearer idea of what might be done about them."[37]

When it turned out that Harlow Curtice had correctly predicted booming sales for General Motors cars and trucks the Curtice legend was "stamped and sealed." Curtice was the "prophet of economic expansionism." "If American business must have such an apotheosis, Harlow Herbert Curtice is just about perfect type casting. At sixty-two he is a trim (five-foot nine, 155 pounds), tailored man who moves and gestures with athletic grace. He has quite the appropriate degree of vibrancy for a man of affairs. A flaming redhead in his youth, his hair and his military mustache are now a distinguished grey. Still, there is enough aquilinity to the nose and the jaw line to unprettify the man and suggest the aggressive perfectionist that he certainly is . . . . But it's practically impossible not to smile when Harlow Curtice smiles."[38]

By the late 1950s and early 1960s some of the old assumptions were being challenged. In 1959, an article in HBR suggested that traditional performance review interviews "are seriously deflating to the employee's sense of importance and personal worth. . . . The fundamental flaw in current review procedures is that they compel the superior to behave in a threatening, rejecting, and ego-deflating manner with a sizeable proportion of his staff."[39]

A scant five years later the demand for a new kind of executive was made unambiguously clear. Those at the top were no longer exempt from interacting with those further down, and executives who failed to master the appropriate skills would pay the price. "As the executives' interpersonal competence decreases, conformity, mistrust, and dependence, especially on those who are in power, increase. Decision making becomes less effective, because people withhold many of their ideas, especially those that are innovative and risky."[40] Democracy in the workplace was the new fashion not because, as Philip Slater and Warren Bennis wrote in 1964, "of some vague yearning for human rights, but because under certain conditions it is a more 'efficient' form of social organization."[41]

At the same time, there was the growing recognition that there were other ways to get to, and stay on, the top. "Egghead millionaires," for example, were brainy types with a "strong yen to be independent about the company they work for, where they live, what they buy, how they play." These new exemplars of American ingenuity were rewriting some of the old rules. Indeed, the growing demand for technical experts produced a new kind of worker: the knowledge worker who advanced in spite of, rather than because of, adhering to the conventional corporate culture. Renegades like Arnold J. Ryden, who in 1957 formed the Control Data Corporation, announced with pride rather than embarrassment that he had "been fired by the best companies in town."[42]

Still, the shift to a new business and industrial culture was an evolution rather than a revolution. In the early 1960s America was still being shaped by "prime movers," men who across the board—in business, politics, art, science, philanthropy, and education—were the top guns. Prime movers were people like John D. Rockefeller III, who was "conceded to be the prime prime mover, and can produce in a few hours a varied and balanced Committee to deal with almost any subject under the sun."[43] Thus, whereas in the 1950s executives were like everyone else, only more so, in the 1960s they could as easily be, in one or another way, separate from the pack. Here is *Fortune* on three of the major players:

> A veteran pilot was reminiscing about the time he went out to dinner with George Theodore Baker, founder and president of National Airlines. "Baker was driving his Cadillac," the pilot recalled, "and no sooner were we off the bridge to Miami Beach than he started driving up a one-way street the wrong way. 'Ted,' I said, 'it's a one-way street.' 'I know,' said Baker, 'but it saves three blocks and I only get a couple of tickets a year this way.'" The story was, we were told, indicative of Baker's style. At fifty-nine, he was "still a lot like the uninhibited, swashbuckling barnstormers who founded the nation's airlines a generation ago. . . . When Baker wants something, he goes directly after it, and if he is balked he lets fly."[44]

> At sixty three, the "bumptious stalwart of aviation," William

Lear, was said to have "shaken the industry with his low-cost executive jet. He's up to his ears in competition and controversy—which is just the way he likes it. On the eve of his sixtieth birthday, Lear gambled his prestige and fortune on a long shot: a small jet plane designed expressly for the corporate market. Sure enough, he became the first man in history to design, build and win certification for a jet airplane—all with his own money. Was this enough for Bill Lear? Not likely. He told his friends that if success did come, "I guess I'll just have to cut out and start all over again."[45]

At the age of fifty-eight John M. Roche became president of General Motors. The antithesis of some of his extravagantly extraverted predecessors, Roche was described as having a placid, "almost priestly" personality. "A modest, self-educated man who had always shied away from personal publicity unless he was convinced that it was genuinely in the interest of GM; a man whose extremely soft-pitched voice . . . is like the murmur of a Cadillac engine; a religious man who customarily attends church before showing up at his office at 8:00 A.M.; and a gracious man who rose to the top in a rough and tough business without ever making a known personal enemy"—this was the new model of leadership in America. This was a leader in keeping with an age that had a decreasing tolerance for the uninhibited exercise of power and authority. [46]

The protests that roiled America in the late 1960s inevitably had an impact on American business. One might reasonably speculate that the hostility during this period toward the nation's chief executive—"Hey, Hey, LBJ, How Many Kids Did You Kill Today?"—was a harbinger. Never again would Americans in high places be immune to close scrutiny. From this point on every authority figure would, sooner or later, become fair game.

The growing doubts about virtually every major American institution led to a period of unaccustomed introspection. The word "conscience" crept into the business lexicon, and major companies such as Alcoa and Chase Manhattan were asking out loud how to balance social responsibility on the one hand with the mandate to make money on the other. At the same time, labor was getting restive. Under the forceful leadership of Jerry Wurf, president of the American Federation of State, County and Municipal Employees, government workers in particular were demonstrating the kind of militancy heretofore associated with miners and autoworkers.

For business executives the days of command and control were coming to a close. As William May, chairman and president of the American Can Company, put it toward the end of the decade, "A chief executive has to persuade as much as command. He has to evoke consent as well as assent among his subordinates, to say nothing of his board of directors. People talk about 'decision making' as if it were some kind of instant action. In actuality, it's a fearfully time-consuming process, because you've got to mobilize people behind those decisions."[47] May could as easily have been talking about being a mayor, or a governor, or, for that matter, president of the United States.

2
The 1970s
Different Drummers

It was impossible during this decade for the private sector to ignore completely what had been happening in the public sector for at least ten years. In terms of the rhetoric at least, the literature on management in business and industry began to reflect some of the trends toward increased democratization that had become a regular part of American political discourse. But the gap in the private sector particularly, between what was said and what was done, was huge. For all the verbiage to the contrary, for many change remained, at best, an unappealing alternative to the status quo. So far as they were concerned, both superiors and subordinates were supposed to remain in place.

POLITICAL LEADERSHIP

The ideas

Given the social and political upheavals of the late 1960s and early 1970s and given a six-year period (between 1968 and 1974) in which two successive presidents were forced out of office, it is hardly surprising that during this time previously held assumptions about leadership in America were thrown into question. In particular, two changes in our political life proved enduring and fundamental. First, the war in Vietnam, the Watergate scandal, and the consequent departures from office of Lyndon Johnson and Richard Nixon cloaked American politics in a mantle of cynicism and doubt that to this day remains in place. The titles of some of the books on politics published during this period tell all: *The Party's Over: The Failure of Politics in America* (David Broder, 1971);[1] *Fear and Loathing:*

On the Campaign Trail '72 (Hunter Thompson, 1973);[2] *Breach of Faith: The Fall of Richard Nixon* (Theodore White, 1975);[3] *Nightmare: The Underside of the Nixon Years* (J. Anthony Lukas, 1976);[4] and *The Culture of Narcissism: American Life in An Age of Diminishing Expectations* (Christopher Lasch, 1979).[5]

The second problem was obviously an outgrowth of the first. The pervasive skepticism led gradually but inexorably to what must now be considered a permanent decline in faith in government. The presidency was tarnished. Politicians in general were increasingly suspect. And the American people became unsure of their own capacity to elect public officials who were honest as well as competent.

During the period 1958–1964 the figures on trust in government had changed little. But in the subsequent six years there was a virtual explosion of antigovernment sentiment. Marked increases in most measures of distrust were observed between 1964 and 1970; and by 1974, after Watergate, the proportion of Americans who felt that most politicians were crooked had climbed to 45 percent. Significantly, these figures did not recede when Watergate did. By the fall of 1980, questions on trust in government were eliciting a cynical response from no less than two out of every three Americans.[6]

The low point was mid-decade, about the time Gerald Ford became president. (Tellingly, the title of his presidential memoir is *A Time to Heal*.)[7] Theodore White wrote of broken myths, "Of all the political myths out of which the Republic was born, none was more hopeful than the crowning myth of the Presidency . . . Richard Nixon behaved otherwise. His lawlessness exploded the legends."[8] Hunter Thompson described Nixon as someone "who represents that dark, venal and incurably violent side of the American character almost every other country in the world has learned to fear and despise."[9] David Broder concluded even before Watergate that the "challenge facing our society and institutions is far more critical than most of us find comfortable to believe." [10] And Christopher Lasch maintained that since people had no hope of improving their lives in any of the ways that mattered, they had "convinced themselves that what matters is psychic self-improvement. . . . These pursuits . . . signify a retreat from politics and a repudiation of the recent past."[11]

The fundamental doubts were also reflected in a literature new to most Americans: that of the Left. This is not to say that in the past Americans had been altogether ignorant of communism and social democracy. It is to say that in the United States the political spectrum had always been quite narrow—even during the post–World War II period when other Western democracies were flirting with communism (for example, France and Italy) and/or embracing social democracy (for example, West Germany and Scandinavia).

Given this history, it is all the more remarkable that the 1970s gave rise to a literature of the American Left, and that this literature found an audience, particularly on college campuses. The search for alternatives to what was now considered disappointing and corrupt meant the most privileged students at the best schools were drawn to an ideology that questioned the most fundamental arrangements, both political and economic, of the American way of life.

Once again, titles tell the tale. In *Class Inequality and Political Order* (1971), Frank Parkin argued that Western capitalist societies are rife with inequalities. He claimed the effects of these schisms are manifest at every level of society, and that in the United States social tensions were acute "at the lower levels of the reward hierarchy." While Parkin's conclusion was in and of itself not startling, his analysis was unabashedly Marxist.[12]

Similarly, in *The Hidden Injuries of Class* (1972), authors Richard Sennett and Jonathan Cobb maintained that the American people were divided by class. Moreover as their title implies, they argued that these class divisions hurt those at the bottom: "The mass of America's white laborers are becoming 'workers' in the classic sense of the term. . . . They are powerless in the hands of the economic and political forces controlling the cities."[13]

The ideology of the New Left also had an impact on the Civil Rights and women's movements. In 1968, Martin Luther King was killed. While one might reasonably argue that King's death is a loss from which the nation has never recovered, it had the effect of prompting some members of the African American community to turn inward, to assume responsibility for their own social and political development.

While the success of this effort is a matter of debate (the African American middle class has gained ground while the underclass is even worse off than it was before), it is nevertheless the case that in the immediate post-King era black political rhetoric underwent a fundamental change. Deprived of King, African Americans substituted grass roots leadership for top-down leadership.

The cry "black power" spoke to this shift. It suggested not only that black power was the equivalent of white power, but that within the black community each individual had the ability to take charge of his or her own life. In other words, black power was on one level a communal stand against racism in America, and on another level a message to every African American man, woman, and child that they can and should be personally responsible for their own behavior.

This emphasis on personal power was perhaps even more apparent in the women's movement. Most feminists involved in movement politics were hostile to the very idea of leaders within their ranks. In the early 1970s in particular, women who made themselves visible were denounced as "elitists."

There was, predictably, a cost to this extremism. As Jo Freeman wrote in mid-decade, the women's movement paid a price for its damnation of leadership. "Given the movement's ideals, the problem of covert power structures was often exacerbated. When informal elites are combined with a myth of 'structurelessness' there can be no attempt to put limits on the use of power because the means of doing so have been eliminated. The groups thus have no means of compelling responsibility from the elites that dominate them. They cannot even admit they exist."[14]

The 1970s, then, were a decade in which the changing order yielded polar opposites. On the one hand were the political activists—those militantly opposed to the war in Vietnam, and those heavily involved in either the women's or Civil Rights movements, and those who took seriously the revived ideal of community organizing (about which more below). And on the other hand was what came to be known as the "silent majority."

Once the shock of the late sixties and early seventies had passed, the question was how to rebuild what had been torn down. How, in other words, could Americans regain their trust in government? (Once again, the title of a presidential memoir is telling. Carter's was called *Keeping Faith*.)[15] In response to this question, and for the first time ever, two political scientists, Glenn Paige and James

MacGregor Burns, wrote books specifically about leadership. (Both were published in the late 1970s.)[16] Exactly why leadership had been so neglected in a discipline to which it would seem to be central has never been clear. In the event, the books by Paige and Burns signalled something of a correction and were almost certainly a response to what appeared to be America's most significant leadership crisis since the Civil War.

Paige's book, *The Scientific Study of Political Leadership*, asked why political scientists had failed to take leadership seriously, and argued for a new interdisciplinary approach to the subject. Burns's tome, *Leadership*, has had considerable influence not only in political science, but in business as well. Burns distinguished between "leaders" and "power wielders." Leaders do their work to reach goals mutually intended by both leaders and followers. Power wielders, in contrast, seek control. "Power wielders," Burns wrote, "may treat people as things. Leaders may not."[17]

Burns makes another key distinction: between the leader whose interaction with followers is transactional and the leader whose interaction with followers is transformational. While the transformational leader is more exotic—"such leadership occurs when one or more persons engage with others in such a way that leaders and followers raise one another to higher levels of motivation and morality"—it is transactional leadership (the exchange relationship) that is more relevant to this book.[18]

At about the same time that *Leadership* was published, psychologist Edwin Hollander wrote *Leadership Dynamics*. Hollander was a leading researcher in the field of leadership (psychologists had long been more interested in the subject than political scientists), and he used the book to convey to a lay audience his theory of social exchange. "When leaders are effective," Hollander wrote, "they give something and get something in return. . . . The leader provides a benefit in directing the group. . . . In return, the group members provide the leader with status and the privileges of authority." [19]

While the theory of social exchange was by no means new, the fact was that gradually leadership became in the popular as well as academic mind a relationship in which both parties could be viewed as equals. Scholars as well as practitioners of leadership were attracted to the idea that what they wanted to believe—that leadership could be a relationship in which both parties stood equally to gain—had at least some "scientific" validity. Moreover this view was in keeping with the temper of the times—times in which presidents fell, loyalties were frayed, and blacks and women led the charge against the old order.

It seems fitting to end this overview of the decade with a look at community organizing. It could be argued that the heyday of the community organizer was some time earlier, when the legendary Saul Alinsky was still around.[20] But in the 1970s community organizers took a more rigorous look at the role of leadership in an activity that was supposedly driven from the bottom up. The irony was that community-based organizations were frequently staff dominated. In other words, rather than developing indigenous leaders, outsiders (professional organizers) researched issues, conducted meetings, and planned actions. Now things were supposed to be different. Local leaders would be trained and taught to fend for themselves.

In his book *Pedagogy of the Oppressed,* Paulo Freire provided the philosophical basis for an era in which participation by the powerless was highly valued. It was Freire who described "cultures of silence," oppressed communities (especially in Latin America), in eloquent detail. And it was Freire who suggested ways in which the politically mute could develop the political consciousness that would, in time, lead to a demand for change.[21]

In a peculiar way, the 1970s were filled with hope and the possibility for change. As we have seen, on the one hand they were years of disillusionment. But on the other hand, the breakdown of the old order gave rise to a sense that the failure of leadership from the top down meant fresh opportunities for leadership from the bottom up. It was a time in which leaders and followers changed roles, and previously held ideas about the exercise of power, authority, and influence in America were open to question.

The reality

In the 1972 presidential election, Richard Nixon won every state in the union save Massachusetts. His lopsided win was misleading. In fact, the country was badly divided. The war in Southeast Asia had created an obvious tear, with the invasion of Cambodia and the shootings at Kent State serving as bloody emblems of the national divide.

The election of 1972 was, therefore, an illusion: it gave the impression of consensus when in fact there was none at all. Watergate reflected the rift between the government and the people. It symbolized a presidency that was increasingly "imperial," and it signalled the end of what was arguably America's age of political innocence. As British commentator Fred Emery put it, "Watergate was a self-destruct tragedy for Richard Nixon [and] for the American people it was a drawn-out ordeal." [22]

So far as political leadership in America is concerned, Watergate mattered on two counts. First, it was the single most severe hammer blow to the people's faith in the president. Whatever the fine points of the Watergate affair, the endgame was incontestable: Nixon was the first chief executive to resign from office because he knew that if he did not leave "voluntarily" he would risk a vote to impeach.

The second reason Watergate matters as much as it does is because it ushered in a new era in American politics. In his big book, *The Power Game*, Hedrick Smith talks about 1974 as the year in which "a political fault line from the Old Washington power game to the New Washington power game" was drawn.[23] According to Smith, change was triggered by three things: political reform, big money, and television.

The reforms transferred power from the executive to the legislative branch of government. But, somewhat paradoxically, they made leadership within the Congress more rather than less difficult. Put another way, although Congress now had more formal power than it did before—for example, to restrain the president from going to war without Congressional approval it had passed the 1973 War Powers Act—its capacity to exercise that power was more limited than it had been previously.

Within Congress, freshman Democrats threw out several established power barons; balkanized the decision-making process by forming scores of new subcommittees; and made clear that they, in contrast to their predecessors, would play down rather than up the importance of party loyalties. Changes such as these were bound to influence the ways in which members of the House and Senate behaved. In particular, they became more aggressive about pursuing their own political agendas which, together with the growing congressional workload, made building coalitions very difficult.

The role of money, especially in political campaigns, was also new. Increasingly, candidates were forced to fill their coffers with contributions from individuals and groups to whom they were then beholden. While in the mid-1970s public financing began to play a more important role in presidential campaigns, this change did not apply to congressional races, which gradually became dependent on contributions from individuals and corporate Political Action Committees (PACS).

Among other things, the money was used to pay for consultants. "Political consultants," Sidney Blumenthal wrote in 1980, "are the new power within the American political system. They have supplanted the old party bosses as the link to the voters."[24] Whereas in the past parties ran and shaped campaigns, by the 1970s the system had changed so completely that these mediating tasks were performed by hired professionals whose primary job was to project the image of the candidate as leader. The implications for relations between governors and governed were obviously considerable.[25]

Arguably, the electronic media had an equally detrimental effect on the political process. Once television became the major source of information about campaigns, American voters no longer relied on input from friends, family members, and work associates. Nor did they any longer want or require materials from political parties or candidate organizations.[26]

Once again, in keeping with past patterns, what had transpired in the 1960s and 1970s made political leadership in America harder to exercise, not easier. First, relations between leaders and led became more distant. Second, faith in leaders by the led was diminished. And third, the capacity for national consensus was weakened. More than two decades later it is possible to see the presidencies of both Gerald Ford and Jimmy Carter as reflections of the trend.

Gerald Ford was never elected vice president or president. Moreover, as Roger Porter has observed, he came to the Oval Office "when the political fabric of the country was frayed, respect for the institution of the presidency greatly diminished, and the nation's economy and foreign relations were in disarray."[27] What to do without an electoral mandate of any kind? How to take control during a time Henry Kissinger later described as the "hysterical summer of 1974"?

Gerald Ford is more important for what he was than for what he did. This is not to say that what he did was inconsequential or ineffectual. It is to say that so far as leadership in America is concerned, it was the man that mattered. There was above all the obvious difference between him and his predecessor. In contrast to "tricky Dick," Ford had always enjoyed an untarnished reputation as a skilled politician and decent man. Whereas Nixon was secretive and suspicious, Ford was open and trusting. Whereas Nixon was the eternally awkward loner, Ford was an extrovert, a sportsman, and to all appearances entirely comfortable with who he was.

His leadership style was also very different from that of his disgraced predecessor. Ford was collegial and he valued staff members who were team players rather than rigid loyalists. He was rather simple in his tastes and he removed from the White House many of the trappings of the imperial presidency. And he actually enjoyed the give and take that characterizes group discussions and collective decision making.

Ford's presidency was in the best sense a caretaker regime. In the end his time in office was too idiosyncratic and too short to reflect his own policy agenda. Thus, he took care of the office. He took care of the American people. He took care not to exacerbate a very bad situation and to provide instead a "time to heal."

Jimmy Carter's tenure in the White House was, like Ford's, a time of transition. It seems clear now that Carter was elected in response to Nixon—a change from the recent past. The trouble was that once the American people really got to know the man (even on Election Day this one-term governor of Georgia was not exactly a known quantity), they concluded they preferred another. Both the president and his policies were somehow too inchoate and demanding to have much appeal.

But, like Ford, and unlike Richard Nixon, Carter was a politician Americans felt they could trust. He was hard working and religious and he was a family man. He was a moralist who preached about, and tried to effect, what he considered the politics of the public good. And he was also, for better and worse, the consummate outsider who railed repeatedly against the ways of Washington and whose distaste for the wheeling and dealing that constitutes political life inside the Beltway was almost palpable.

But while the politics of good character worked for President Ford, standing him in good stead during his brief two years in the

White House, by the time Jimmy Carter became president the act was wearing thin. Clearly, one of Carter's attractions as candidate was the fact that he was an authentic outsider. In distinction even to President Ford he was unsullied by Washington's ways, and he did not come across as hungry for power. Unfortunately, before very long, it became apparent that many of the traits that seemed so engaging in candidate Carter were less so in President Carter.

Of the several problems Carter had as president, two stood out: his tendency to preach rather than persuade and his reluctance to play the game of politics. Carter's rhetoric was slightly too pious and nearly joyless. The United States was chided for being "the most wasteful nation on earth." Americans were warned of impending "painful sacrifices" and threatened with "catastrophe" if they did not swallow the president's "bitter medicine." Moreover he disdained horsetrading. As James David Barber wrote, "Carter had little taste for dealing—'not much of a trader,' he called himself—and he too often found Congressional delays and machinations not merely mistaken, but also 'disgusting.'" [28] In short, President Carter alienated precisely those whose cooperation was essential to his purposes.

What became obvious is that the presidency had been gravely weakened by the politics of the late 1960s and early 1970s. By 1980 not only were Americans no longer worried about what less than ten years earlier had been tagged "the imperial presidency," now the concern was quite the opposite—that the office was powerless to cope with growing problems both domestic and foreign. President Carter's inability to end the Iranian hostage crisis and bring down inflation led to the conclusion that presidential power had been eviscerated.

Still, it must be reiterated that the six years of Ford and Carter in the White House did provide a critical counterpoint to the six years of Richard Nixon. They reassured the American public that the Republic was stable, and that political leaders, while not necessarily effective, were not necessarily corrupt. It is impossible to overestimate the significance of this contribution.

It should also be noted that in spite of the fact that LBJ had quit Washington, for a time at least the mentality of the Great Society persisted. During the 1970s, growth in government continued, even when a Republican was in the White House. Between 1970 and

1975 the percentage of the Gross National Product spent on income maintenance programs such as social security, unemployment, and public housing went from 6 percent to 8.5 percent, and by 1980 it had climbed to over 9 percent. The Housing and Urban Development Act of 1968 alone accounted for 600,000 new or rehabilitated units over the subsequent four-year period.

But in other ways the seventies were a time to scale back. Political leaders across the United States were chastened by events of the recent past, and the American public was willing to settle, at least for a while, for governors who were perhaps more honest than accomplished. The Congress was similarly affected. The mood of the moment was to stress the limitations of, rather than the possibilities for, legislative leadership. In a book published mid-decade, *Leadership in Congress,* Robert Peabody makes the point. "The party leadership's contributions to most . . . legislative endeavors is marginal at best: they schedule legislation, work out appropriate floor strategy, and corral a few votes here and there." In sum, as a consequence of the continuing decline in their power, congressional leaders were reduced to falling back on more subtle forms of influence such as personal persuasion.[29]

Lesser mortals were also chastened by the difficulties increasingly associated with leadership in America. Women and African Americans still had trouble reaching the playing field, despite a decade or more of heightened political activity. The 95th Congress (1977–78) had only one more woman than the 87th Congress (1961–62), and even in areas that traditionally favored women, such as school boards, the numbers remained low (13 percent nationwide). Blacks fared no better. For example, in 1975, among thirty union locals with black members in the San Francisco Bay Area, only ten had blacks in leadership positions in proportion to their membership, and in ten others there were no black leaders at all.

Withal, leadership from the bottom up continued to flourish. It could be argued in fact that there was a relationship between them: when top-down leadership was least edifying, Americans were motivated to form their own interest groups and draw on their own sources of power and influence.

The late 1960s and 1970s were a particularly fertile time for community organizers. The reasons for this burst of activity include the fading dream of the War on Poverty, the egalitarian ideologies of the Civil Rights and women's movements, stagflation and urban decay, and a cadre of committed men and women who were ready, willing, and able to get involved.

Ernie Cortes was a case in point. A graduate student at the University of Texas, he quit school in 1964 to work with farmworkers in the Rio Grande Valley. He helped form COPS (Communities Organized for Public Service), which became the largest urban community organization in the country. Cortes "began with existing leadership in churches, local PTAs, boy scouts groups, women's clubs. He tried to involve what he called the 'central core leadership' of the Mexican-American community, drawn from the range of neighborhoods. He interviewed two thousand people to find the nuances and themes of community opinion. And he set up a rigorous training schedule. Leaders learned how to break down problems into manageable parts that they could act on. They learned to research issues, plan strategy for action, conduct an action, and evaluate the results. After building a neighborhood base, COPS addressed a complex of issues that affected the entire Mexican American area, as well as many other constituencies in San Antonio."[30]

A man like Ernie Cortes confirmed that leadership in America was still possible, even without formal authority. Cortes lacked conventional resources such as money and position; nevertheless he was able to create change through hard work at the grass roots. Cortes is significant in another way. He points to the importance of personality. Leadership theorists are always arguing about the significance of the "hero in history." How much of a difference can any single man, or woman, make? Are individuals the most important historical determinants? Or are they merely swept along by the tides of history? Cortes seemed to provide evidence that sometimes one man matters.

Similar conclusions were drawn at the national level. Change had made the importance of character, or personality, clear. They included

• Congressional reform. Changes in the legislature weakened party leaders. Now their personalities and skills, strengths and liabilities, were the single most important determinants of their ability to create change.[31]

• The decline in importance of political parties. This put a premium on personal qualities, and on the capacity to create political organizations loyal to individual candidates rather than to the major parties. The growing importance of money and political consultants exacerbated still further the tendency to focus attention on individuals rather than ideas.

• The changing culture of the press, both print and electronic. Private lives, once off limits, were increasingly considered fair game. The rules changed so that leaders were exposed "warts and all." As it happened, knowing more about our leaders' predilections metamorphosed into a preoccupation with them.

Our shifting attentions, from institutions to individuals, made possible the rise and reign of one of the most popular politicians in American history, Ronald Reagan. America's loss of faith in what Theodore White called the "crowning myth of the presidency," was in a peculiar way responsible for its love affair with a man who, whatever else may be said of him, wore the mantle of his office with considerable grace under considerable pressure.

BUSINESS MANAGEMENT

The ideas
By the turn of the decade, the upheavals that had characterized American politics in the late 1960s began to have an impact on American business. In fact, from that moment on what happened in one sector was increasingly important to what happened in the other.

The year 1970 began with a bang. Robert Townsend, a businessman with impeccable credentials (he had led the formidable Avis challenge to Hertz), wrote a book that broke the mold. *Up the Organization: How to Stop the Corporation from Stifling People and Strangling Profits* turned the grey flannel suit inside out. The book was short and punchy, cynical and castigating, witty and irreverent, pedantic and pointed. Townsend made the following points: the traditional corporate hierarchy was dated; most organizations were cumbersome and inefficient; and most CEOs were stuck, clinging to old managerial ways even though they no longer worked.

Townsend was the Abby Hoffman of big business. He tossed grenades, hoping to demolish the old and build something new.

In fact, rather like Hoffman, Townsend had a particular problem with men in authority who resisted rather than fostered change. In particular, he chided CEOs who still insisted on ruling from the top down.

- "All decisions should be made as low as possible in the organization."
- "Many give lip service, but few delegate authority in important matters. And that means all they delegate is dog-work."
- "Most people in big companies today are administered, not led. They are treated as personnel, not people."
- "We aren't producing leaders like we used to. A new chief executive officer today, exhausted by the climb to the peak, falls down on the mountaintop and goes to sleep."[32]

Up the Organization clearly hit a nerve. Everyone who was anyone was compelled on one or another level of consciousness to consider the radical implications of Townsend's treatise. The book made it impossible for executives to go about business as usual while politicians were being publicly eviscerated. By the early 1970s establishment organs such as the *Harvard Business Review* published articles that confirmed a sea change was taking place. In a 1971 piece titled "Who Wants Corporate Democracy?" David Ewing asserted that phrases such as "bottom-up control," "employee activism," and "corporate democracy" were being heard with increasing frequency. Wrote Ewing, "All the signs point to an ever-more persistent drive on the part of employees to participate further in the making of corporate policy. . . . Pressures are building to change the ground rules of governance."[33]

Another HBR article from the same period conveyed a similar message. It was titled "Make Way for the New Organization Man." Who was this new man? A highly evolved white-collar worker who required a new kind of leader. In the past, Mack Honan wrote, executives made solitary decisions, issued commands, and supervised their execution. In the brave new world of the 1970s, such behavior would not wash. "The new organization man requires a different kind of leadership style simply because he represents a different form of 'followership' potential: he reacts to ideas rather than orders."[34]

The new game in town was collaboration. The assumption was that the overwhelming majority of CEOs and upper-level managers were white, middle-aged men who had been educated and socialized during a time when the rules were different from what they were after the invasion of Cambodia and the shootings at Kent State. There was, it was felt, a real need to teach the old dogs new tricks.

A book by Chris Argyris titled *Increasing Leadership Effectiveness* illustrates the point.[35] Based on the assumption that adults could actually be taught to think and act in new and different ways, the book argued that this instruction could be applied to leadership. At the time Argyris was James Bryant Conant Professor of Education and Organizational Behavior at Harvard. In other words, he was able to use his impeccable credentials to proselytize for a new kind of leadership—one that was collegial and flexible rather than hierarchical and rigid. CEOs were taught to be less defensive, more collaborative, and better able to cope with the uncertainties that inevitably result from the diminished restrictions on what to say and how to behave.

About the same time, Peter Drucker also weighed in with a "landmark study of management as an organized body of knowledge." *Management: Tasks, Responsibilities, Practices* was noteworthy above all for the level of its ambition.[36] That is, what it said was arguably less startling than the claim it made to present a codified body of knowledge. It was a bold enterprise, based on the assumption that in the developed world the major way of doing work was in large organizations and that these organizations were, perforce, run by managers.

Again, the function of the book was one of instruction. Drucker assumed that if managers would only take the time to think they would inevitably be better at what they do. Interestingly, Drucker made it a point to address the turmoil in American politics. "It is fashionable today," he wrote, "to talk of a revolt against authority and to proclaim that everybody should 'do his own thing.' This, then, I have to admit, is a most unfashionable book. It does not talk about rights. It stresses responsibility."[37]

In response, perhaps, to the temper of the times, which was increasingly hard on those in high places, there was a parallel literature that sought to instruct on how to retain power and maintain control. Writing in HBR in 1973, Robert N. McMurry got right to the point: "The most important and unyielding necessity of organizational life is not better communications, human relations, or employee participation, but power."[38] Clearly, McMurry disdained all those references to the new organization man who required a new kind of leader. Rather he was an unrepentant old-timer, whose hero was none other than Niccolò Machiavelli. "Without power there can be no authority," McMurry cautioned. "And without authority there can be no discipline."[39]

Four years later, John Kotter, who has since become one of the most widely read scholars of leadership and management, published an article that, while more genteel, had a tone not too different from McMurry's. While acknowledging the antipower mentality of the times, Kotter nevertheless insisted that large, complex organizations required managers who were skilled in the acquisition and use of power.[40] Here is what Kotter claimed successful managers had in common.

1. They are sensitive to what is considered acceptable behavior in the acquisition and use of power.
2. They have a good intuitive understanding of the various types of power and methods of influence.
3. They develop all the types of power and use all the methods of influence.
4. They establish career goals and seek out managerial positions that allow them to develop and use power.
5. They use all of their resources to develop still more power.
6. They engage in power-oriented behavior in ways that are tempered by maturity and self-control.
7. They accept as legitimate that they influence other people's behavior and lives.[41]

Perhaps nothing demonstrates the impact of politics on business as much as the attention paid at this time to the matter of "full equality in employment" for women. Business and industry were clearly being pressured to improve on what had been an abysmal record of discrimination against all those other than white males.

Now men were told to hire women because they were required

to do so by the 1964 Civil Rights Act, and because in 1972 an order was issued requiring government contractors to initiate affirmative action programs, and because it was determined that "Equal Opportunity for Women is Smart Business." As General Electric put it in a pamphlet distributed to all managers, "The [women's] movement is not a fad or an aberration, but a major social force with great and growing impact on business and other social, political and economic institutions. As such, it must be taken seriously by business managers; its future potential must be foreseen and constructive responses must be designed to meet legitimate demands."[42]

Again, much of the attention was devoted to instruction: how to teach white male managers who had been socialized during a time when such things didn't matter to make the personal and organizational changes necessary to bring women on board. Affirmative action programs were designed to "show the steps which organizations must take to foster equal treatment of the sexes." Studies were set up to overcome the belief that "young males are still considered better risk for entry-level managers than young females." Initiatives were detailed for organizations that claimed they were interested in "employing more women managers." And men were furnished with proof that even though they thought they made decisions and evaluations "that are not sexually biased, just the opposite is probably the case."

One of the best books in the area reads almost as well today as it did when it was first published. Rosabeth Moss Kanter's *Men and Women of the Corporation*, while very much a product of its times, nevertheless still pertains.[43] Of course Kanter had an agenda. As she said at the outset of the book, "I was also motivated by my involvement in the women's movement to seek understanding of the fate of women as well as men in organizations."[44] But she was careful to insist that change on behalf of women and minorities would also benefit everyone else. Moreover, she claimed, minority rights would be good for business.

Kanter focused on power. "I am using 'power' in a sense that distinguishes it from hierarchical domination. As defined here, power is the ability to get things done."[45] She also provided hints on how power could be gained. (Clearly, as she defined it, power was a widely available resource.) They included making useful social connections; soliciting mentors; initiating peer alliances; and informing women about the biases and stereotypes that had always held them back. In the end, Kanter's work was not very different from Townsend's. Both concluded that the old power structures had become fossilized, and that in the future managers would have to become planners and professionals rather than merely watchdogs.

Toward the end of the 1970s, Abraham Zaleznik made an important early distinction between leaders and managers. In a piece written for HBR, he claimed that because they were different personality types, "managers and leaders differ fundamentally in their world views." These differences, Zaleznik wrote, were evident in their goals, in their attitudes toward work, in their interpersonal relations, and in their orientations toward themselves.[46]

These differences would be much discussed in the coming years. In any case, the legacy of the 1970s was clear. On paper at least the top tier had been brought down a notch (or two), and those in the middle and at the bottom of the organizational pyramid became part of the dialogue on corporate governance. As Argyris noted in 1973, traditional management theories had produced slow but steady deterioration. The goal now was the improvement of organizational life and the creation of a more "human" work environment that would also, surely, boost company performance.[47]

The reality

Despite the rapidly changing rhetoric that characterized the literature on management during this period, in reality things moved more slowly. Women and African Americans in particular found the 1970s promised far more than they delivered.

This is not to say progress was insignificant. In 1973 General Electric reported that as a consequence of changes in how executives were judged and compensated, it had raised minority employment at all levels by an impressive 57 percent. Moreover, theorists continued throughout the decade to work on the problem of how to bring about change more quickly. In 1976 two Harvard Business School professors wrote that practically no company had yet achieved full equality in employment for women and minorities because "it is doubtful that many government officials or business executives fully understand the real dynamics of the problem." They argued for a "flow of women and minority-group men through each management level."[48]

Still, in general, reports from the trenches were less than encouraging. One of the problems with which women had to contend was the training they received. While companies reported they planned to hire significantly more women in the 1970s, they expected new hires to have majored either in accounting or business. Yet in 1971 only 2.8 percent of all women graduates received degrees in these fields—compared with 22 percent of all male graduates. Moreover, women continued to be far more likely than men to drop out of the labor force, which meant that recruiters continued to think of women hires as something of a gamble.

Once they reached positions of authority, women were still at a considerable disadvantage. By 1978, women who had received their MBAs from Harvard in 1973 discovered that they were slower than men to emerge as "stars"; that men were twice as likely to hold upper-level management positions and be involved in setting organizational policy; and that men were earning significantly more money.[49]

In short, good intentions notwithstanding, women continued to have little access to leading roles in American business. In 1978 only one woman—Katherine Graham, who had inherited the *Washington Post* from her father and husband—was CEO of a major American company.

Predictably, African Americans fared no better. Estimates were that in 1972 less than 3 percent of the line managers and officers in industry were black, and that most of them were in the lower reaches of management. Only a tiny number of African Americans held vice presidencies, and no major corporation had a black CEO.

More significant, perhaps, was the degree to which those African Americans who did "make it" felt uneasy. Dr. Stuart Taylor, a black psychologist who taught at the Harvard Business School, concluded on the basis of a two-year study that "as blacks in management jobs are pulled one way by corporate conformism, and another by the growing desire to assert their separate black identity," their level of stress increases.[50]

Frequently African American executives found themselves assigned to areas in which they dealt largely with other African Americans—such as urban affairs, community relations, and "special" (read African American) markets. As Ernest Holsendolph wrote in *Fortune* in 1972, "These jobs are black islands in white industry. The executives who occupy them are often well paid, but they have little or no impact on company profits, and little or no prospect of getting onto a track that leads to the top levels of management."[51]

An autobiographical article published by *Harvard Business Review* in 1973 confirmed the problem. Edward W. Jones Jr. described the experience of being a black manager who sought to climb the corporate ladder in a white organization. "During those years, I found myself examining my actions, strategies, and emotional stability. I found myself trying desperately to separate fact from mental fiction. I found myself enveloped in almost unbearable emotional stress and internal conflict, trying to hold the job as a constant and evaluate my personal shortcomings with respect to it."[52]

Clearly, change in the private sector was slow. With few exceptions, corporate leaders in the 1970s were what they had been previously: white Christian males. Moreover, the traits that characterized them rang familiar. Case in point? Dave Mahoney. The $350,000-a-year CEO of Norton Simon had a track record to be envied. "Anyone farsighted enough sixteen years ago to have parlayed a $20,000 bet on corporate jockey David J. Mahoney, by successively investing in the companies that hired him, would have made a killing by now," breathed *Fortune*. Described as "an engagingly self-confident man whose bravado masks layers of shrewd calculation," Mahoney had the "attributes for success in the public arena. He is a gregarious man, open-faced, hearty, with a visible curiosity about the people he encounters." Moreover he was tall, "with greying brown hair and a bronzed, slightly battered looking face. . . . At forty-nine, he is a bit flabby about the waist, but his bearing is almost military, and he has the quality that actors call 'presence.' He dominates his surroundings."[53]

Fortune was similarly smitten with Edward Carlson, credited with the turnaround of United Airlines. Unlike his predecessor, a man named George Keck, whom *Fortune* charged with the cardinal sin of being "an introvert, a loner," Carlson was reported to be "warm and outgoing." He knew "how to talk to people, how to make them feel good, and how to do the little things for them that will win their good will. He is a politician, and one of the best, although too gentlemanly to be a backslapper. He drops in from the friendly skies and acts as if he was really interested in every employee."[54]

For all their old-fashioned virtues, both Mahoney and Carlson also demonstrated a more modern capacity: the ability to connect with men and women at all levels of the organizational hierarchy. Both were praised for what appeared to be their genuine interest in other people, and both were credited with being responsive to those around them.

The tensions permeating American business during the 1970s were apparent in one of the nation's leading firms: the Ford Motor Company. On the surface, the past prevailed, with Henry Ford II presiding over the company to considerable acclaim. In 1978 Ford completed the three best years in its history; in terms of earnings it ranked fourth among all U.S. industrial companies. But at corporate headquarters in Dearborn, Michigan, things were less placid than they appeared. It was not at all clear that Henry Ford was the man to lead the company into the 1980s, or even that the leadership of the Ford Motor Company should continue to be a function of family ties.[55]

What was certain was that one of America's leading industries, automobiles, was about to face a new kind of competition from abroad. Were "the big three"—Ford, General Motors, and Chrysler—equipped to meet the challenge? Of his own tenure Ford said, "thirty-three years is too long." Yet he made no provision for his succession, and had only recently fired, in an unexpected outburst, the man considered likely to replace him, Lee Iacocca.

There was another straw in the wind at another one of America's great companies, E. I. du Pont de Nemours & Co. Du Pont was then the twenty-third largest industrial enterprise in the world. It had been in existence one hundred and seventy-five years, and had during this entire time only one CEO not related to the Du Pont family. In 1974 the board appointed a second chairman of the board and chief executive officer who was not a clan member. But this time the choice was utterly improbable: the son of a poor Jewish shopkeeper who, along with his wife, was a Lithuanian immigrant.

The selection of Irving Shapiro as head of Du Pont sent two signals. First, it indicated that Du Pont, like Ford, was in a period of transition. The increasingly complex domestic and international environments within which Du Pont now had to compete demanded a leader of a different kind, a leader with the training and experience to cope with new legal, political, and technological complexities.

Second, the choice of a man like Shapiro, although still uncommon, suggested that tradition was loosening its iron grip. Shapiro's strength was his expertise. His rise to the top at Du Pont indicated that in some quarters at least, the need for a new kind of corporate leader was being recognized.[56]

In the end, however, the 1970s were more remarkable for what was said than what was done. The rhetoric spoke to change, but the amount of change that actually took place was meager. To be sure, there was a newfound emphasis on relating, on interpersonal skills. As the chairman of the Bendix Corporation, W. Michael Blumenthal, put it, "You can't operate successfully in any organization if you're cut off from your people. You've got to reach out toward them . . . and let them know they can reach you when they feel they have to."[57] There was also a modest push to democratize, to flatten the business hierarchy. International Harvester, for example, was reorganized in ways that prefigured the corporate landscape a decade and a half later.[58]

But when all was said and done CEOs such as Shapiro and Blumenthal were the exception rather than the rule. In general, despite what was happening in the public sector and despite the new corporate ideology that promised something new and different, those at the top resisted rather than embraced change. While young Turks chafed at the bottom of the corporate ladder, most of those who remained in charge were not very different from their predecessors. Slow to decipher the handwriting on the wall, and personally comfortable where they were, by and large America's top business leaders had to be pushed, kicking and screaming, to another place. (Arguably, this push came from the East. "The Japanese are Coming—With Their Own Style of Management," trumpeted *Fortune* mid-decade.")[59]

Robert Townsend insisted that decisions should be made toward the bottom of the organizational hierarchy rather than at the top. And Chris Argyris warned that traditional management theories produced organizational atrophy. But while old habits began to give way during the decade, they did so only slowly and grudgingly. Women and African Americans were still almost entirely excluded from the boardroom. Those running American businesses looked very much like those who had been running American businesses all along. And decision making was only marginally more democratic than it had been heretofore. The fact of the matter is that most business leaders stayed stuck. Unable to bend with the shifting wind, they, and millions of workers obliged to follow their lead, eventually paid dearly for insisting on keeping things more or less as they were.

3
The 1980s
Narrowing the Differences

The 1980s were fixated on leadership. Ronald Reagan did no less than change the American political discourse; and Lee Iacocca proved that U.S. business had a future even in an age of increasing global competitiveness. Between them they defined a decade that, for all the newfangled talk of constituents, followers, and subordinates, was still distinguished by its obsession with how great men can do great things.

POLITICAL LEADERSHIP

The ideas

During the 1980s I myself wrote and edited no less than five books with the word "leadership" in the title: *Leadership: Multidisciplinary Perspectives;*[1] *The Political Presidency: Practice of Leadership;*[2] *Women Leaders in American Politics;*[3] *Political Leadership: A Source Book;*[4] and *Leadership and Negotiation in the Middle East.*[5]

For better or worse, I was hardly alone. There was a veritable explosion in the 1980s of books and articles about leadership. There was even a distinction between the beginning of the decade and the end. Between 1980 and 1983 an average of three books a year on leadership were published; by the end of the eighties the number had climbed to twenty-three.[6]

Why the proliferation? Changes in business and industry that suggested the old ways of doing business would no longer suffice. Changes in American politics that created new, more tenuous, relationships between leaders and led. Changes in the American culture

61

that threatened previously established authorities. Changes in technology that altered the way leaders and led conversed. And Ronald Reagan.

In the event, for all the increase in the quantity of books on leadership, qualitatively they in most ways resembled their predecessors. The definitions were familiar.[7] And the literature as a whole continued to fall into the two conventional categories—books and articles that focused exclusively on leadership in the public sector and books and articles that focused exclusively on management (now, increasingly, called leadership) in the private sector.

Those with an interest in political leadership were particularly taken with a slender volume by Robert C. Tucker titled *Politics as Leadership*.[8] Tucker claimed that leadership is the very essence of politics—a view that grew out of his extensive work on the Soviet Union. In fact, *Politics as Leadership* emerged from an earlier essay titled "The Dictator and Totalitarianism" in which Tucker argued that in some circumstances at least—for example, in the case of Stalin— the impact of personality on politics is great.[9]

Tucker made another important point. While psychologists had long understood that leaders do not necessarily hold formal positions of authority, it was not a concept that had really reached those who study politics. Tucker broke ground by writing about "nonconstituted leaders"—persons who are political leaders "without possessing power or occupying high political office." (Examples Tucker gave included Mohandas Gandhi, Martin Luther King Jr., Dr. Albert Schweitzer, and Andrei Sakharov.)

Another student of communism also pointed to what political scientists in general were slow to recognize—that sometimes leaders really matter. In her 1981 book *Do New Leaders Make a Difference?* Valerie Bunce concluded that "particular leaders do seem to matter when they are in their honeymoons. In this sense, while environment is always important, it is more malleable and more supportive of elite direction and innovation during the honeymoon in office."[10]

The interest in political leadership during this period spawned a new type: the political entrepreneur. In a book titled *Public Entrepreneurship,* Eugene Lewis looked at what he called the "organizational lives" of Hyman Rickover, J. Edgar Hoover, and Robert Moses. He concluded that they (and selected others, of course) were a breed apart. They were "persons who create or profoundly elaborate public organizations so as to alter greatly the existing pattern of allocation of scarce public resources."[11] Lewis pointed out that public entrepreneurs have a high degree of autonomy and flexibility while at the same time they are able to limit outside interference in their affairs. He did not use the word *leader* to describe his public entrepreneurs, but clearly they were men who created far greater change than their less enterprising and more conventional counterparts.

Later in the decade (1987), Jameson Doig and Erwin Hargrove came out with an edited volume related to Lewis's work. In a collection titled *Leadership and Innovation: A Biographical Perspective on Entrepreneurs in Government,* they covered change agents from James Forrestal to Nancy Hanks.[12] Interestingly, Doig and Hargrove made a point of distinguishing themselves from colleagues who played down the role of the individual leader. For example, they took issue with the well-known political scientist Herbert Kaufman, who had argued that even agency heads who hurl themselves into the fray make their marks in inches, not miles.[13]

All this attention to leadership prompted a return to the charismatic leader. The idea of charismatic leadership was developed, of course, in the nineteenth century by the renowned German sociologist, Max Weber. In the 1980s Ann Ruth Willner revived the notion in a book titled *The Spellbinders: Charismatic Political Leadership.*[14] To be sure, the term "charisma" had been in the marketplace for some time, at least in the United States. Since John Kennedy, any politician with any appeal at all was said to possess that ineffable something that came to be known as charisma. But the original definition of "charisma" was narrower. As Willner points out, if the relationship between leaders and followers is genuinely charismatic, followers believe their leader to have nearly superhuman qualities. They go along with the leader's directives simply because he (rarely is a charismatic leader a "she") asks them to, and they respond to the leader with a fervor more typically associated with religion than politics.

Because of the devotional nature of genuine charisma, it was generally considered to have gone out of fashion in the twentieth century. After all, what place is there for an authentic charismatic leader in an era enamored of science and technology? Certainly, until Willner, no American social scientist had updated the concept and applied it to modern political leaders ranging from Adolph Hitler to the Ayatollah Khomeini. But clearly the time was ripe for a fresh inquiry—particularly into the question of how charismatic leadership came to pass in an age when, to all appearances, it should have been irrelevant.

If charismatic leadership says, perhaps, more about the psychology of followers than leaders, psychohistories (or psychobiographies) do just the opposite. A good psychobiography seeks to answer the riveting Freudian question: What makes this man tick? (Again, few psychobiographies are about women.) While the 1980s' penchant for books on leadership did not result in major new psychobiographies, they did solidify a related trend: one in which details of leaders' personal lives were laid bare, presumably in the lofty expectation that their true characters would thus be revealed.

In truth, the decade gave rise to little more in this regard than the elevation of *People* magazine and, eventually, the *National Inquirer* to mainstream journalism. Americans became hellbent on learning what they could about the private lives of those who would lead them.

To be sure, the evolution was a gradual one. In the 1930s and 1940s the American people scarcely knew that their president could not walk unassisted. And they certainly were in the dark about FDR's great love affair with Lucy Mercer. In the 1960s the Kennedys were still lying to the American people about the condition of (lobotomized) sister Rosemary, and John Kennedy's by now well-known penchant for bedding women other than his wife Jacqueline remained a well-kept secret. It was First Lady Betty Ford who in the 1970s pushed the envelope: She told us she talked about sex with her daughter; mentioned marijuana in connection with her son; and disclosed to all the world that she had breast cancer. (After leaving the White House Betty Ford also made public her addiction to drugs and drink.)

By the late 1980s the gloves were off. Our popular and political culture had "progressed" to the point where sex, drugs, and rock and roll were fair game—largely because it was somehow assumed that too much of a bad thing at the individual level was too much of a bad thing at the national level. As Gary Hart's brief fling with the presidency demonstrated, by 1988 a single slip—Hart was caught playing games with Donna Rice who was not, as it happened, Mrs. Hart—could be politically lethal.

The personalization of political leadership coarsened the political process, but it also worked to the advantage of those rare specimens who shone in the hot glare of the limelight. Indisputably, one such leader was the man who dominated American politics in the 1980s: Ronald Reagan. Reagan became known as "the Teflon president" precisely because no matter what he did, or what went on around him, he personally remained nearly immune to criticism. Put another way, in an era in which high-visibility leaders came under growing scrutiny, Reagan managed to emerge virtually unscathed.

His origins as a movie actor notwithstanding, Reagan's greatest impact was actually in the realm of ideas—ideas about how Americans thought about politics, and ideas about how they thought about the presidency itself. So far as ideology is concerned, the term "Reagan Revolution" says it all. Reagan's notions about downsizing government, about devolution, and about the importance of individual responsibility were no less than a radical departure from the liberal mindset that had dominated American political thought since the New Deal.

Reagan was nothing so much as a throwback to an earlier time when the simple verities held. They included

• American exceptionalism. According to Reagan, "Someone once said that the difference between an American and any other kind of person is that an American lives in anticipation of the future because he knows it will be a great place."[15]

• American self-help. As biographer Lou Cannon put it, Reagan imagined that "the American nation had been carved from wilderness by pioneers unrestrained by the forces of nature or the power of the state."[16]

• Limited government. Cannon writes that Reagan complained constantly that government "does not solve problems, it subsidizes them."[17]

• Congenital optimism. Reagan was a true believer. He combined disarming modesty with brash self-assurance and he believed all things were possible. "If there is one thing we are sure of, it is . . . that man is capable of improving his circumstances beyond what we are told is fact."[18]

Reagan's ideas presaged the convergence of private- and public-sector leadership. For example, his push to downsize what he considered a bloated federal bureaucracy popularized the idea of efficiency in government. Amazing! For the first time in a long time the nation's chief executive resembled nothing so much as a private-sector leader determined to keep the organization lean and mean. And with regard to his push for decentralization, Reagan did no less than transform the executive role. As Aaron Wildavsky observed, "In Reagan's time the Presidency [became] the institution of 'last resort,' entering the fray only when others abdicated."[19]

Remarkably, in spite of his limited intellectual capacities, Reagan also had an impact on our conception of the presidency itself. The eight years of Ronald Reagan did no less than reaffirm the fact that a single leader can make a major difference. Before Reagan the American presidency had for two decades been under attack. Kennedy was shot. Johnson was obliged to retire after only one full term. Nixon was compelled to resign in disgrace. Ford was denied his own tenure. And Carter was kicked out after four years.

To the surprise of nearly everyone, then, Ronald Reagan was able to accomplish two major feats. He became the first president since Dwight Eisenhower to serve two full terms in the White House; and he redirected the ship of state. In short, Ronald Reagan singlehandedly reversed our conception of what late-twentieth-century presidents could accomplish if they were both skilled and lucky.

In an early assessment of the Reagan presidency, Fred Greenstein wrote: "Reagan and company reversed the notion that presidency was becoming increasingly powerless."[20] By the time Reagan left the White House there was near consensus. He had maintained control of the national political agenda, "in part by concrete accomplishments, but also by exuding confidence and self-assurance."[21] Moreover Ronald Reagan had provided "about as much direction as the existing American anti-leadership system can support."[22]

Was it, in fact, the Reagan presidency that inspired at least some of the many books on leadership published during the 1980s? Hard to say. What is clear is that by the time the 1980s were over the study of leadership was respectable. As Jean Blondel put it, "The detailed study of . . . political leadership is more than mere curiosity about the behavior of the men and women who rule the world: it is directly and inextricably linked to the attempt to ensure that political leadership improves in the generations to come."[23]

The reality

In 1980, *Washington Post* columnist David Broder published a book titled *Changing of the Guard*. Broder argued that leadership in America was changing and that the "next ones in the leadership succession" had experiences different from those who preceded them.[24] In the last chapter of the book Broder describes an "extraordinarily intense" young congressman from Georgia by the name of Newt Gingrich. Even as a freshman legislator Gingrich attracted attention. Why? Because he had the vision and drive to push his agenda—to achieve the majority that had eluded House Republicans since 1952.[25] His plan was to make government more efficient by reducing the federal bureaucracy and cutting taxes and spending.

One of the early signs of Gingrich's political genius was his use of television. In particular, he capitalized on the House schedule. At about seven P.M., after its regular business ends, the House goes into "special orders"—which means individual members are free to give long speeches because most of their colleagues have gone home. Gingrich seized that moment to preach his politics. With C-Span still operating, he eventually had a daily television audience of more than 250,000.[26]

In fact, it was becoming nearly impossible to exercise political leadership at the national level without using television. To be sure, television had played a role in presidential politics since the 1960 presidential campaign. But never was a chief executive so good at milking the medium as the "Great Communicator," Ronald Reagan. (During his years in the White House, Reagan also had a regular radio show. He used air time to take strong stands on a variety of issues, knowing that by and large he was addressing listeners who relished sermonettes on topics as diverse as farm problems, tax legislation, Communist subversion abroad, and modern morality.)[27]

The Reagan White House also understood that television was, of course, more about pictures than words. The president's trip to Normandy was a case in point. Having arranged that he would arrive on the fortieth anniversary of D-Day, Reagan's image makers took advantage of the occasion. The site they chose for the delivery of his carefully crafted speech was Pointe du Hoc, an enormous rock that jetted out to the sea. Moreover, they positioned the president smack in front of a memorial to the U.S. Army Rangers who during World War II had actually scaled the 130-foot cliff. Finally, they handpicked their audience: aging veterans who decades earlier had done the deed and who naturally wept when listening to Reagan's words.[28]

For a student of leadership, it is difficult to overestimate the importance of Reagan's skill as a communicator. As Hart pointed out, "By the time he entered office, Ronald Reagan was well prepared to cope with the 'rhetorical reflex.' Indeed, he may well have been chosen for the office precisely because he possessed this reflex."[29]

Of course, in order for Reagan to accomplish what a previous string of presidents had failed to do required more than rhetorical skills. He also possessed

- Clarity of purpose. Reagan's agenda was short and simple and he stuck to it unwaveringly.
- The capacity to implement. Reagan put together a generally strong team that, especially during the first term, was able to put into practice what had previously been preached.
- The ability to be ingratiating. Never pompous or self-important, Reagan retained the innate simplicity and modesty that had served him well since his early days in Hollywood.
- Pleasure in, and a capacity for, politics. Unlike his immediate predecessor, Reagan enjoyed, understood the need for, and excelled at personal politicking.
- Congenital optimism. Reagan believed the United States was the best of all possible places in this best of all possible worlds. Problems could be solved and endings would be happy.
- Skilled use of power. Because he appeared both democratic and friendly, it was relatively easy for him to sell himself in the political marketplace. Of how many presidents can it be said that they were able to drive a "velvet steamroller" through the Congress and "flatten" their opponents in such a way that it was "almost painless."[30]

Reagan's success in the White House gave rise to fresh optimism about the ability of those at the top to create change. During the 1980s books on the presidency had titles like *The President's Agenda*,[31] *The Strategic Presidency*,[32] and *Presidents, Politics, and Policy*.[33] Each was based on the assumption that, in the words of one of the authors, "The conduct of the presidency does depend to a great extent upon the mind and character of the president."[34] In other words, along with everyone else, scholars who saw Reagan in action concluded that a gifted chief executive could still exercise considerable power and influence.

However, political leaders in institutions other than the presidency had a more sobering experience. For all the fresh attention to leadership, and for all the rediscovery of clout in the White House, leaders in different places found it increasingly difficult to get others to go along. The Senate, for example, continued on a course established at least a decade earlier. That is, it was more open, fluid, and decentralized than it had been before—which made life difficult even for those with the most power. To be sure, majority and minority leaders had the most influence. In particular, more than anyone else, the majority leader retained the right to set the agenda. But, as Senator Robert Byrd's (Democrat from West Virginia) extended tenure as both majority and minority leader testified, and as another majority and minority leader, Senator Robert Dole (Republican from Kansas), confirmed, "The leadership is powerless unless the senators are willing to give them authority."[35]

Byrd was either majority or minority leader from 1977 to 1988. Nevertheless he remained a loner. He relied less on personal popularity than on hard work, ideological pragmatism, and deep institutional loyalty. As Ross Baker wrote, "While having no close personal friends among members and little aptitude or inclination for sociability and intimacy, a leader such as Byrd is capable of being perceived as a friend because of his ability to inspire trust, work hard, and provide accurate assessments of political and legislative outcomes, conferring by doing so a sense of security upon both the institution and the individual senator."[36]

Still, Byrd found it hard to get others to go along. To be sure, the larger political context within which he operated did not help. During the years Byrd was majority leader (1977–79 and 1987–88), the White House was occupied either by an ineffectual Democrat or by a popular Republican. And during the years Byrd was minority leader, Reagan was in his prime. Still, the fact of the matter is that for all his experience Byrd found it hard to lead. The number of reasons even Democrats had for following the party line were simply dwindling.

The exceptionalism of the Reagan experience was further confirmed at the grass roots. In particular, African Americans found it impossible to replace fallen heroes such as Martin Luther King and Malcolm X. To be sure, individual black leaders made major strides—for example, in 1983 Harold Washington was elected mayor of Chicago and Wilson Goode mayor of Philadelphia. Moreover Jesse Jackson's 1984 and 1988 presidential campaigns increased the level of participation by African Americans across the board. Nevertheless, the black community was increasingly divided. Growing distinctions between the black middle and lower classes threatened to split the community, and not even Jackson and his well-publicized "Rainbow Coalition" was able to bridge the various gaps.

Women had a similarly frustrating experience during the 1980s, particularly with regard to their inability to pass the Equal Rights Amendment (ERA). In March 1972, the ERA sailed through the Senate by an overwhelming margin (84 to 8). In addition, in the ensuing ten years a majority of Americans continued to favor passage. Yet on June 30, 1982, the deadline for ratification passed. When push came to shove, only thirty-five of the required thirty-eight states were on board for the ERA.

The failure of the women's movement to develop an effective leadership cadre played a role in its defeat. It hampered the ability of women to organize within their own ranks, and inevitably reduced their capacity to reach out to constituencies other than their own.[37]

By mid-decade, Reagan notwithstanding, there had emerged in America the widespread impression that government was not working very well. It seemed that most political leaders were, for whatever reasons, incapable of fixing what was broke. Put another way, in addition to the frustration of leaders who found it increasingly difficult to get things done, followers now felt that leaders were part of the problem. Explanations for the growing level of dissatisfaction abounded. They included

- Divided government;
- Gridlock;
- Increasingly nasty political discourse;
- Increase in independent voters and ticket splitters;
- Decline in party discipline;
- Growing gap between campaigning and governing;
- Increased attention to image;
- Decreased attention to issues;
- Rise of lobbyists and political consultants;
- Interest group politics;
- Decline in civic engagement;
- Television;
- Metamorphosis of politicians into celebrities;
- The "me decade."

This last point bears repeating. In their classic book on American life in the 1980s, *Habits of the Heart*, Robert Bellah and his colleagues discuss the culture of individualism—and its relationship to leadership. "For all the lip service given to respect for cultural differences, Americans seem to lack the resources to think about the relationship between groups that are culturally, socially, or economically quite different." This collective inability to cope with difference led "many to believe that only effective 'leadership,' with the assistance of technical expertise, can meet the problems of our invisible complexity."[38]

As the 1980s drew to a close, George Bush was in the White House. It soon became clear that in general his leadership skills were weak (his performance during the Gulf War was a notable exception), and his standing in the polls declined accordingly. So far as political leadership in America was concerned the mood of the moment was bleak and the "changing of the guard" to which Broder had referred when the decade was young had yet to be realized. Bush was a veteran of World War II and he grew to political maturity in the heyday of the Cold War. Neither he nor, for that matter, any of his contemporaries seemed equipped to lead America into the twenty-first century. The question remained: Who were "the next ones in the leadership succession" and when exactly would they take the perennial bull by its perennial horns?

BUSINESS MANAGEMENT/LEADERSHIP

The ideas
By the mid-1980s, leadership was definitely "in." No longer did the captains of business and industry speak of "executives" or "managers." The word *du jour* was "leadership" and it was on the lips of everyone who was anyone. As *Fortune* put it in 1983: "It's in the air, trend spotters, just about ready to precipitate in the swirling clouds of economic change, and rain down on us in a thousand articles and speeches. . . . This soon to be very hot subject is leadership."[39]

The attention to leadership was, above all, a manifestation of the sense that all was not well. By the 1980s it had become clear that the world was changing in ways that threatened the well-being of a corporate sector that at least since the end of the World War II had dominated not only the American economy but the global economy as well. In fact, this sense of unease, and the accompanying data that seemed to confirm it, permeated nearly every book on leadership that was published during this period.

In her 1983 book *The Change Masters: Innovation and Entrepreneurship in the American Corporation*, Rosabeth Moss Kanter made the point. "Not long ago," she wrote, "American companies seemed to control the world in which they operated." Now we were in a much scarier world, one in which factors such as the control of oil by OPEC, foreign competition, inflation, and regulation "disturb the smooth workings of corporate machines and threaten to overwhelm us." Kanter went on to talk about the American economy "slipping into the doldrums," noting that "economists argue about whether the first letter in the economy of the early 1980s is *R* (recession) or *D* (depression)."[40]

In his 1988 book *The Leadership Factor*, John Kotter held more or less the same view. He described what he called the growing "competitive intensity." In some cases this was because strong foreign firms had invaded other domestic markets—for example, in automobiles. In others, change was the consequence of deregulation—for example, in the airline and insurance industries. And in still other cases the greater competition was the result of market maturity or overcapacity. Kotter continued, "Whatever the source, the new competitive intensity has destabilized companies and even whole industries. It has . . . created a level of turbulence that is sometimes extraordinary, especially when compared to the 1950s and 1960s."[41]

But not every problem was thought to be a consequence of objective change. In *Leaders: The Strategies for Taking Charge,* Warren Bennis and Burt Nanus blamed leaders themselves. If ever there was a moment when a strategic view of leadership was needed, the authors wrote, "this is certainly it." (The book was published in 1985.) But, Bennis and Nanus contended, leaders were falling short. "These days power is conspicuous in its absence . . . . Institutions have been rigid, slothful, or mercurial. Supposed leaders seem ignorant and out of touch, insensitive and unresponsive."[42]

The reasons for America's growing inferiority complex were complex, but so far as the private sector was concerned they can, arguably, be summed up in one word: Japan. American business was thrown for a loop by the swiftness and sureness with which Japan had forged ahead. Japan provided stiff competition for the United States in the production and distribution of goods; and it also seemed to have new and better ideas on leadership and management. In other words, such an inferiority complex as Americans did suffer was specifically vis-à-vis the Japanese.

Consider the introduction to the 1980s mega-hit by Thomas Peters and Robert Waterman, *In Search of Excellence: Lessons from America's Best-Run Companies.* The monster out to get us was clearly Japan.

- "We hear stories every other day about the Japanese companies, their unique culture and the proclivity for meeting, singing company songs, and changing the corporate litany."[43]
- "Finally, it dawned on us that we did not have to look all the way to Japan for models with which to attack the corporate malaise that has us in its viselike grip."[44]
- "Good management practice today is not resident only in Japan."[45]

In fact, as the above statement in particular indicates, perhaps the single best explicator of the enormous success of *In Search of Excellence* was its very premise: that Americans could beat the Japanese at their own game. It was not true, Peters and Waterman argued, that Americans had lost it. On the contrary. In fact, there were in the United States many companies that were being splendidly run and managed, and that were able to shine even in an environment of "competitive intensity."

For all the new buzzwords that had permeated the literature on leadership and management since at least the early 1970s, when push came to shove, as it did during the 1980s, the answer to our problems still was thought to be leadership by a select few. Here was the pattern. The patient, the United States, was diagnosed as being in serious condition. The cure for what ailed us? Good leadership. The leadership literature's newfound attention to followers notwithstanding, as before, good leadership was thought to be all about the ability of a select few to do the right thing at the right time in the right way.

To be fair, the nature of leadership had presumably changed. It was no longer possible for corporate titans to rule from on high, remote and inaccessible. In order to succeed in the new climate, in which change was as much political as it was economic, leaders had to interact with constituencies including employees, board members, and leaders in other organizations.

Tellingly, although they were talking to business, Peters and Waterman borrowed from politics. They drew on James MacGregor Burns's concept of the transforming leader who, of course, had emerged from the political realm. "We are fairly sure," they write, "that the culture of almost every excellent company . . . can be traced to transforming leadership somewhere in its history. . . . The transforming leader is . . . the value shaper, the exemplar, the maker of meanings." [46] Peters and Waterman also played up, as Burns did, the need for what they called a "leader-follower symbiosis." Without it, they claimed, such important leader attributes as believability and excitement would be nearly impossible to convey.

What is striking here is an irony first described by Joseph Rost. In *Leadership for the Twenty-First Century,* he has a chapter called "Leadership Definitions: The 1980s." The chapter is replete with definitions of leadership ranging from leadership as management (old-fashioned) to leadership as transformation (new, hip). But at the end of the chapter Rost comments that while he once believed that Burns had begun the process of reformulating our understanding of leadership, by the late eighties he had changed his mind. Leadership was still being cast "as great men and women with certain preferred traits influencing followers to do what the leaders wish."[47]

This curious combination of being simultaneously leader-centric ("individual executives who have developed specific skills create superior organizational performance") and follower-centric ("excellent companies create environments within which people can blossom, develop self-esteem, and otherwise be excited participants in the business and society as a whole") characterizes the 1980s leadership literature. It is, to understate it, confusing. Still, it is a confusion that must be mastered in order for the convergence between public-sector leadership and private-sector management to become clear.

Nearly every important book on business leadership that came out in the 1980s reflects this fusion. Whether or not Reagan fuelled the phenomenon is uncertain. One may reasonably speculate, however, that a president who was both a visionary and a communicator contributed to the increasing frequency with which leaders were seen to be, simultaneously, directive and responsive.

The strategies of leadership outlined by Bennis and Nanus reflect the trend. Three out of the four focus on the leaders' capacity to engage their constituencies—getting their attention, gaining their support, and earning their trust. (Only strategy #4 focuses entirely on the self—on creating what is termed positive self-regard.)[48] Kanter and Kotter also address the need for change masters to build coalitions. Kanter writes about lining up supporters, bestowing favors in exchange for support, and securing the blessings of others;[49] while Kotter describes network building as one of the cornerstones of effective leadership in complex organizations.[50] Finally, in his popular text titled *Leadership in Organizations,* Gary Yukl describes relationships with others—subordinates, peers and superiors—as the single most important leadership variable.[51]

Quite clearly, definitions of good private-sector management began during this period to look remarkably like what was supposed to constitute good public-sector leadership. It was no accident that Burns's "transforming" political leader made his way to the head of the class in the corporate world. For a complex set of reasons that ranged from changes in the economy to changes in the culture, business leaders felt increasing pressure to develop the political skills of their public-sector counterparts.

There is, however, one aspect of the literature on leadership in business that is not at all evident in the literature on leadership on politics: self-help. While the notion of self-help may be variously defined, it surely relates to what Bennis and Nanus call "the creative deployment of self." (This includes recognizing strengths and compensating for weaknesses; nurturing skills and developing talents; and acquiring "emotional wisdom.") If all this sounds curiously "new-agey," or vaguely psychotherapeutic in nature, that's because it is. Borrowing rather heavily from some of the know-thyself and work-on-thyself thinking that was so popular during the 1980s (and indeed still is), Bennis in particular evolved during this period into a strong advocate of leader self-awareness. In his (1989) book titled *On Becoming a Leader,* Bennis preaches the lessons of self-knowledge such as, "you are your own best teacher," and "true understanding comes from reflecting on your own experience."[52] He concludes a chapter on "knowing thyself" with the following equation: "Self-awareness=self-knowledge=self-possession=self-control=self-expression."[53] (To understand Bennis's approach to leadership, which has been highly influential in corporate America, it is helpful to know that, among his other experiences, he had six years of psychoanalysis.)

In the 1980s, leadership training programs that particularly emphasized personal growth began to flourish. According to Jay Conger, a Professor of Organizational Behavior who evaluated many different leadership programs, those that emphasized personal growth were generally based on the assumption that leaders are individuals who are "deeply in touch with their personal dreams and talents and who will act to fulfill them."[54] The Leadership Development Program at the highly successful Center for Creative Leadership in Greensboro, North Carolina, is an example. As Conger relates it, throughout their time at the Center leaders and managers receive feedback from both staff and peers. Finally, "armed with information on an array of dimensions, participants return home with insights into how their behavior affects themselves and others. It is assumed that after the program, participants will have the personal motivation to improve."[55]

The degree to which the notions of self-knowledge, self-help, and self-improvement permeated the literature on leadership in large organizations during this period is confirmed in a book written by

Perry Smith titled *Taking Charge*. Smith is not just another business school type trying to ride a trend. Rather, he is Major General Perry Smith, USAF Retired, who for many years headed the National War College in Washington and developed its professional leadership program. While most of *Taking Charge* is a brisk and practical guide on how to run an organization, two of the chapters turn inward. In the first, Smith argues that personality assessment tools and health testing can be helpful to the executive in a number of ways. And in the second he maintains that the mature executive "works hard to become introspective and to get feedback, and to take corrective action where appropriate."[56]

The notion that leaders can help themselves and improve performance has remained confined to the private sector. In fact, the very proliferation of leadership training programs during the 1980s was testimony to the widespread conviction among those in business and industry that leaders can learn. Apparently those in the public sector did not then—nor do they now—generally share this optimism.

The reality

The 1980s were in many ways a time of high anxiety. Despite the happy face of Ronald Reagan, a stock market that went more or less straight up, and the collapse of communism, in the private sector at least tensions were high. The winds of change were breezing through the corridors of corporate America and the consequence was unease.

We have already seen that much of the leadership literature was based on the proposition that American business was in trouble and that only strong men (and maybe an occasional woman) could save the day. In the real world, however, this hypothesis seemed somewhat weak. The evidence was that even those at the highest levels of leadership and management were struggling to stand firm on the shifting ground. Consider this sampling of titles from a single issue of *Fortune,* dated December 1982: "Corporate Strategists Under Fire"; "A Dangerous Time for Economic Policy"; and "Incredible Shrinking Travel Budget." Together they spoke to a wide range of difficulties including the risks of macroeconomic policy, the pressures to become leaner and meaner, and the personal and professional vulnerability of even those at the highest rungs of the corporate ladder.

The sense that leaders themselves were precariously situated permeated the literature they were most likely to read. A *Fortune* article that appeared in September 1982 typified the trend. Titled "Hard Times Catch Up With Executives," the piece detailed the recent decline in executive compensation and clout. It was noted that in the 1970s top managers had grown accustomed to "hearty pay increases and an ever richer banquet of benefits."[57] Now corporations were freezing and cutting salaries, postponing and reducing raises, and suspending cost-of-living allowances, bonuses, and matching contributions to savings and profit sharing plans. More ominously, perhaps, executives were being offered early (read forced) retirement or cut loose altogether.

The bottom line was the bottom line. As profits dwindled in key sectors such as automobiles, heads of companies felt they had to downsize to survive. The numbers told the story. Executives cost their companies roughly double their annual salaries. Therefore, getting rid of a $100,000-a-year manager, and not replacing him, would save an employer about $200,000.

The threat to executives was palpable. An article in *Fortune* detailed John De Lorean's "long downhill ride," going into chapter and verse about how the onetime superstar at General Motors had slid into a life of shady deals and drug busts.[58] Another piece in the same magazine dwelled on the catastrophic fire at a conference center in New York that killed thirteen top Arrow Electronics executives, including the forty-four-year-old chairman and the forty-one-year-old executive vice president.[59]

But problems in American business transcended mere individuals. As the decade matured, systemic solutions themselves became problematical. For example, Japanese management methods, which had been seen as something of a magic bullet, were now called into question. As *Fortune* put it, "Lots of U.S. companies have tried to import quality and productivity magic from across the Pacific. Some are finding that the unions don't like it, the workers and boss can't hack it, and the factory's the wrong shape and size in the wrong place."[60]

Ironically, given the homage now paid the idea of democracy in the workplace, many of the problems pertained to worker participation. Companies had trouble starting such programs, and then they had trouble sustaining them. When General Motors first attempted to introduce quality circles (1977) they failed to enlist the all-important support of the local union. Moreover, sustaining employee involvement proved downright tricky. In fact, employees themselves proved more resistant than originally anticipated. When push came to shove, those supposedly profiting most from increased worker participation often had trouble adjusting to their new levels of activity and responsibility.

Of course, managers also had to get on board. As *Fortune* noted mid-decade, "Too often the human resources department, hot with the new gospel, will come in and set up the circles without securing commitment in deed, as well as word, from the managers who have to work with the circle's recommendations."[61] A scant two years later another piece appeared that reconfirmed the difficulties. Titled "The Revolt Against Working Smarter," its main point was that managers were resisting participative management programs such as quality circles and work teams precisely because they were often effective—in which case they were a threat to the very supervisors who were supposed to support and maintain them. In other words, in fact the primary blame for why some 75 percent of such participatory programs failed lay not with workers but with management: upper, middle, and lower.[62]

Those who in theory at least were supposed to be among the direct beneficiaries of the democratization of business and industry seemed little better off than they had been previously. African Americans in particular still struggled; indeed in the 1980s attention to them dwindled. Women, on the other hand, were still high on the agenda. The trouble was that their hopes too were, if not exactly dashed, certainly muted.

To be sure, there were pockets of progress—for example, women in banking were doing far better than they had been before. Still, in general the situation was not good. There were basically two reasons for the disappointing performance: the nature of women and the nature of the system.

For their part, women were bailing out. One out of four of the best women MBAs in the class of 1976 had quit her managerial position to start her own business, work part time, or simply stay home. A full 25 percent of the top women MBAs were opting for alternatives other than the long hard climb up the corporate ladder.

Nor was the system changing in ways that made it more responsive to women in particular. In 1984 Katherine Graham was still the only CEO of a major American company.[63] Lesser mortals still had trouble breaking into senior management. The "glass ceiling" was real for many thousands of women who did well for eight or ten years as middle managers, but who then found it difficult if not impossible to keep moving onward and upward. In 1984, only four of the 154 spots at the Harvard Business School's Advanced Management program went to women. Since the thirteen-week program was designed expressly for executives selected to go on to greater heights, the numbers were telling.

The reasons why women then and now are doing less well in the private sector than might have been anticipated only ten or twenty years ago are complex and open to debate. In the event, at least three factors pertain. First, girls are socialized differently from boys, and they are given throughout their lives fewer opportunities to exercise leadership than are their male counterparts. Second, there is evidence to suggest that women may be less motivated to lead than men. Whether this is because they have primary responsibility for bearing and raising children, or because they have different life experiences, or because they have an innately different need for power and/or achievement, remains unclear. The point is that so far as the drive for leadership is concerned, women and men may not be one and the same. Finally, there is the matter of hospitality. Even in the United States, which in comparison with most of the rest of the world has a relatively high number of women in positions of authority, the barriers to progress for women in the upper echelons of corporate America remain formidable.

Given the failures of traditional American management, it comes as no surprise to learn that during this period private-sector heroes were, in one way or another, marginal men. They were not, in other words, grey flannel types who had always played by the rules only to emerge in the right place at the right time. Rather, this was a decade during which the free-wheeling entrepreneur was top dog. Graduates of the nation's leading business schools eschewed conventional corporate careers in favor of entrepreneurial adventures, and the stars of the decade were a handful of men who had taken a flier only to emerge very rich and very much in control of their very own corporate empires.

Attention was already riveted on one William H. Gates III, then a mere stripling of twenty-eight, who was described in 1984 as wanting to make Microsoft the General Motors of the industry by taking command of a much bigger and more promising market segment. (Microsoft already dominated the market for the software that ran the 1980s generation of business microcomputers.) Gates himself was viewed as anything but a conventional businessman: "He is a remarkable piece of software in his own right. He is childishly awkward at times, throws things when angry, and fidgets uncontrollably when he speaks. . . . Gates is fantastically committed to Microsoft, working 90 hours a week and driving his 500 employees (average age: 26) just as hard."[64]

A different model, arguably America's most successful entrepreneur at the time, was Ken Olsen, a former engineer and Sunday school principal, who in twenty-nine years took the Digital Equipment Corporation from nothing to $7.6 billion in annual revenues. This achievement notwithstanding, Olsen remained very much the engineer, tinkering with the nuts and bolts of DEC computers, and wearing clumsy, thick-soled black shoes below his expensive, well-cut suits.[65]

But by the time the decade drew to a close another shift was taking place. Sick of self-flagellation, and of the relentless hostility to traditional notions of management, corporate America returned to the notion that old-fashioned leaders—for example, James R. Houghton of Corning Glass—might not be so bad after all. The October 24, 1988, issue of *Fortune* described Houghton as "a model of how to develop and communicate a leader's vision."[66] According to the article, Houghton stated his goals and how he planned to reach them, moved quickly to shed losers and develop long-term financial objectives, established the concern for quality as the company's central long-term value, and motivated involved employees by listening to them and responding to their ideas.

If by the end of the decade more traditional ideas about leadership were back in fashion, the middle years had in fact been captured by one Lee Iacocca. For most of the 1980s Iacocca was king of the hill. He triumphed in the quintessential American business: cars. He had finagled government into being the instrument of Chrysler's rescue. He was perched at the pinnacle of power and influence in America. And he wrote all about it in a best-selling autobiography that sold a zillion copies.[67]

Iacocca was not cut from the same WASP cloth as other captains of American industry. His name ended in a vowel and he came from nothing—the son of immigrant parents whose hard work, love for their two children, and abiding faith in America were the underpinnings of their son's remarkable success. But Iacocca had a great balancing act. He was at the same time a company man and a renegade, a manager and an entrepreneur, a car-maker and deal-maker, and a capitalist who embraced corporate socialism when it suited his needs. Iacocca was in fact so successful in business that the question came up: If he's so great at the leadership game, why doesn't he play in government? Why doesn't Iacocca run for president of the United States?

Nothing ever came of the idea, although it was bandied about for years. As for Iacocca himself, he never said much about running for office, but his book, interestingly, ends not with a discussion about American business, but rather with a six-point program for the federal government. While the specifics of Iacocca's ideas are not relevant here, they bear on the thesis of this book. Iacocca's work exemplified, and his book further developed, the proposition that leadership in business and leadership in government had begun to converge. In fact, Iacocca's own experience testified to the ways in which players from one sector could benefit by mingling with players from the other.

In the first three chapters of this book I have traced trajectories of leadership and management between the 1950s and the 1980s. As we have seen, whereas in the 1950s the distinctions between the public and private sectors were dramatic, by the 1980s they had begun to fade.

Beginning in the mid-1960s it was public sector attitudes toward leadership that led the way. The push to democratize American politics, to put flesh and bones on abstract concepts such as pluralism and participation, inevitably if only gradually had an impact on ideas about command and control that had up to then dominated American business. To be sure, corporate America also changed in response to the increasingly competitive global environment. But even before the economic threat from abroad became readily apparent, traditional corporate notions of how people can and should be managed had started to give way.

By the mid-1970s America had lost, along with its innocence, its post-World War II optimism. Too much had gone wrong and the nation's politics would never again be the same. The mood was one of growing distrust and declining faith in those institutions and individuals that had always been the bedrock. In what would appear at first glance to be a paradox, the interest in leadership grew. As America's political leaders grew weaker, Americans became more interested in defining what exactly leadership was.

At the same time, business began to sing government's song. Top-down leadership was under increasing assault. Followers, workers, were supposed to get some respect. And the demand for diversity was heard loud and clear.

Still, for all the newfangled rhetoric, change was slow. In fact, it was during the 1970s that the gap between what was said about leadership and what was actually done first became obvious. Both the public and private sectors were plagued by what in some circles had already come to be known as a "credibility gap."

In the 1980s, the distinctions between leadership in government and leadership in business diminished. America's political and corporate leaders now shared a general loss of confidence in what they did, an increased interest in who they were and how they behaved, the demand that they communicate with their followers and demonstrate at least modest interpersonal skills, and the growing awareness that in some ways at least their work was related.

Still, the differences between the two sectors remained considerable. Most strikingly, perhaps, leaders in business grew self-conscious, even self-aware. Unlike political leaders, who to this day are not exactly known for reflecting on their craft, or evaluating their own performances, business leaders developed a powerful interest in self-improvement. Since the 1980s it has become impossible to look at leadership in corporate America without simultaneously looking at leadership education.

It would take another decade for the similarities between public and private sector leaders to rival the differences. This further narrowing of the distance between politics and business was the consequence of changes in the international and national environments in which both domains are necessarily embedded. These changes—and it is to them that we now turn—also yielded a world in which the historical divide in America between political leaders and their corporate counterparts was rendered largely obsolete.

Part II

COMING TOGETHER

4

The Winds of Change
Politics, Economics, and Technologies

Having just made the point that changes in the international and national environments in which political and business leaders are necessarily embedded have driven them closer, two questions arise: Just what are these changes? And how exactly have they changed leadership roles so as to make them more similar than they are different? The next two chapters will seek to answer these questions by surveying the landscapes of politics, economics, technology, business, organizations, and culture.

INTERNATIONAL POLITICS

As we approach the year 2000 there is a sense that global changes are pervasive and that they are depositing us in realms new and unfamiliar. To be sure, such shifts are difficult to chronicle with precision. When exactly do they occur? What exactly is happening? Who exactly is being affected, and in which ways?

What we do know is that we are not where we were before. We are post-Soviet, or post-heroic, or post-Cold War, or post-modern, or post-something. We also know that times of transition are scary. Nothing makes us quite as uneasy as uncertainty and, by definition, moving from one era to the next is fraught with not-knowing. We are in virgin territory as concerns nearly every aspect of the human condition: science and technology, politics and economics, culture and consciousness. As a result, there is the gnawing sense that mastering the world in which we now live will be difficult, if not impossible. The rate of change is so fast that competence dates like quicksilver and knowledge becomes quickly obsolete. Before our very eyes, what we think we know metamorphoses into something else—something that in its new guise is, quite simply, foreign.

An equally disquieting circumstance is our inability to predict the future, even in a general way, and even in the near term. Historian Richard Pipes has written acerbically about the failure of even the best and brightest to foretell the end of communism: "The collapse of the Soviet Union was a catastrophe for Sovietologists and, more broadly, the entire discipline of political science. Never has so much money been allocated to study one country; never have so many academic and government specialists scrutinized every aspect of a country's life. . . . Yet when the end came, the experts found themselves utterly unprepared. . . . They missed everything."[1]

There are, in fact, no more significant changes in international politics than the ones just alluded to—the collapse of communism, the demise of the Soviet Union, and the end of the Cold War. It is impossible to overestimate the magnitude of these events; nor have we even begun really to adapt to them. Old institutions such as NATO continue to dominate our foreign policy discourse. (NATO is a *military* alliance, originally formed in 1949 only to counter the Soviet threat.) Dated enmities continue to shape our perceptions. (As Bill Clinton's attempt to enlarge NATO testified, Russia is still seen as a potential foe, even though the country is now famously weak.) And outdated models persist in determining both our defense budgets and foreign policy apparatus. (Current military budgets still average 85 percent of Cold War levels.) We have not yet, in other words, come fully to grips with the new realities of the postcommunist era. Nor have we begun to formulate a new way of thinking about the world that would enable us to pursue a coherent foreign policy.

At first glance, the end of the Soviet empire would seem to be for most Americans strictly a matter of foreign politics, one of little consequence to domestic politics. It might also seem that the demise of the Soviet Union is a matter of concern primarily to the public sector, rather than to the private one. As we shall see, however, such assumptions are premature. Changes in global enmities and alliances have already had a profound impact on our domestic agenda; and they have already and in many obvious ways affected those who run, and are employed by, American business and industry.

Perhaps the single most obvious consequence of the end of more than fifty years during which the United States was engaged in the equivalent of hand-to-hand combat with another great global power has been the turn inward. As the presidential campaigns of 1992 and 1996 attest (all major candidates gave foreign policy short shrift), Americans these days are far more concerned about the economy, crime, and health care than they are about Bosnia, China, or the Middle East.[2] Clearly, the lack of a visible and dangerous enemy has changed the content of our national discourse, even as the continued spending on military hardware constrains to some degree our national options.

Of course, the collapse of communism has also had an enormous impact on the private sector. Economic and trade policies are at the top of the national agenda. Global competition for the sales and distribution of products and services shapes the direction of corporate America. And the international marketplace is now without question the playing field on which captains of business and industry must prove their speed and agility.

What are some of the consequences of global change? The list that follows is testimony to the fact that whatever their exact nature, they matter to leadership in the twenty-first century because they matter to how our collective work at both the national and international levels can be accomplished.

1. Global political awakening.

In the past, for reasons both political and technological, most of the people in the world were nearly ignorant of what was happening beyond the terrain with which they were personally familiar. For much of the twentieth century the grip, successively, of Nazism and communism precluded many on even a continent as relatively advanced as Europe from having a clear understanding of what was happening in international affairs. Along parallel lines, until the recent revolution in telecommunications, the peoples of Asia, Latin America, and Africa were quite ignorant of cultures other than their own. Now, though, literacy is spreading, populations are increasingly urbanized, and telephones, television, fax machines, and the Internet are in effect eliminating barriers to audio and visual communications world wide. The net effect is not only to facilitate and accelerate the spread of information and ideas, but also nearly to eliminate the secrecy that until recently was a fact of political life.

Whatever else may be said about the "ethnic cleansing" that was part of the war in the former Yugoslavia, it cannot be claimed that the rest of the world did not know about it.

2. The American shift away from Europe and toward Asia.

Until the last decade or so of the twentieth century, the United States was as it had always been—disposed to Europe. Ideas that constituted the American Creed were rooted in countries such as England and France. The overwhelming majority of white Americans came from European stock. America's culture was shaped by Europe's manners and mores. And America's foreign affairs—political, military, and economic—were dominated by its long and close ties (friendly and hostile) to various regions, institutions, and individuals on the European continent.

In the 1990s, though, the connection weakened. Perversely, perhaps, this fraying of old ties was accelerated by the fact that there was no longer a dreadful and mighty European foe. When the Soviet Union collapsed, so did the last vestiges of our fixation on Europe. It is Asia that now newly engages us—in the recent past particularly Japan, in the present and future particularly India and China.

3. Nationalism and Balkanization.

Recent history has been characterized by a balance of power. Europe in particular was divided into two large camps, each consisting of several nations unified in their opposition to each other. Thus, during the forty-plus years after the end of World War II, our foreign policy universe was, in effect, bipolar. The countries of the Soviet bloc were on one side, and those of the "Free World" were on the other.

Now the world is less simple. The disintegration of the Soviet empire unleashed in East Europe and Central Asia waves of nationalism that to varying degrees destabilized populations that, while under the thumb of strongmen such as Stalin, Khrushchev, Brezhnev, and Tito, had no choice but to toe the line. The bloody strife in the former Yugoslavia is only the most obvious manifestation of the revival of ethnic and tribal tensions. But to witness this phenomenon, Americans need not roam nearly so far. To the continuing astonishment of its neighbor to the south, Canada is by no means immune from the threat of Balkanization. The possibility that Quebec will ultimately secede from the rest of the country remains real.

4. Diminished U. S. influence.

On the surface it seems that the end of the twentieth century should be the time of greatest American impact. This is "the American century"—a term that is particularly apt now that the great struggle of the last fifty years, between capitalism and communism, has been won by the West, with the United States in the lead.

But in some ways America's victory is hollow. The United States often finds it difficult to exercise more influence around the world than it did before, and it is unable to profit in any obvious way from its political victory. One might even argue to the contrary. Since the end of the Cold War, the rest of the "Free World" no longer needs the protection it once did from the ideological threat of communism and the military threat of the Soviet Union. Despite the fact that the United States is now the only global superpower—it has no peer militarily, economically, ideologically, or culturally—it is in the peculiar position of finding that its ability to persuade other nations to go along has been reduced rather than enhanced.

America's huge military arsenal is virtually irrelevant, and on the new battlefield in foreign affairs, the global marketplace, America is in some ways at a disadvantage (for example, in its high labor costs). Finally, so many of America's cultural exports are associated with the decline of Western civilization—money, sex, drugs, rock and roll—that even in this domain it is difficult to experience a sense of unmitigated triumph.

5. Vanishing ideologies and the clash of civilizations.

During the great wars of ideas—when fascists fought democrats and communists took on capitalists—principles were the coin of the realm. National leaders could claim that their decisions were based on ideas and ideals. But with the defeat of fascism and communism, the need for moral passion has disappeared. Both democracy and capitalism are, to varying degrees, facts of life in most of Europe, Asia, and the Americas. As Zbigniew Brzezinski has observed, "Apart from the Islamic world, where fundamentalist political tendencies are quite marked, the global political scene is dominated by rhetoric and values that are primarily consumption oriented, and that stress personal self-gratification as the primary purpose of political action."[3]

Unfortunately, this does not mean a world free from strife.

Samuel Huntington has written, famously, about the "clash of civilizations." Suffice it to say here that he foretells a world beset not by traditional national, economic, or ideological rivalries, but rather by competing cultures. His argument is grounded, if you will, in the globalization of international politics. In the past, the conflicts with which we were familiar, and into which we were drawn, were conflicts within Western civilization and between nation-states. Now, though, with the Cold War over, foreign affairs is world affairs, and they are more complicated than, merely, inter-nation interaction.[4]

Again, the complex war in Bosnia is an obvious case in point. It was a new kind of conflict, one in which armies and peoples were often indistinguishable from each other, and states were replaced by militias or other informal groupings whose ability to use sophisticated weaponry was limited. Such wars tend to be intractable. Television images of suffering, seen around the world, sap the will to conduct a conclusive military campaign, and the absence of effective central governments makes such struggles difficult to end through conventional negotiations.

6. Globalization.

While the notion that transnational trends have already overtaken us is exaggerated, national boundaries are in fact more porous and, arguably, less significant than they used to be. With the Cold War over, old assumptions, patterns, boundaries, and institutions are giving way.

Military rivalries have been replaced by commercial competition. National security issues now include terrorism, overpopulation, pollution, and disease. And a host of transnational players are emerging to cope with the brave new world—at the expense of the power and authority of the traditional nation-state. Multinational corporations and banks, global communications networks, international institutions and agreements such as UNESCO and NAFTA threaten the nation-state all of us know and some of us love.

This train will not be stopped. Too much has changed. As Paul Kennedy has observed, "These various trends from global warming to twenty-four-hour-a-day trading are transnational by nature, crossing borders all over the globe, affecting distant societies, and reminding us that the earth, for all its divisions, is a single unit."[5]

7. The emergence of new challenges and priorities.

Implicit throughout this discussion has been the assumption that since the world is no longer bipolar, and since as a consequence there is no longer a need to protect against a conventional military threat, attentions will shift. They will focus on new concerns that in different ways put people at risk. They include:

• Burgeoning World Population. The numbers are staggering. At mid-century the annual increase in world population was estimated to be about 47 million. By the year 2000 this figure will rise to about 112 million. Almost without exception the increase is taking place in developing countries, and putting a preternatural burden on resources such as food, clothing, and shelter.

• Pollution and Declining Natural Resources. In large part because of our great numbers, the threat to the environment is unprecedented. The air we breathe is dirtier, the water we drink more polluted, and the soil in which we grow our food further eroded. It is impossible to exaggerate the magnitude of damage already done to what Paul Kennedy calls the "earth's thin film of life."

• Teacup Wars. Leslie Gelb has written about the difficulties of developing a post-Cold War foreign policy. He concluded that while nuclear proliferation, Russian uncertainties, new Chinese ambitions, and trade wars all present U.S. foreign policy makers with major challenges, the biggest problems may well arise from "wars of national debilitation."[6]

• Unstable markets. By late 1998 the Asian crisis, the economic collapse of Russia, and the swoon in European and U. S. stocks had served notice: the global marketplace could threaten both individuals and institutions.

• Terrorism and Nuclear Proliferation. Terrorism is nothing new and the degree of terrorism in the 1990s is not unprecedented. But events such as the bombing of a federal building in Oklahoma City have brought the threat of terror to America in ways previously considered unthinkable. We live in an age when instructions on how to make a pipe bomb are available on the Internet and when the possibility of nuclear catastrophe is taken seriously, even beyond Hollywood.

8. New national actors take center stage.

In an article that appeared in May 1995, Thomas Friedman, writing in the *New York Times*, made fun of the G-7. The annual meetings of the Group of Seven—the United States, Britain, France, Japan, Italy, Germany, and Canada—used to make history. Now, Friedman wrote, "they make tourism." Mocking the notion that this particular group of seven constituted the world's leading economic powers, Friedman argued that it was ridiculous to have a summit of this kind without including China (likely to be the world's largest economy by 2010), India (likely to be the world's most populous country in another decade, and also one of the most technically advanced), and Brazil (which has emerged as the most powerful country in the Western Hemisphere outside the United States and accounts for nearly half the G.N.P. of South America).[7]

With regard to bilateral relations with China in particular, the United States must do better in the future than it has in the past. The United States has seesawed uneasily between flogging the Chinese for their poor record on human rights and cozying up to them on matters relating to production and trade. America has been far behind Japan, for example, in developing a coherent policy toward China on matters both geopolitical and economic, and it has failed so far in both the public and private sectors to develop a strong cadre of China experts.

NATIONAL POLITICS

The degree of political change abroad is nearly matched by the degree of political change at home. Here it will suffice to list only some of the shifts that have impacted on how leadership in the public sector is exercised.

1. How men and women run for office.

Changes in political campaigns—in particular, the decline of political parties, the increased importance of primaries, and the need for big bucks in order to win on Election Day—have fundamentally altered the way we recruit and select those who would be our governors. While they have had many consequences, among the most important is surely the gap between what it takes to campaign and what it takes to govern.

For example, the point of primaries was to increase popular participation in the selection process. But the ways in which they determine nominations have had unintended consequences. Candidates are compelled to take positions different from those they might otherwise espouse; they are expected to demonstrate a superhuman capacity for running around the country at a frenzied pace on little sleep and bad food; and they are obliged to run in what inevitably becomes a simple horse race. The "I-win you-lose" mentality that now pervades political campaigns coarsens the political process and downplays the importance of hard thinking about public policy.

Our campaign financing laws have further damaged a system in which image matters most. Major campaigns are big business and they demand big bucks. Put another way, running for office has become the ultimate act of salesmanship, and the product being sold is the candidate himself. Inevitably, then, candidates are demeaned by having to make a pitch at every turn. Inevitably, then, the electorate is suspicious. Inevitably, then, when candidates become governors their stature has long since been diminished.

2. The increased importance of polls.

We like to think that leaders seek to effect policies and practices in which they genuinely believe. Alas, we now know better. We know American presidents live by their ratings and die by the polls.

Paul Brace and Barbara Hinckley describe Richard Wirthlin's role in the administration of Ronald Reagan. Wirthlin was a public-opinion expert who was paid by the Republican National Committee, which shared his services with the White House. "For an estimated $1 million per year, Wirthlin provided polls, special techniques, frequent consultations with Reagan, and almost daily consultations with Chief of Staff Donald Regan. His techniques included a 'speech pulse,' by which people holding special computerized dials could test-market presidential speeches. The dials not only tapped positive and negative reaction but also measured very specific things, such as response to the speaker's credibility. They measured reactions moment by moment and word by word."[8]

The Clinton presidency—even before the question of impeachment came up—has arguably been worse. Described by Elizabeth Drew as "poll-driven and consultant-ridden," the Clinton White House was filled with public opinion experts who had unparalleled influence on both foreign and domestic policymaking. Drew wrote, "Previous Presidents had pollsters and other outside political advisers, but never before had a group of political consultants played such an integral part in a Presidency. Clinton's consultants were omnipresent, involved in everything from personnel to policymaking to the President's schedule."[9]

The problems associated with being too dependant on polls include survey results that are inaccurate and misleading; cycles that because of their predictability should be largely discounted; and the "rally 'round the flag" syndrome associated with international crises that nearly always boost a president's popularity. (President Carter's approval rating jumped twenty points during the early stages of the Iranian hostages crisis and again when the Soviets invaded Afghanistan—even though on both occasions his immediate response was to do nothing!)

But the knottiest problem associated with polling is the balancing act that constitutes governing in a democratic system. There is merit, of course, in having leaders listen to what their followers say. We the people have a right to be heard and to expect that there will be a certain level of responsiveness to our preferences. In addition, popular support is a powerful political resource. Presidents who have it get more of what they want.

The question is, Where does it end? At what point is it appropriate for a leader to listen to the sound of his *own* voice? Clearly, there is no single answer to this question, but it can be said with some assurance that in general we want leaders who have clarity of vision and certitude of purpose. Truman had the lowest poll ratings of any president. But he confounded the pollsters by defeating Governor Thomas Dewey in 1948 and history has treated him especially well. The fact is that part of Truman's appeal is that he didn't give a damn about polls—and he didn't care who knew it.

In a speech delivered at Princeton University in 1890, some twenty-four years before his election as president, Woodrow Wilson spoke to the issue. It is no small irony that during his final years in the White House his words came back to haunt him. "I do not conceive the leader a trimmer, weak to yield what clamour claims, but a deeply human man, quick to know and to do the things that the hour and his people need."[10]

3. The Balkanization of America.

Some argue that the United States is no more fractured now than it used to be.[11] Michael Lind claims that although the United States is diverse, it in fact has—like Mexico, and unlike Canada—a common culture and identity. Still, there is the widespread impression that in recent decades the highly touted melting pot has broken apart. Conflicts dividing Americans generally fall into two categories: those among groups (for example, races, religions, nationalities, classes, genders, generations, classes) and those over issues (for example, affirmative action, abortion, gun control).

Class is perhaps the most interesting of the many fault lines, for it is arguably the most threatening to what is traditionally considered the American way of life. Robert Reich has not tired of reminding us that as the economy grows, people who work the machines and clean the offices and provide the basic goods and services are supposed to share in the gains. But since this has not happened, even in the booming economy of the 1990s, he goes on to caution that if "we lose our middle class and become a two-tiered society, we not only risk the nation's future prosperity, but also its social coherence and stability."[12]

Conflicts over policy are sometimes exaggerated because of the attention they now receive. For example, there is a real divide over the question of legalized abortion in the United States between those who advocate free choice and those who call themselves pro-life. But the way information is distributed and events are covered heightens existing tensions and precludes what might otherwise be a more civil debate. (In 1995 the National Association of Radio Talk Show Hosts gave its Freedom of Speech Award to G. Gordon Liddy. Liddy is the convicted Watergate burglar whose right-wing radio show is heard on nearly 300 stations nationwide. He is merely one of the more egregious examples of those who have access to the air or Internet, and who apparently think nothing of yelling "Fire!" in a crowded theatre.)

4. The political agenda.

For reasons that include the information revolution, shifting demographics, global competitiveness, the end of the Cold War, and a decline in public civility, as the United States approaches the millennium it faces new challenges that will require political leaders to break with the old ways of doing business.

In recent years, several of the best and brightest have written about what they consider the most significant challenges facing the United States at this turning point in history. The following list draws on Zbigniew Brzezinski's *Out of Control: Global Turmoil on the Eve of the 21st Century*[13] and Paul Kennedy's *Preparing for the Twenty-First Century*.[14]

- Trade Deficit—forces United States to borrow and threatens key sectors of production and employment.
- Low savings and investment—results in a relative decline in America's investment in research and development.
- Inadequate health care—still leaves millions unprotected.
- Poor schools—America's youth is woefully undereducated, especially in comparison with its European and Japanese counterparts.
- Widespread urban decay and deteriorating national infrastructure.
- Greedy wealthy class—insists on tax breaks and corporate welfare.
- Excessively litigious society—divisive and costly.
- Deepening race and poverty problem—too many homeless, too many poor, too many African Americans living below the poverty line.
- Too much crime and violence—exacerbated by easy access to lethal weapons.
- Drug culture—especially in the nation's cities.
- Growing underclass—traps young urban blacks in particular.
- Excessive sexual activity—too many babies having babies, too many sexually transmitted diseases, too many one-parent families.
- Moral corruption by the media—sex and violence in the home, at the movies, and on the air.
- Decline in civic engagement.

- Multiculturalism and political correctness—undervalue the very attributes that unify (e.g., common language, shared historical traditions).
- Political gridlock—the inability of the system to fix what's broke.
- Bloated national defense budget—saps capital, materials, and skilled labor from nonmilitary production.
- Demographic changes—more elderly, more diversity, more people.
- Environmental concerns—global warming, shrinking rain forests, pollution.
- Inadequate planning—especially for twenty-four-hour-a-day financial flows, electronic trading, and the globalization of business and communications.[15]

The lists generated by Brzezinski and Kennedy are suggestive rather than complete. (For example, they pay scant attention to problems of nuclear proliferation.) With regard to leadership, in any case, the point is clear: The problems are as pressing as they are daunting, which means that leaders who ignore them do so at their peril.

ECONOMICS

It has become clear in recent years that many issues once considered part of the political realm are driven now by economic forces. In a world at least as preoccupied with economic competition as it is with military threat, the line between politics and economics is increasingly difficult to draw. All the more reason, then, for public- and private-sector leaders to master more or less the same bodies of knowledge. Political leaders will be no more exempt from the demand for economic expertise than corporate leaders will be from the demand for political skill.

In his book *Post-Capitalist Society*, Peter Drucker claims we are poised at the brink of a "divide" that occurs only once every few hundred years in Western history. In the post-capitalist society the institutions of capitalism survive, he argues, "but the center of gravity in the post-capitalist society" is different. The basic economic resource is no longer capital, or natural resources, or labor. It is knowledge.[16] For example, "the actual product of the pharmaceutical industry is knowledge. Pills and prescription ointments are no more than packaging."[17]

The implications of this shift are enormous. The primary *economic* challenge to the postcapitalist society is the productivity of the knowledge worker. The primary *social* challenge is the dignity of the service worker in an environment in which such work is devalued. The primary political challenge at the *national* level is to make public policy that supports the need to be globally competitive. And the primary political challenge at the *international* level is the reorganization of world politics during a time when the nation-state is rivaled by transnational organizations and the free flow of capital, production, markets, and communications.

America's domestic and foreign politics have clearly been transformed by the imperatives of globalization. While the president of the United States has to some degree always been held responsible for the performance of the American economy, the issue has never been as pervasive as it is on the rim of the new millennium. Nearly every domestic policy decision the chief executive now makes is driven by economic as well as political considerations. In addition, since the end of the Cold War and the collapse of communism, the nature of international competition has changed. Bill Clinton has spent far more time worrying about the North American Free Trade Agreement (NAFTA), and opening up the Japanese market to American cars, than he has about Inter-Continental Ballistic Missiles.

In keeping with the times, the president's economic advisory team has expanded exponentially (as has that of Congress). Once upon a time there was only one executive branch agency that played a major role in the financial affairs of government—the Department of the Treasury. Now we have the Federal Reserve Board, the Office of Management and Budget, and the Council of Economic Advisers. Since the 1970s the increase in the number of players and advisory structures has accelerated even further. President Ford had his Economic Policy Board; President Carter his informal economic policy group; and Presidents Reagan and Bush had cabinet councils.

President Clinton went his predecessors one better. Convinced from the start that in the 1990s economic policy would become more important than it had been before, he established the National Economic Council. Its purpose: to serve as overall coordinator of economic policy. The first chair of the NEC came to Washington from Wall Street. The highly respected Robert Rubin was described by Elizabeth Drew as a "slim fifty-four-year-old man with soulful brown eyes and a soft voice and slightly greying hair,"[18] and credited by many with having a hand in the booming nineties. (Rubin eventually succeeded Lloyd Bentsen as Secretary of the Treasury.)

The fact that economic issues are now of overriding importance to political decision makers, at the state and local levels as well as at the national one, is another sign that the public and private sectors are converging. For example, some economists argue that in order to remain competitive the United States must do what private enterprise does—increase savings and investment rates and invest in research and development. Moreover, in order to have a positive impact on prices American producers can charge, and on the wages of American workers, the government has no choice but actively to manage trade policy. (To be sure, other economists claim that nations and corporations cannot be compared. Paul Krugman reminds us that if a corporation cannot afford to pay its workers, suppliers, and bondholders, it will go out of business. "Countries on the other hand, do not go out of business. They may be happy or unhappy with their economic performance, but they have no well-defined bottom line. As a result the concept of national competitiveness is elusive.")[19]

Despite the growing confluence between government and business, the United States does not now have, nor did it ever have, a formal industrial policy. Still, a loud minority continues to argue that greater cooperation between those in politics and those in business would be to our collective advantage. As Clinton cronies Ira Magaziner and Robert Reich wrote in *Minding America's Business*, our standard of living can rise only if capital and labor increasingly flow to industries that add greater value per employee, and if we maintain positions in these businesses superior to those of our international competitors.[20]

Economist Lester Thurow concurs. He points out that those who lost jobs in autos and machine tools as American firms lost market share at home and abroad typically took a 30 to 50 percent wage reduction—if they were young. If they were over fifty, they were usually permanently exiled to the periphery of the low-wage, part-time labor market. Losses like these may not be significant at the national level, but on a personal level they are important to the millions of affected workers and their families. "The correct redress for their problems, however, is not to keep Japanese autos or machine tools out of the American market, but to organize ventures such as the government-industry auto battery consortium that seek to expand the American auto industry's market share by taking the lead in producing tomorrow's electric cars."[21]

The heated debate over NAFTA reflected the increasingly complicated interweave between government and business. A trade agreement is, by definition, an economic agreement. But the process of reaching it is political. In addition, accords such as NAFTA are saddled with assumptions made by both sides that are impossible to prove. In this case they included: 1) NAFTA will create the world's biggest and richest market—a $6 trillion market of 360 million consumers; 2) Free trade will spur a massive relocation of American factory jobs to Mexico, which will, in turn, become an Asian-style exporter; 3) NAFTA will enable Japan to build plants in Mexico, its new duty-free "back door" into the American market; 4) NAFTA is good for the United States because it will stop Mexican immigration; 5) NAFTA is a fine idea in theory, but in practice it will punch a $40 billion hole in the federal budget.

It is the connections that are of particular interest here—between politics and economics, government and business, and political leaders and their corporate counterparts. The journal *Foreign Affairs* may be viewed as an indicator. This most prestigious of the various publications on American foreign policy was until recently confined largely to the realms of Kremlinology and nuclear deterrence. Now it is filled with articles of rather a different sort: "Competitiveness: A Dangerous Obsession," "The Truth About NAFTA," "The Pacific Century," "Clinton's Emerging Trade Policy," "Latin America: The Morning After," "The Shrinking Dollar: Let it Slide?" and "Japan's Financial Leviathan."[22]

Moreover the fact that economists have an uncertain reputation for precision and prophesy has not stopped them from playing a growing role in national affairs. The reasons are obvious. First, national economies are growing exponentially. As populations increase world wide, Western markets continue to expand and many other countries, once considered part of the "Third World," are joining the fray of industrialization and consumerism.

Second, the nature of the game has changed in ways that demand the wisdom of the experts—even if the experts disagree and are frequently wrong. The globalization of the marketplace in particular, and the accompanying free flow of capital, have altered the landscape in ways that test the mettle even of those few political leaders who are economically savvy. Coca-Cola is now sold in 195 countries with 5.2 billion people. Intel sells about half of its computer chips abroad. U.S. imports exceed $600 billion. Foreigners own more than $350 billion worth of U.S. stocks. And when Mexico is in crisis, the dollar plunges.

Finally, economics is quite simply the most exciting game in town. With the decline in interest in national security as traditionally defined, economic issues have moved front and center. In fact, the meaning of national security itself has changed to include the notion of economic preparedness. Is the United States able to fend off the "Japanese Leviathan"? Can the United States compete against Asia? Can American workers survive cheap labor from Mexico? And what about China? Are trade agreements with China likely to help American producers, or will they instead decrease our leverage vis-à-vis this most challenging of all our competitors?

The weapons of economists are ideas and access. Without ideas there is no reason to give them access; without access their ideas have no impact. But those economists equipped with both have had in recent decades a significant impact on public policy. In the past, political players who were economists by trade included names such as John Kenneth Galbraith, Arthur Burns, Paul Samuelson, Walter Heller, Milton Friedman, James Tobin, Kenneth Arrow, and Michael Boskin. In the nineties Federal Reserve Chairman Alan Greenspan dominated the scene, and two women reached the upper ranks: Alice Rivlin, who in fact had been a Washington player for years, and Laura D'Andrea Tyson, who, when she was appointed by President Clinton to chair his Council of Economic Advisers, was a forty-five-year-old economics professor at Berkeley.

But it is an economist by the name of F. A. Hayek who catches the spirit of the end of the twentieth century perhaps better than any one else. Hayek was never in government but he has been a favorite of those who preach to leaders in business. He disparaged economic planning of any kind, and argued instead that "order generated without design can far outstrip plans men consciously contrive."[23] Management guru Tom Peters is a big fan, and in his book *Liberation Management* expounds on Hayek's ideas. "Why spend so much time on Hayek?" Peters asks. "Simple. To fail to appreciate—in the fullest sense of that term—the richness, passion, and raggedness of the market mechanism is to be unprepared to lead a firm (or a regional or national economy)—especially in today's unhinged global marketplace. There is no doubt that economists and planners don't much like bawdy capitalists."[24]

It is Peters's parenthetical comment that is of particular interest. His argument is that whatever rules govern leadership in business, should govern leadership in government as well.

TECHNOLOGIES

Technology is, ostensibly, the great equalizer. Telephones, television, copiers, fax machines, personal computers, the Internet—all of them everywhere, providing instant access to the same information to anyone able to get their hands on the necessary hardware. The telecommunications revolution has changed everything. There is no nation, group, or individual that cannot obtain, in theory at least, access to "the basic economic resource . . . knowledge." (In fact, while the cyberspace revolution began in the United States, Europe, and a handful of other countries such as Japan, its greatest impact over the next few years may well be on the authoritarian states of Asia—home to two-thirds of the world's population and its fastest growing economies. Authoritarian governments will have to address the obvious dilemma: that to get their economies to grow at the desired rate, they will have to import precisely those technologies that make the control of information difficult if not ultimately impossible.)

Of course, the private sector in particular depended on information processing machines and systems long before the invasion of the computer. From new filing systems to new ways of organizing production, business and industry found that making money required careful control not just of people and materials, but also of information. However, it was the introduction in the 1980s of the personal computer (originally developed during World War II for military and scientific use) that changed everything. Now it was a tool sitting in the office *and* in the home. Every member of the family presumably had access to it, and every member of the family could use it to process, organize, and exchange information.

More than two million personal computers were sold by 1981. By 1982 the figure more than doubled. By 1995, 56 percent of American homes had computers. One year later the number went up another 10 percent. Moreover, children as young as two and three were being taught to be computer literate. Schools and libraries across the land, especially those located in wealthier communities, had computers installed for children of all ages, and software was developed even for toddlers.

Of course, there is no revolution without a counter-revolution. So for every futurist who saw computers as all about community, freedom, and economic progress, there were others who wondered what the fuss was all about—or went so far as to predict that computers would end civilization as we know it. In fact, by the mid-1990s the technophobia seemed to some to be extreme. A piece that appeared in *New York* magazine in July 1995 was emblematic. The cover illustration was of a hand holding a pistol to a computer, and the story was titled "Die, Computer, Die." Clifford Stoll (in *Silicon Snake Oil*) was quoted as saying that the Internet was subverting traditional notions of intimacy, conversation, and letter writing. Sven Birkerts (in *The Gutenberg Elegies*) asserted that "we are living in a state of intellectual emergency—an emergency caused by our willingness to embrace new technologies at the expense of the written word."[25] And in a 1995 television interview, the author of *The Surrender of Culture to Technology*, Neil Postman, claimed all new technologies were a "Faustian bargain."[26] He was particularly worried about computers in schools. What will happen to the socialization process when students depend on computers for instruction? But Postman was whistling in the wind. The computer has already transformed the social and academic lives of students on college campuses across the United States. Dormitory lounges have been carved up for clusters of computers, student unions have been declining as gathering places, and dorm rooms are high-tech caves.

Of course, the best answer to the question of whether the trillions of dollars invested in information technology is worth it is, "It depends." As Steven Lubar has observed, sometimes computers have simply been put to work at the wrong jobs. "Useless paperwork done by computer simply produces more useless paperwork. Badly managed jobs done by computer are still badly managed. It doesn't increase productivity."[27] The point is that some institutions and individuals use computers to automate their problems, not to solve them.

Whatever the reservations, by the mid-1990s technomania was irreversible. In a special issue of *Newsweek* that came out in February 1995, the editors concluded "The revolution has only just begun, but already it's starting to overwhelm us. It's outstripping our capacity to cope, antiquating our laws, transforming our mores, reshuffling our economy, reordering our priorities, redefining our workplaces, putting our Constitution to the fire, shifting our concept of reality and making us sit for long periods in front of computer screens while CD-ROM drives grind out another video clip."[28]

Needless to say, the more feverish the technomania, the more heated the debates it inspires: control versus decentralization, surveillance versus privacy, censorship versus free speech, linear versus interactive education, reality versus virtual reality. And then there is this: Will computers create yet another division? Will the United States be further sundered by promoting those who are computer literate and shutting out those who are not?

The numbers are telling. While in the schools the divisions are arguably less than anticipated, at home they are considerable. In 1998, 44.3 percent of white children had a computer at home; for black children the number was only 29 percent. The sharp racial divide is especially evident among households below the median income. Lower-income white households are twice as likely to own a home computer as black households. (The federal government is not oblivious to the disparity. In 1996 the Federal Communications Commission recommended that schools and libraries across the country be made eligible for discounts of from 20 percent to 90 percent on the cost of telecommunications services, including access to the Internet and connections among classrooms.)

In *Being Digital,* Nicholas Negroponte described how information technology is transforming our lives. Even now, he wrote, atoms are still the basic stuff of human interaction. For example, digitally recorded music is distributed on plastic CDs, with huge packaging, shipping, and inventory costs. But this is changing rapidly. "The methodical movement of recorded music as pieces of plastic, like the slow human handling of most information in the form of books, magazines, newspapers, and videocassettes, is about to become the instantaneous and inexpensive transfer of electronic data that move at the speed of light."[29]

Negroponte predicted the switch from atoms to bits would change everything. In fact, he claimed, the information age itself is as good as over. Now we are in the post-information age in which the target audience is reduced to one. Everything is made to order and information is personalized. Even the concept of place will change. If instead of literally going to work, your work is done electronically, by logging into the office, where exactly do you work? If a doctor in Houston performs surgery on a patient in Alaska, where is the doctor based? If you have an account with America Online, Compu-Serve, or Prodigy, you know your e-mail address, but you do not know where it physically exists. As Negroponte points out, your e-mail address is more like a Social Security number than a street address. It is a virtual address.[30]

Since technology is already in the process of transforming the way we live and work, the question is what really matters during this time of transition and uncertainty? Three answers come to mind. First, the future is then, not now. Whatever changes eventually characterize the post-information age, they are not yet clear, nor are they here. It will take decades for the technological revolution to sort itself out and for us to decipher which changes will fundamentally alter they way we live and work.

Second, the revolution in information technology is slower to have an impact on the public sector than on the private one. Political leaders have lagged behind their corporate counterparts in dealing with the cyberspace phenomenon. Even as I write, in 1998, many of our elected officials remain computer illiterate. (President and Mrs. Clinton only recently learned to use e-mail to communicate with their daughter Chelsea, who in the fall of 1997 began attending Stanford University.) To a degree, this is a function of the generation gap. Most public office holders did not grow up with computers. But some of the ignorance is willful—willful in the sense that by and large politicians have not yet taken the time and trouble to learn the fundamentals of information technology.

Finally, we are now faced, constantly, with hard decisions about which technologies in which to invest. In other words, we must learn to discriminate between those that are good (useful) and those that are bad (wasteful, unnecessary). The information revolution is positive in that it yields more data, faster, in more diverse forms, to more people, than has ever been possible before. However, it is bad in that it can be misleading. What technology spews clearly satisfies the cravings of inveterate "information junkies." But enormous quantities of data do not necessarily enhance our capacity to address a range of problems that have historically proved intractable—crime, starvation, disease, pollution, overpopulation, racism. In fact, it might reasonably be argued that since in many circumstances computers favor the individual over the community, we will in time be even less well equipped than we are now to do the collaborative work required to address the most complex social, political, and economic issues.

LEADERSHIP AND CHANGE

This chapter began with two basic questions: In which ways have the international and national environments changed? And how have these changes affected public and private leadership roles so as to make them more similar than they are different?

Up to this point we have considered politics, economics, and technologies. Whether or not the changes in these areas are as sweeping as they were at other points in human history is impossible to determine. What is clear is that they are of major consequence, and that they therefore impact—or should impact—on how both political and business leadership is exercised. In particular, the size and scope of change in recent years has so affected the larger environment within which all leadership takes place, that the requisites for public and private leadership have converged.

• Political and business leaders were faced with the collapse of communism and the demise of the Soviet Union—as well as the new world order (or disorder) these seismic events inevitably generated. Markets and politics have been profoundly affected by the international context, which is very different in the late 1990s even from what it was in the late 1980s.

• Political and business leaders now engage in domestic politics in ways that make them increasingly interdependent. The growing importance of money in politics makes politicians much more sensitive to the needs and wants of their corporate counterparts than they used to be. Moreover, the fact that politicians are now driven by polls compels them to take account of "customer" preferences in ways that resemble nothing so much as business leaders hawking their wares. In fact, the advertising that now riddles America's political campaigns is merely the most obvious indicator that Madison Avenue itself has learned to straddle the line between selling people and selling goods. Finally, the problems faced by elected officials and their corporate counterparts are increasingly one and the same. For example, as Texaco's CEO will testify, racism is scarcely confined to the public sector—any more than collective concerns such as trade deficits, rising costs of health care, poor schools, and crime can properly be addressed either by public officials or business executives acting alone.

• Political and business leaders now meet, regularly, at the intersection of politics and markets. Elected officials have to concern themselves far more aggressively than they did in the past with selling American goods in the global marketplace; and the politics that underlie international markets has compelled business leaders to master the political process both at home and abroad. The convergence of politics and markets in the saga that was passage of the North American Free Trade Agreement provides a fine example of how two domains, public and private, that in the past were thought of as distinct no longer are.

• Public- and private-sector leaders have had to (or will have to) cope with the revolution in information technology. Computers have changed the ways politicians run for office and govern once in place; and they have changed the ways corporate leaders conduct their business, sell their products, and manage their employees. Leaders in both domains are increasingly expected to master technology in all its aspects, its pitfalls as well as its promises. Moreover the debates technology inevitably inspires—for example, surveillance versus privacy, control versus decentralization, censorship versus free speech—inevitably straddle the lines between the public good and private interests.

Writing in the *New York Times* in November 1996, foreign affairs columnist Thomas Friedman drafted a job description for Secretary of State in President Clinton's second term. I can think of no better way to end a chapter that argues for the convergence of politics and markets than to quote from Friedman's piece. "The successful applicant for this job will understand just how much the world, and therefore this job, has changed since the end of the cold war. Historically there have been two kinds of foreign affairs: the commercial foreign affairs conducted by the Secretaries of Commerce and Treasury—and conflict-resolution foreign affairs conducted by the Secretary of State. . . . The distinction between these two is no longer valid. We have moved from a world dominated by superpowers to a world dominated by both superpowers and 'supermarkets.' In this new world, the bond and stock markets of Wall Street, Tokyo, Singapore, Shanghai, Paris, London, Frankfurt, Zurich and Hong Kong can be as influential in shaping the behavior of states as the traditional foreign policy engines."[31]

5

The Winds of Change
Business, Organizations, and Culture

In the previous chapter we explored changes in politics, economics, and technologies, and the ways in which these changes contributed to the converging roles of leaders in politics and business. In this chapter the song is the same but the lyrics are different. The argument for convergence continues, but to further make the case this time the domains are business, organizations, and culture.

BUSINESS

Men who in the 1950s, 1960s, and 1970s took jobs of one kind or another in business and industry thought they knew the rules of the game. How could they have guessed that in short order the rules would change so much that the game itself was nearly unrecognizable?

In the last ten to fifteen years the private sector has been swept by changes that were by and large unforeseen. The reasons for what amounts to a sea change in work in America may be summed up with surprising economy: the technological revolution and the globalization of markets. The two are linked, of course, and they, in turn, have generated other changes—such as downsizing and the weakness of labor vis-à-vis management—that themselves are interconnected. The fact, in any case, is that changes both in technology and the global marketplace have left everyone slightly unnerved, trying to stay a step ahead of the next guy by anticipating what's next.

Actually, our record as prognosticators in this regard is something less than splendid. In fact, such predictions as do surface are typically more descriptive than prescriptive. An article that appeared

111

in *Fortune* in May 1993 is typical. With a straight face the author proclaimed that there were six trends that "will reshape the workplace":

1. The average company will become smaller, employing fewer people.
2. The traditional hierarchical organization will give way to a variety of organizational forms.
3. Technicians, ranging from computer repairmen to radiation therapists, will replace manufacturing operatives as the worker elite.
4. The vertical division of labor will become obsolete.
5. The paradigm of doing business will shift from making a product to providing a service.
6. Work itself will be redefined: constant learning, more high-order thinking, less nine-to-five.[1]

The only trouble with this list was that rather than being an indicator of what would be it was a description of what already was. The title of the article notwithstanding ("Crystal Ball"), the workplace had already been "reshaped." As the list does, however, suggest, the "six trends" had an impact on two levels: corporate and individual. Particularly in the last decade or so, both organizations and those who people them have had to make major adjustments.

To begin at the beginning is to begin with the workplace. By now it is conventional wisdom that business and industry have long since been transformed by the information revolution. Here is only a partial list of what the private sector has had to contend with.

• The technology. All change is difficult, and it is especially difficult when organizations are forced to teach those who inhabit them something entirely new. While there are those in the workplace who thrive on every innovation, there are others for whom mastering the new technologies has been difficult, time consuming, and frustrating.[2] As a consequence, organizations have had to invest major resources merely into helping along the millions for whom technology is not second nature.

• The expense. Technology costs money. A lot of it. Between 1985 and 1995 American companies spent nearly $1 trillion on fancy computer systems.

• Instant change and constant obsolescence. The $1 trillion would not have been so hard to absorb if it had been spent on something enduring. But in the interests of greater speed, more information, and faster communications, organizations feel obliged regularly to "upgrade" systems in which they have only recently made a heavy investment. Moreover, sometimes innovation takes totally unanticipated turns. Originally, the consensus on the information superhighway was that it would be a souped-up cable-TV network. As things turned out, however, the delivery system is the Internet.

• The productivity paradox. To maintain their competitive edge, organizations have spent large sums of money on technology and endured rapid obsolescence. It would all have been worth it if productivity had increased. During most of the 1980s this was not, however, the case. Productivity in U.S. service industries grew an anemic 0.7 percent annually. To be sure, by the 1990s performance started to improve—but at a cost. While American business learned how to use the new technologies in ways far more suitable and sophisticated, the by now familiar price to be paid was that whole ranks of the employed became unemployed.

• Speed. The speed with which information is now gathered and disseminated; the speed with which individuals and groups now communicate with each other; and the speed with which decisions are now being made, products changed, services delivered, and customer wants, needs, and wishes satisfied.

• Information. More information than you ever imagined. Faster information. Cheaper information. Information that can be instantly distributed. However, even the information revolution has a downside: information overload. By the mid-1990s Americans possessed 148.6 million e-mail addresses, cellular phones, pagers, fax machines, voice mailboxes, and answering machines—up 365 percent from seven years earlier. "Throw in 170 million standard issue telephones," wrote *Fortune,* "and you've got the full picture of what we'll dub Infobog: a pervasive, invasive information infrastructure that is as much a part of our lives as religion was for medieval serfs."[3]

• Communications. In some cases, changing communications means no less than changing the way the work is done. Medicine provides a compelling example. Until recently, getting a diagnosis meant getting it from a physician in the same room with you. Now, computer-linked interactive video systems enable a specialist in one place to make a diagnosis on a patient in another.[4] Moreover, advances in robotics and digital communication give specialists the power to treat and even operate on patients thousands of miles away.

The globalization of markets has affected business and industry as much as the revolution in the delivery and dissemination of information. Predictably, Coca-Cola has been in the vanguard. The company dominates the global soft drink market, shipping more than eleven billion cases of soda each year. Coke is available in over 195 countries—that is, in nearly every sovereign state on the face of the earth—and four of its brands (Coca-Cola, Diet Coke, Fanta, and Sprite) are among the five best-selling drinks in the world. And there's more to come. Coca-Cola's top sixteen markets account for 80 percent of its business, but they account for only 20 percent of the world's population. No wonder recent growth has been especially high in places as diverse as Thailand, Chile, and Hungary. No wonder Coca-Cola's late, legendary CEO, Roberto Goizueta, salivated when recalling that after a sixteen-year absence his company had reentered the Indian market (nearly a billion people strong). No wonder he was forever reminding his troops that "every single one of the world's 5.6 billion people will get thirsty every day."

McDonald's brand name is the world's second most recognized (after Coca-Cola), and the company adds to its holdings two new restaurants every day—two-thirds of them in locations outside the United States. Iceland, Israel, Saudi Arabia, and Slovenia are just a few of the countries that have recently surrendered to Big Mac attacks. Similarly, Texaco, the third largest U.S. oil company, is looking to pump up profits by pumping up more foreign crude. It expects to double its European production by the turn of the century; develop major projects in Indonesia, China, and Thailand; expand on an agreement with the Russians to explore fields beneath the Arctic circle; and upgrade its refineries and improve its marketing network in the fast-growing Asia-Pacific region.

But when it comes to capitalizing on globalization, no one can beat the old American standby Procter & Gamble. Cincinnati-based P&G is the largest daily use consumer products company in China (although it is losing out to its archrival, Unilever, in India and

Indonesia). Contrary to all expectations, P&G now sells half of all the shampoo bought by those once known as the "Red Menace." How did P&G do it? With strategies designed to impress the most hardened general. They spotted the enormous potential for an effective dandruff shampoo and used advertising to draw attention to the condition. They ignored common sense Sinology—that only affluent Chinese could afford foreign brands. They besieged the market with the kind of aggressive dedication reminiscent of nothing so much as a military campaign. (One former P&G manager called it "the early application of overwhelming force.") They outspent their rivals (they bought more advertising than any other company in China). They took on the government when it made sense to do so. They trained a small army of Chinese to think the American way. And they pushed for "total retail coverage"—American lingo for getting P&G's shampoo and detergent in every shop.[5]

In fact, the United States was late to the table. The Europeans and Japanese understood before the Americans did that promoting national trade policies was tantamount to promoting the national interest. Only during the Clinton administration did the debate over how to strike an appropriate balance between trade issues and more traditional foreign policy concerns move to center stage. Under the direction of Under Secretary of Commerce Jeffrey Garten, a concerted effort was made to use U.S. political power to support American efforts to win contracts and business opportunities abroad. In 1994 the Department of Commerce built a "war room"—a space where more than 150 major contracts around the world were tracked daily. As the *New York Times* reported, it was from there that Mr. Garten called on American officials, from President Clinton on down, to promote the trade policies of the United States, much the way the Germans and Japanese had done for years.[6]

By now, of course, it is widely recognized that companies that fail to adapt are threatened with extinction. One of the more striking responses in sectors such as banking, entertainment, and telecommunications has been the wave of mergers, dissolutions, and redistributions. And there's something else that's new—at least to the private sector: federalism. As Charles Handy argues, since federalism offers a well-recognized way to deal with paradoxes of power and control—such as making things big by keeping them small—it is especially well suited to the late-twentieth-century way of doing business. "Change a few of the terms," Handy writes, "and these political issues can be found on the agendas of senior managers in most of the world's large companies."[7]

Percy Barnevik, former CEO of Asea Brown Boveri, described his sprawling enterprise of 1,100 separate companies and 210,000 employees as a federation (although in 1997 the topdown decision was made to cut fully 10,000 jobs in Europe and invest in Asia instead). Basel-based Ciba Geigy moved from a management pyramid to an organization with fourteen separate businesses that controlled 94 percent of all company spending. In other words, corporations around the world (including General Electric, Johnson & Johnson, and Coca-Cola) are combining local autonomy with central controls. They are like nations that have strong federal governments and also large measures of state and local autonomy.[8]

Given the various changes, it was hardly surprising that CEOs and upper-level managers found the going tough. Even the best and brightest corporate leaders discovered that the ways they had been taught to do their jobs no longer applied. Old haunts were called into question, and in 1993 *Business Week* had the temerity to question Mecca: "Harvard B-School: Is It Outmoded?" The cover story was critical from start to finish. "Harvard isn't just failing to show management how to confront these and other vital issues [e.g., globalization, diversity], the school's critics say. In its insularity and rigidity, it might well be breeding insular, rigid managers, to the detriment of the corporations they'll help run. 'The more Harvard succeeds, the more American business fails,' says Henry Mintzberg, a management professor at McGill University."[9] A year later *Fortune* chimed in. "These days every business school dean worth his baggy tweeds is agonizing over what exactly it is that an MBA—or anybody else—will need to know or do to be effective in business a decade from now. And is it teachable? Business education's current plunge into self-analysis is the deepest in thirty years."[10]

Most of us did not, however, lose a lot of sleep over those at the top. By and large, high-level executives have been protected against changing times. For those further on down the corporate ladder, however, the story has been different. In general, the 1980s and 1990s have not been easy. As *Fortune* put it in the article cited in the beginning of this chapter, "More and more of the population will be caught up in the defining activity of the age: scrambling.

Scrambling for footing on a shifting corporate landscape. . . . Scrambling to upgrade their software, their learning, their financial reserves. Scrambling even to carve out moments of tranquility under a banner blazoned FIGHT STRESS, a banner flapping like a Tibetan prayer flag in the gale of change."[11]

Above all, American workers have had to cope with the relentless downsizing of American business. Millions who had a different future in mind have been—are being—thrown out of work in the, arguably, necessary quest to make American corporations as lean and mean as possible in the increasingly competitive global marketplace. In the three years ending mid-1994, five companies—IBM, AT&T, GM, Sears, and GTE—announced layoffs totalling 324,650 employees. As a survey of corporate executives by the American Management Association confirmed, for many companies, payroll trimming had metamorphosed from quick fix to permanent strategy.

Until the mid-1970s the average number of employees per company increased. But by the 1990s it had become impossible to go more than a couple of weeks without reading about one or another major American corporation eliminating thousands of jobs. Richard Barnet nailed it early in *The Nation*: "The global job crisis of the 1990s results from the interactions of the dramatic advances in labor-saving technologies and the equally remarkable expansion of the international labor market. 'Competitiveness' is the mantra of this new economy, and the winning strategies involve 'downsizing' labor costs and increasing market power through corporate takeovers. A global pool of bargain labor is available to companies making virtually anything and, increasingly, to corporations selling insurance, data of every description, and legal, engineering and accounting services."[12] To add insult to injury, investors looked favorably on payroll slashing. When Chemical Bank merged with Chase Manhattan they calculated they could eliminate 12,000 jobs. The news—there would now be 16 percent fewer workers—sent the value of the two bank stocks up 11 percent.

Since about one-third of the jobs in the United States are at permanent risk to the growing productivity of low-wage workers in China, India, Mexico, and elsewhere, there has been an inevitable and generally pervasive downward pressure on wages and working conditions. Strikes, once the most powerful club in labor's arsenal, are only rarely effective now precisely because management is able to threaten: Take it or we're out of here. Indeed, the double whammy of the technological revolution and globalization has generally had a devastating effect on the labor movement. Barnet pointed out that in the mid-1990s the proportion of the U.S. workforce in private industry organized for collective bargaining, now about 11 percent, was smaller than it was in 1936, the year after enactment of the Wagner Act, the principal New Deal labor law reform.

Management is not, of course, entirely to blame for labor's ills. Some of the blame must be shouldered by labor itself. The once vigorous and even fiery movement—in the 1950s fully one quarter of all private-sector employees were union members—had withered badly under the well-meaning but largely ineffectual leadership of Lane Kirkland who was forced out (kicking and screaming) in 1995. During his time in office

- union membership had declined precipitously;
- labor's hardest-won rights (to reclaim a job after a strike, to company-paid health benefits, even to a living wage) were increasingly jeopardized;
- strikes were losing their effectiveness;
- unions' financial reserves shrank badly;
- labor was on the losing side of nearly every political battle (for example, it had campaigned against the North American Free Trade Agreement and for a law that would have forbidden industry to fire workers who strike).

Of course, labor has not been entirely emasculated. Even in the last decade there were situations in which unions took a stand. But the overall climate in which they did so was hostile and union gains were generally few and far between.

Public-sector employees were also targeted. For example, teachers unions found themselves under assault as never before—victims of Republican electoral successes, disenchantment with public schools, and the weakened state of labor in general. In Michigan, California, Illinois, Indiana, Pennsylvania, Wisconsin, and other states, teachers unions fought measures designed to curtail members' bargaining power and job security.

The trend toward privatization is another ominous sign for those in public sector jobs. With voters pressing for lower taxes and smaller government, the lure of privatization means public employee unions are giving up even more leverage as they attempt to bargain for wages and benefits. In New York City, Mayor Rudolph Guiliani used the threat of privatization in negotiations with sanitation workers, school custodians, and schoolbus drivers. In New York State, a Department of Social Services memo recommended privatizing services, consolidating units, and laying off 400 workers over two years. And in New Jersey, Governor Christine Todd Whitman took on the Communications Workers of America, who represent 34,000 of the 65,000 unionized state workers. She shifted twenty-three Division of Motor Vehicle offices to private hands, at the expense of 334 union jobs. Moreover, Whitman let it be known that she was determined to continue turning state functions over to private contractors. Hetty Rosenstein, executive vice president of CWA Local 1037, which represented the Department of Motor Vehicle workers, said she saw "something very scary happening" in the way the job losses came about. "We tried reaching out" to state negotiators, she claimed. "But they weren't interested."[13]

Clearly, the nature of work in America has changed.[14] The unwritten social contract—be good and you will be rewarded with lifetime employment—has been broken.[15] The problem is clear: Ironclad job security does not produce the agile and competitive work force today's global economy demands. In fact, the "job" itself may be dead. Warns William Bridges, "The reality we face is much more troubling, for what is disappearing is not just a certain number of jobs—or jobs in certain industries or jobs in some part of the country or even jobs in America as a whole. What is disappearing is the very thing itself: the job. That much sought after, much maligned social entity, a job, is vanishing like a species that has outlived its evolutionary time."[16]

The difficulties are compounded by the fact that business leaders have a hard time telling the truth and nothing but. ("We don't want to fire you. But if we have to, we will.") In fact, by and large employers have assumed precious little responsibility for the dilemma in which employees find themselves. It is the workers themselves who are expected to reinvent their professional lives. An admonition in the *Harvard Business Review:* "In an economy where ideas and knowledge have replaced products and services, work begins with the self."[17] Cautionary notes from *Fortune:* "New Technology Means New Career Ladders" and "Planning a Career in a World Without Managers."[18] Advice from the *New York Times:* "New Secret of Success: Getting off the Ladder."[19]

The result of what amounts to a contractual change in the relationship between business and labor is predictable: scrambling— scrambling to carve out moments of tranquility under a banner blazoned FIGHT STRESS. And in fact, coping with stress has become big business. According to *Personnel Magazine,* the cost to American business of stress-related illnesses is approximately 90 billion dollars a year. In transportation, communications, and utilities, no less than 50 percent of all managers are reported to "appear stressed." (The numbers in manufacturing, retail, and finance are only slightly lower.) Strategies designed to soothe beleaguered American workers range from biofeedback to psychoanalysis to assertiveness training to diet modification. And carefully crafted lists identify elements of a stress-free workplace such as talking openly, humor in the workplace, flexible hours, and child care programs.[20]

Of course, as suggested above, not everyone is suffering. Throughout what has been a difficult time for employees, CEOs have done remarkably well. In 1993, twenty-three of the nation's twenty-seven top job-slashers received raises averaging 30 percent; and in 1997, IBM chairman Louis Gerstner was paid no less than $8,000,000. Moreover, the phenomenon of phenomenally high pay is not confined to the private sector. Top executives at nonprofit organizations are also getting a piece of the action. CEOs of the largest charities and foundations often earn $250,00 a year or more. In 1995, the president of the Ford Foundation was paid $548,371, the president of New York University was paid $350,000, the CEO of Mount Sinai Medical Center $900,000, and the head of the American Red Cross $200,000. (To be sure, this handsomely paid group did not come close to matching its corporate counterpart. In the same year, the president and CEO of General Motors was paid $3,425,000, the chairman and CEO of Philip Morris $1,904,000, and the chairman and CEO of AT&T $3,499,000.)

Not everyone finds this ennobling. Derek Bok, the former president of Harvard University, was troubled early in the cycle by what he found. He pointed out that during the 1970s and 1980s federal civil servants saw their pay decline by 25 percent, and teachers barely held their own. During the same period the earnings of leading managers soared. Wrote Bok: "Inflated pay checks strain the social fabric at a time when Americans need to work together to help the country resolve a formidable set of common problems. In a globally competitive, knowledge-based economy powerful forces are already at work to raise the relative pay of highly educated people. It is dangerous to increase these differences even further at the very time when tens of millions of less educated Americans have been watching their own earnings decline significantly."[21]

Perhaps in response to the growing gap in wages between high level executives and those who work for them (especially hard to stomach when executive performance is poor), there has been in recent years a surge in shareholder activism. Increasingly, those who run business and industry are being called to account for what they do and how well they do it.

A survey of more than 1,000 independent and inside directors of the nation's top public companies found that 75 percent said their boards set clear objectives for evaluating CEO performance. Moreover, 26 percent reported that they themselves were reviewed on an annual basis; and 18 percent said that several board members had resigned or not run for reelection because the board as a whole considered them ineffective.[22]

Heads of companies such as Eastman Kodak, American Express, W. R. Grace, ITT, Baxter International, Westinghouse, General Motors, K-Mart, and AT&T have all felt the sting of shareholder activists. This is noteworthy because until the 1990s the shareholder rights movement was largely an academic exercise. Only in the last few years have shareholders become increasingly convinced that as individuals and collectives they had a right, a duty even, to exercise power. Rather than accepting the proposition that the businesses in which they are invested are the fiefdoms of chief executives and their hand-picked boards, such investors (often they are fund managers) insist that corporate leaders, like their political counterparts, be accountable to the demand for better performance.

ORGANIZATIONS

Since virtually all major private-sector enterprises are structured along organizational lines, it follows that changes that have had an impact on business in general, have also had an impact on the organization in particular. (Because public-sector organizations have been slower to change than their private-sector counterparts, the following discussion pertains more to business than to government.) Consider the impact of speed, information, and networks.

• Speed has already been mentioned as a competitive weapon— one that sometimes enables one company to best another. The implications of the demand for speed are enormous. Above all, the need for near-instant responses demands a more flexible management style that allows employees to act on their own initiative.

• The easy access to information has also had an impact, particularly on how people work in relation to each other. Networks connect people to people and people to data. They allow information that once flowed through hierarchies to pass directly between us. In other words, information accelerates the process of cutting slices from the old wedding-cake bureaucracy.[23]

• Networks establish easy links between departments that were previously considered functionally distinct. The advantages of such interactivity are obvious: faster response times; smoother operations; greater innovation; increased competitiveness and cost reductions; and higher levels of satisfaction in the workplace.

The demand for speed, the glut of easily available information, and the facility with which people can communicate with each other has inevitably led to changes in organizational structures and systems. In the past, organizations in business and industry prided themselves on tradition, on custom, on managing change in a manner that was as orderly as it was judicious. Haste was frowned on, dramatic moves considered reckless, and stability prized perhaps above everything else.

Moreover, men who were managers were educated, trained, and socialized in a fashion that was in keeping with the organizational cultures and hierarchies that had prevailed since the dawn of the modern corporation. The man in the grey flannel suit evoked in the beginning of this book was the very model of rationality, stability, and predictability that was prized until only rather recently. The task was to control change, not to trigger it.

But now vertical structures are out and in their place are far messier notions of what organizations should look like. Tom Peters's 1992 book, *Liberation Management* (which appeared ten years after *In Search of Excellence*), is still a good exemplar of the fashionable (a word Peters loves because it implies rapid obsolescence) approach to late-twentieth-century organizations. Consider the title. The very notion of liberation implies freedom from the past, freedom from control, freedom from what is expected, and freedom to act on your own initiative. The subtitle of the book, *Necessary Disorganization for the Nanosecond Nineties,* makes a similar point. It suggests that there is a premium placed on breaking with traditional hierarchical organizational structures, and it highlights the demand for fast responses to fast-changing times.

In the world according to Peters

• Everything is fashion, fickle, ephemeral. He quotes approvingly from a Japanese designer for Matsushita: "Japanese consumption is a continuous cycle of new products replacing old products, everything is in a process of change, nothing endures. We do not seek permanence."

• Independent profit centers are the future. "Small-scale, independent units—even a 'unit' of one—will play the lead role in responding to a fickle marketplace."

• Being lean is key. Describing ABB's now former CEO Percy Barnevik, Peters writes: "Barnevick has gotten the business of reducing central staff down to a near-science. He insists the head count in any headquarters activity can be cut by 90 percent the first year . . . . But that's just the start."

• Hustle is a virtue. "The idea of—and necessity for—doing everything faster is hard to challenge."

• Information is everything. "Organizations that have learned how to learn, that are engaged by electronic bulletin boards with outsider organizations to which they are just slightly related, that are hooked into universities and other learning centers—they alone will thrive."

• Vertical hierarchies are dead weights. There should be no traditional hierarchy, no organization charts, no job descriptions, no policy manuals, no rules about managing client engagements, and no guidelines for promotion.

• Vertical integration is out; networks are in. Organizations are now more about relationships than structures, more about problem solving than control.

• Hang loose and get lucky. Ask dumb questions. Empower. Don't back away from passion. Constantly reorganize. Listen to everyone. Don't listen to anyone. Decentralize. Decentralize again. Destroy hierarchies. Open the books. Start an information deluge. Take off your coat and tie. Get out of your office. Avoid moderation in all things.[24]

Clearly, the model of what an organization should look like has changed. In fact, even the geography of the workplace has changed. In the past, going to work invariably meant going, physically, to a central workplace. But now the virtual office competes with the traditional office as a place from which employees conduct their business. Although the office away from the office has usually been thought of as a boon to those excused from reporting to work every morning (especially for parents with children), the initiatives often come from companies eager to save both money and wear and tear on their employees. According to a study completed in 1996, 42 percent of companies of various sizes have workers that telecommute. (The figure is up from 33 percent one year earlier.) Of course, telecommuting is not for everyone; in fact one in five such arrangements fail.[25] Many workers want to go to the office, enjoy hanging out by the coffee machine, and worry that if they would be out of sight they would be out of mind. For its part, on the whole, management also remains a bit queasy. Put simply, employers have less control over those who work out of the office than they do over those who work in it.

This brings us to the question of leadership and management. How do leaders and managers cope with organizational structures and practices that are changing so fast? How do those who were trained to run one kind of an enterprise adapt to another? Books such as Rosabeth Moss Kanter et al.'s *The Challenge of Organiza-*

tional Change: How Companies Experience It and Leaders Guide It; journals such as the *Harvard Business Review;* and magazines such as *Fortune* and *Forbes* all seek to address what Kanter calls the "challenge of change."

Since the nature of change varies, the quality of good management depends, of course, on the kind of change the organization is experiencing. Kanter and her colleagues identify three types of change: changes in the relationship between the organization and its environment; changes that involve units within the organization; and political changes in which competing interests are involved. As well, they distinguish among various changemakers: strategists, implementers, and recipients.[26] But in the end, they, like nearly all those who write about leadership and change in the late twentieth century generate more or less the same ideas about how to be a good leader. They include

- Create a vision.
- Level with everyone.
- Communicate everything—and then some.
- Rethink motivation.
- Foster diversity.
- Empower. Everyone.
- Create networks.
- Form teams.
- Go horizontal.
- Decentralize.
- Hang loose.
- Always learn.

What will be readily apparent should be stated outright once again: the gap between organizations in the public and private sectors is large. The changes to which we just referred by and large apply to organizations in business and industry; they are less applicable to government bureaucracies. This is not to say that no government enterprise has responded to the changing times. It is to point out that because their professional lives are not at risk, public-sector leaders are far slower than their private-sector counterparts to adapt to what is new and different.

The efficiency gap between government and business was the subject of David Osborne and Ted Gaebler's influential book, *Reinventing Government.* Osborne and Gaebler pointed out that to remain competitive in the new global marketplace, American corporations had no choice but to move to flattened hierarchies, a focus on quality, and a fresh focus on customer satisfaction. They further noted that voluntary, nonprofit organizations also managed to "come alive with new initiatives."

In contrast, they charged government organizations with being "like luxury ocean liners in an age of supersonic jets: big, cumbersome, expensive, and extremely difficult to turn around." Government bureaucracies developed during the industrial era once worked well enough, Osborne and Gaebler conceded. But somewhere along the line, they became bloated, wasteful, and ineffective. "And when the world began to change, they failed to change along with it. Hierarchical, centralized bureaucracies designed in the 1930s or 1940s simply do not function well in the rapidly changing, information-rich knowledge-intensive society and economy of the 1990s."[27]

In short, it is widely recognized now that many public sector organizations have become stale. Whereas in the past they and the tasks they were expected to accomplish constituted a reasonably good fit, no one is arguing that in the late twentieth century this happy circumstance still prevails.

CULTURE

In the past, culture was considered a group, tribal, or national phenomenon. The distinctions among peoples were so sharp that to speak of, say, Americans and Brazilians in the same breath made little sense. Now these gaps are starting to close (although the extent of this change is a matter of debate). For example, for reasons that go back to our shared history and, more recently, to the homogenizing effects of information technology and the global marketplace, North Americans and West Europeans now share many of the same characteristics and concerns.

Nevertheless, the discussion that follows will focus on the United States. While few characteristics of contemporary American life would seem unfamiliar to those living in, for example, Amsterdam or Athens, there is something about culture that remains elusive unless it is specific, and so we will focus on how such change is experienced in the United States.

The reasons so many Americans feel that life is different now than it was merely a generation ago start with the family. Those of us who are in our forties and fifties grew up in a society in which fractured families were a rarity, whereas now they are commonplace. As Judith Bruce, author of a 1995 study on family decay, put it, "The idea that the family is a stable and cohesive unit in which father serves as economic provider and mother serves as emotional care giver is a myth. The reality is trends like unwed motherhood, rising divorce rates, smaller households, and the feminization of poverty. . . . [28] The major findings of her report confirm the obvious:

- Whether because of abandonment, separation, divorce or death of a spouse, marriages are dissolving with increasing frequency. In developed countries such as the United States, divorce rates doubled between 1970 and 1990.
- Parents in their prime working years face growing burdens caring for children, who need to be supported through more years of education, and for parents, who are living longer into old age.
- Unwed motherhood is common virtually everywhere. In the United States nearly one third of all births are out-of-wedlock. (In Northern Europe the figure is even higher.)
- Children who live with one parent are more likely to be poor than those who live with two.
- Even in households where fathers are present, mothers are carrying increasing economic responsibility for children.

Of course, there is a relationship between the changing family structure and the changing role of women. It is not necessary to chronicle here what has obviously been a revolution in the way women live and work. In general, women have benefited from the changes, which afford them choices unimagined only a short time ago. But they have also placed on them, us, additional burdens. Women tend to work significantly harder than men (at home and on the job), and their economic contributions are increasingly important to the family's well-being. [29] Moreover, women usually contribute a larger proportion of their income to the household than do men, and men keep more than women for their personal use.

In addition to the decline of the two-parent family, and of institutions such as the nation's public schools, what other factors contribute to the impression that the quality of American life has gone down? Two important ones are the impoverishment of our community life and the debasing of our public discourse.

Community life in America is not what it once was for a variety of reasons. They include urban decay (departure of the middle class), the rise in crime (keeps us at home), television and computers (keep us at home), increased work loads (decreased leisure time), and, of course, the aforementioned changes in the American family. Moreover often, in place of real organic communities, we now have instant communities. In late-twentieth-century-America private associations are a growth industry. In 1970 there were 4,000 private neighborhood groups (not including condominiums and cooperatives); by 1990 there were 66,000. By mid decade the fastest growing residential communities in the country were private; usually gated; governed by a thicket of covenants, codes and restrictions; and designed to provide those with the money to pay the secure, homogeneous sense of connection that was becoming increasingly elusive in the rest of America. More than four million Americans now live in such closed-off developments, and about twenty-eight million more live in areas governed by private community associations, including condominiums and cooperatives. During the next ten years, these numbers are expected to double.

It is not that exclusive communities such as these are new. But in the past they were peopled either by the very rich or by retirees. What is different now is that a considerable proportion of middle-class families in largely white areas of the country have chosen to wall themselves off, opting for private government, schools, and police. Urban experts generally agree that for a nation that has historically prided itself on combining individualism and community, such enclaves are undesirable. Says the director of a nonprofit group that works to build community links among new suburbs, "The worst scenario for America with this trend would be to have a nation of gated communities where each group chooses to live among people just like themselves and ignores everyone else." [30]

Exactly how the deterioration of our community life relates to the deterioration of our public discourse is difficult to say. What is clear, in any case, is that both have been on a trajectory that is consistently downward.

In virtually every corner of American life the definition of what is considered fit to print and say has expanded. Accelerated by the "inappropriate" relationship between President Clinton and former White House intern Monica Lewinsky, and pressed by the tabloids, even the most prestigious of our daily papers cover private lives in a manner that would have been unacceptable even a few years ago. In addition, television is riddled with sleaze, available even to the youngest viewers at virtually every hour of the day and night. And radio, that previous bastion of tradition, is now a veritable haven for coarseness in public discourse.

Yet another sign of the times is the nasty rhetoric that characterizes much of our political discourse. Campaigns have become downright dirty. Candidates are guilty by association. (Remember Willie Horton?) Their personal lives are cannon fodder. And their views and behaviors are derided in vulgar shorthand: "racist," "elitist," "leftist," "anti-women," "gestapo tactics," "womanizer," "tax-cheat," "liar," and so on. In a 1995 cover story on Pat Buchanan, *Time* magazine gave a reason for why in recent elections the rules have changed. "The disappearance of a cold war enemy invites politicians to take aim at internal targets that were once protected by the rules of patriotism. . . . Psychologists have encouraged the trend by demonstrating that voters retain negative messages four to six times as readily as positive ones." [31]

Moreover, our national legislature, the Congress, once known for the courtly manners of its members, has also become less civil. The 1995 budget discussions resembled nothing so much as a lowly brawl. Said Representative Henry Hyde, an old-guard Republican elected in the 1970s, "I think this trend is terrible, deplorable. We all need a two-week hiatus, but that's the last thing we're going to get. This is a trend that's developed over the last six or seven years. It's grown out of the success of negative campaigning." In turn, the Democrats blamed the Republicans, particularly the scrappy and occasionally mean Speaker of the House, Newt Gingrich. Charged Massachusetts Democrat Barney Frank, "Gingrich is the role model. He decided early on that the way to take power was to delegitimize your opponents and, instead of simply airing policy differences, to characterize them as bad people. Success breeds imitation." [32]

Of course, the yelling and screaming reflect intergroup tensions. Abortion, immigration, welfare, gay and lesbian rights, affirmative action, taxes, and crime are merely some of the issues that provoke passion and blame all the way around. And then there is race, the divide that was widened even further by the late, great O. J. Simpson case. The verdict in the criminal case triggered real bitterness between white Americans and black Americans, and some astonishment that at the end of the twentieth century different races still see things so differently.

Racial tensions notwithstanding, the argument has been made that what really divides us is not race but class. It is, in fact, possible that when the history of this period is written, the big story will be about what is sometimes referred to as the vanishing middle class.

For some reason, despite a spate of articles that appeared mid-decade such as the one in the October 16, 1995 issue of the *New Yorker* titled "Who Killed the Middle Class," or the one in the July 31, 1995, issue of *Newsweek* titled "The Overclass: Is a New Elite of Highly Paid, High-tech Strivers Pulling Away from the Rest of America?" or the one in the August, 1995, issue of the *Atlantic Monthly* titled "The Structure of Success in America," Americans have been slow to recognize the new reality. In defiance of statistics and common sense, 90 percent of adults persist in identifying themselves as "middle class." But, as John Cassidy noted in late 1997, between 1980 and 1996 the share of total household income going to the richest 5 percent of the families in the United States increased from 15.3 per cent to 20.3 percent. Meanwhile, the share of the income going to the poorest sixty percent fell from 34.2 percent to 30 percent. The fact of the matter is that the middle class is being squeezed even as I write. [33]

The decline of the middle class would not be quite so troubling if it did not exacerbate the gap in the United States between those who have a great deal and those who have far less. As the above statistics testify, the divide between rich and poor is virtually certain to grow. The question is whether the term "middle class" will eventually lose its meaning. [34]

Given the isolations and divisions that characterize so much of

American life on the cusp of the twenty-first century, what is the glue that still holds Americans together? How does the national culture persist? Or does it?

In the beginning of the century, the industrial revolution provided togetherness—mass production, mass consumption, mass media, mass education. Now, though, as Alvin and Heidi Toffler have pointed out, centrifugal forces are winning out. We are experiencing the customization, the individualization, of practically everything. Customized production. Micro markets. Five hundred channels. And instead of common cause, hundreds of single-issue interests. [35]

Several ways of repairing the national fabric have been proposed. The Internet brings together congenial types, playing roles from matchmaker to classroom teacher. But it is, let's face it, virtual togetherness. The Internet does not provide face time, and so the extent to which it can really satisfy the need to belong and to connect is limited. Similarly, recently hatched communitarian movements have made scarcely a dent in our national consciousness.

Maybe, then, it is values that will save us from ourselves. Maybe in the very arguments values generate lie the best hope of shoring up in the United States the flagging sense that for all the differences among us, we're in this (however "this" is defined) together. In the 1990s stories on values have been featured often in national magazines—for example, a *Newsweek* cover with a kid in a duncecap and a lead story titled "Shame: How Do We Bring Back a Sense of Right and Wrong." [36] And books on values have, to the surprise of many, sold like the proverbial hotcakes. William Bennett's *Book of Virtues, The Moral Compass,* and *The Death of Outrage,* Francis Fukuyama's *Trust,* and Ben Wattenberg's *Values Matter Most* were all big sellers in the 1990s and, it is fair to say, part of the national debate.[37] (According to Wattenberg, some of the hot-button issues were abortion, amnesty, busing, capital punishment, condoms in the classroom, crime, dependency, school discipline, drugs, family values, feminism, flag burning, gays in the military, gun control, homelessness, homosexuality, illegitimacy, infidelity, multiculturalism, permissiveness, political correctness, pornography, prayer in schools, quotas, race, sex education, and welfare.)[38]

Whether or not values will matter most to early-twenty-first-century American politics is debatable. What does seem clear, however, is that as money increasingly divides us, values may become an even more important tool for holding us together. The degree to which our political leaders have the capacity to keep most of us near the ideological center may, in the end, determine America's ability to forestall the balkanization that otherwise threatens further to fray the national fabric. [39]

LEADERSHIP AND CHANGE

Like its immediate predecessor, this chapter addressed two basic questions. Here, question number one was, What are the key changes in business, organizations, and culture? And question number two was, How do these changes affect the convergence of political and business leadership? In other words, I am claiming once again that the larger environment within which both public- and private-sector leaders are embedded is changing in ways that demand they have increasingly similar skills and employ increasingly similar tactics. As well, there is a growing necessity for more interaction between leaders in politics and leaders in business—despite the fact that for a variety of reasons they are still considered more different than alike.

• Political as well as business leaders have had to contend with change in corporate America. This is, of course, not an entirely new phenomenon. But for a variety of reasons—in particular the information revolution and the globalization of the economy—we have reached a point where significant change in corporate America is likely to have political as well as economic consequences. For example, both the downsizing of the labor force and the growing income gap between those at the top of the corporate ladder and those further down played a role in the 1996 Republican primaries. For months, Pat Buchanan, in his guise as angry populist, dominated Republican presidential politics. Conversely, when Texaco's personnel practices were exposed as racist, CEO Peter Bijur took to media outlets such as CNN to fight the growing backlash, which had been orchestrated by political leaders such as Jesse Jackson. Bijur's level of media exposure at that moment was reminiscent of nothing so much as a prominent politician caught in the line of fire.

• Political as well as business leaders are now expected to demonstrate managerial virtues such as competence and efficiency. The success of Osborne and Gaebler's *Reinventing Government,* and Vice President Al Gore's subsequent dedication to reducing the size of the federal bureaucracy while simultaneously increasing its level of productivity, are only two of the more obvious examples of the drive to have government look more like business. To some degree, this quest for greater efficiency has been driven by budgets. With less money at their disposal, governments have felt compelled to improve their management of increasingly limited resources. But there was also what we might call "the corporate effect." When the private sector was forced to become lean and mean in order to remain globally competitive, the attention it received for making what turned out to be a largely successful effort was bound to have an effect on the public sector. If corporate America can do more with less, why can't government do the same?

• Finally, political and business leaders are embedded in the same national culture, which, in turn, affects them in ways that are vaguely analogous. Both politicians and corporate executives have had no choice but to address in one fashion or another changes such as the decline of the family, more women in the workplace, the pressure to diversify, group conflicts, and the heated debates over values. Public- and private-sector responses to cultural shifts such as these have not, of course, been identical. But neither politicians nor their executive counterparts have been able to escape spending time on the knotty problems cultural changes inevitably generate.

Without wishing to push the point too hard or too far, one general conclusion seems inescapable: The changes touched on in this and the preceding chapter—in politics, economics, technology, business, organizations, and culture—have had an impact on how both political and business leaders spend their time. Both are now expected to demonstrate some of the same traits and skills, and both are now expected to employ some of the same leadership tactics. Put another way, the overlap between what leaders in both domains are supposed to be, and how they are expected to behave, is far greater now than it was in the past.

6
The 1990s
Side by Side

By the late twentieth century, the notion that public- and private-sector leaders were different species on different planets was exposed as a fiction. Although the studies of leadership in government and business generally remain separate exercises, the theory and practice of leadership have converged in ways unimaginable even a decade or two ago. Not only is the ideology of leadership in business nearly indistinguishable now from the ideology of leadership in government, leaders on both sides of the divide are having to perform in ways that are remarkably similar. These similarities are hardly surprising. On the cusp of the new millennium, the two domains intersect at nearly every turn, and both are shaped by the larger national and international contexts that themselves govern how and when leadership is exercised.

POLITICAL LEADERSHIP

The ideas

Once Ronald Reagan left the scene, the problems bedeviling political leadership in late-twentieth-century America seemed to resurface. For much of the 1980s, there was a respite of sorts—several years during which it seemed those in positions of political authority managed to steer the ship of state to where they wanted it to go. But by the early 1990s, the optimism started to wane. Colored by what was widely perceived to be the disappointing presidency of George Bush, it soon became clear that political leaders faced challenges best described as daunting.

So far as the theorists were concerned, the problems fell into four groups.

- Problem #1: Being stuck. Here we are, scholars like Joseph Rost argued, at the start of a new era, but still tied to old models of how leadership should be exercised. "The crisis in leadership is . . . that our school of leadership is still caught up in the industrial [rather than in a postindustrial] paradigm."[1] Although they were not writing about leadership per se, in *Reinventing Government* David Osborne and Ted Gaebler reached more or less the same conclusion: "The kind of governments that developed during the industrial era . . . no longer work very well."[2] Political scientist Paul Light confirmed the bloated bureaucracies. He found that between the early 1960s and the early 1990s the number of senior executives and presidential appointees had increased by no less than 430 percent.[3]

- Problem #2: "A pessimistic minimalism in democratic thought and practice."[4] America now has an electorate best described as largely apathetic. In the 1996 presidential election, less than 49 percent of eligible voters bothered to go to the polls. (Benjamin Barber has proposed an antidote to this pessimistic minimalism: "strong democracy."[5] This is not to say that in a strong democracy leaders are dispensable. Rather it is to propose the model of a facilitating leader, who makes participatory institutions work well and who promotes social cohesion and community.)

- Problem #3: Followers, or, to use the politically correct term, constituents, who are functionally if not legally disenfranchised. American politics has, by default, become leader-centric. We focus too much on those in positions of authority, and too little on those who are not. While on the surface it would appear that leaders might benefit from a circumstance in which they are nearly always the center of attention, in fact our obsession with what they think and how they behave (in their private as well as public lives) does them a disservice. It forces them to assume virtually all the responsibility for our collective well-being—a circumstance that is neither functionally advantageous nor, in fact, fair.

Ronald Heifetz has written of this proclivity, which is especially pronounced when there are problems for which no adequate response has yet been developed—for example, poverty and racism.

Under such circumstances, Heifetz writes, "We look to our authorities for answers they cannot provide. What happens then? Authorities, under pressure to be decisive, sometimes fake the remedy or take action that avoids the issue by skirting it."[6]

Scholars of the presidency have become all too aware of this leader-centric (president-centric) mentality and have generally distanced themselves from it. Stephen Skowronek, for instance, has taken a historical approach, describing patterns that recur no matter who is in the White House. "John Adams and Thomas Jefferson, John Quincy Adams and Andrew Jackson, James Buchanan and Abraham Lincoln, Herbert Hoover and Franklin Roosevelt, Jimmy Carter and Ronald Reagan—this repeated pairing of dismal failure with stunning success is one of the more striking patterns in presidential history, and accounting for it forces us to alter the way we have been thinking about that history."[7] Similarly, Charles O. Jones, in his book *The Presidency in a Separated System,* asks why our president-centric mentality persists. "It is not clear," Jones writes, "why those who should know better cling to this perspective in light of the historical fact and daily reminders of separationism as the central feature of our government."[8]

• Problem #4: The flawed nature of the leader-follower relationship. The American presidency and the American people are an obvious case in point. If words have meaning, presidents, being leaders, are supposed to lead; and their constituents, being followers, are supposed to go along, at least most of the time. (Remember Wilson: "I do not conceive the leader a trimmer, weak to yield what clamour claims.")[9] However, American politics being what they are in the late twentieth century, political leaders seem to have trouble hearing the sound of their own voice. What registers instead is the sound of polls. Paul Brace and Barbara Hinckley describe a "public-relations presidency," and a president who is interested primarily in maintaining and increasing public support.[10] (Of course, even if presidents were to forgo self-interest for the national interest, the media would make such dedication difficult. Network television, leading newspapers, and national magazines commission polls that measure the president's popularity at every turn.)

What is to be done? Given the fact that leadership experts have identified at least four major problems facing political leaders at the end of the twentiety century, what do they propose to do about it? How, in other words, can change be created when change is in order?

Several ideas have been generated.

• Solution #1. Strengthening ties between leaders and followers. There is in the 1990s what we might call a cult of followership. As if in penance for their previous obsession with leaders—now seen as wrongheaded and elitist—leadership theorists have rediscovered followers with a vengeance. In fact, the righteous anger at how followers have been treated in the leadership literature is a frequent nineties theme. Gary Wills, for example, is nearly beside himself. In his book *Certain Trumpets,* he decries what he perceives to be the rank injustice. "The followers are, in the [leadership] literature, a hazy and not very estimable lot—people to be dominated or served, mesmerized or flattered."[11]

To be fair, however, Wills notwithstanding, the notion that followers matter has not entirely escaped leadership scholars. In fact, in spite of the tag "Leadership Studies," most of the work on leadership makes clear that there is no leadership of any kind without followership of some kind. As psychohistorian Bruce Mazlish put it, the leader does not even exist before the encounter with the group he or she is to lead.[12] Moreover, it might even be argued that in the literature of the 1990s, followers have moved to center stage. In his book, *The Power of Followership,* Robert Kelley makes the point. While some followers are merely joiners, Kelley says, others become full-fledged collaborators, an integral part of the change process. Leaders and followers, Kelley insists, are no less than "co-adventurers embarking on a worthwhile journey together [and] relying on each other to arrive there safely and successfully."[13] Rost concludes simply that the activities of leaders and followers "are two sides of the same coin, the two it takes to tango, the composer and musicians making music, the female and male generating new life, the yin and the yang."[14]

• Solution #2. Collaborating. This remedy for what ails us is similar to the one proposed just above—but takes it, perhaps, one step further. It suggests less a direct link between two distinct species, leaders and followers, than it does a kind of holistic effort in which everyone is involved. While social commentators like Robert Putnam talk more about the "civic community" than they do about leadership per se, their argument has profound implications for how leadership might be exercised. Putnam claims that networks of engagement "allow dilemmas of collective action to be resolved."[15] Again, the point is not that collaboration eliminates the need for leadership. Rather, it demands a different kind of leadership—one that encourages work by the community as a whole. David Chrislip and Carl Larson have concluded that collaborative leaders must inspire commitment and action; they must be problem solvers; they must generate broad-based involvement; and they must sustain hope and participation.[16] Incidentally, there is no reason why those in positions of high authority cannot collaborate. Sometimes collegial leadership at the top is formalized (as in the Supreme Court); and sometimes collegial leadership at the top is simply informal (one individual has authority but decisions are nevertheless reached through collaboration.)[17]

Finally, before leaving the collaboration solution, I should note that it has also been applied to work at the international level. In an article published in 1990, Harlan Cleveland, one of the few who has been both an outstanding theorist and practitioner of leadership, explored the conditions under which national leaders might collaborate for the benefit of the international community. Here are a few of what Cleveland called the "priceless ingredients" necessary for such work: consensus on desired outcomes, a game that is win-win, a "cocktail of fear and hope," modern information technology, and individual agents of change.[18]

• Solution #3. Fostering public entrepreneurship. Although Osborne and Gaebler got credit for the idea that the entrepreneur has a place not only in the private sector but in the public one as well, in fact, as we have seen, the notion of political entrepreneurship is older than the success of their relatively recent book would suggest. In Eugene Lewis's 1980 book *Public Entrepreneurship,* he demonstrated that even the most rigid bureaucracies are vulnerable to brilliant, determined, and entirely idiosyncratic change makers.[19]

The notion of idiosyncracy is also central to Osborne and Gaebler's entrepreneurs, for if they do nothing else they break the mold. Above all, public entrepreneurs distinguish themselves by their capacity to see things in a new way; by their ability to define problems differently from their predecessors; and by their willingness to develop entirely fresh solutions to old problems. "For the past 50 years," Osborne and Gaebler write, "most public leaders have assumed that government's role was one-dimensional: to collect taxes and deliver services. . . . But today's entrepreneurial leaders unhook themselves from the tax-and-service wagon."[20]

• Solution #4. Doing adaptive work. Ronald Heifetz has been particularly interested in how so many groups, like so many individuals, manage to avoid doing the work that really needs to be done. As he sees it, it is the leader's task to expose and orchestrate conflict, and then to help the group learn a new and different way of doing work. Adapative leaders do not provide answers. Rather they enable group members to dig out on their own.[21]

It seems clear that as the twentieth century draws to a close the experts believe they have two basic tasks: First, to learn how leadership in America got broke, and second to figure out how leadership in America might be fixed. The degree to which they—we—are on the right track will be explored as the discussion moves from theory to practice.

The reality

It is apparent that the nation's politicians are not hanging out in the nation's libraries. There is little to suggest that what is being preached by even the best scholars of leadership is being practiced by those in a position to do so. There are exceptions, of course. *Reinventing Government* was read in Washington, and in a few places such as Harvard's Kennedy School of Government and the University of Maryland's Academy of Leadership public sector leaders are learning new ways. But in general, the gap between what is being advocated and what is being done is enormous. Most leadership scholars speak only to their own kind and then wonder why their, our, voices fail to resonate beyond the halls of academe.

The fact of the matter is that those who practice politics in America rarely reflect on what it is they do. Are politicians simply too busy to approach their leadership tasks in ways other than those already familiar? Do they lack access to new ideas on how leadership at the turn of the century might be practiced? Or is it that we persist in electing officials who, by their very natures, are resistant to contemporaneous notions such as collaboration, entrepreneurship, and adaptation? Whatever the reasons, the truth is that by and large those who now practice politics bear a powerful resemblance to those who did practice politics.

The top sets the tone, and each of the two men who have served as president in the 1990s has been marred by a major deficiency: George Bush was considered inept, and Bill Clinton has been seen as sleazy.

At the time of the 1992 Republican convention, Richard Morin of the *Washington Post* wrote, "President Bush staggered into . . . Houston this week as the most unpopular incumbent president to seek re-election in the past five decades." Morin ticked off the humiliations: the greatest sustained drop in presidential popularity ever recorded, the lowest job approval rating of any president at a similar point in his presidency, and the highest disapproval rating of any incumbent president seeking reelection.[22] Charged Walter Dean Burnham, Bush "displayed a striking mixture of rigidity and policy zigzags, all in an overarching context of profound indifference."[23]

Bill Clinton's problem was evident from the start. Indeed, charges about his character circulated even before the 1992 New Hampshire primary. He was, it was said, an adulterer. He was, it was said, a draft evader. And he was, it was said, a liar. ("I didn't inhale"). Thus we had on the national stage "Slick Willie"—"a man of dubious honesty but indubitable glibness who claimed innocence on technicalities and could not give a straight answer to a question."[24]

Doubts about Clinton's character never went away, even after he was elected president the second time. There was Whitewater, a thorn in the president's side that threatened also to pierce the First Lady. There were scandals such as "Travelgate" and "Filegate"—in which Hillary Rodham Clinton was, in fact, also involved. There were charges of illegal campaign fundraising. There was Paula Corbin Jones, a one-time Arkansas state employee who claimed that when the president was governor he exposed himself to her in a Little Rock hotel.[25] And finally there was Monica Lewinski.

Of course, there were objective reasons for some of Clinton's political problems. For example, in 1992 he was elected with only a 43 percent plurality; ran behind most members of the House and Senate; and had less party support in Congress than other recent Democratic presidents. Moreover, initially at least, his domestic agenda was nothing if not overly ambitious, especially his health care plan. Still, the evidence suggests that voters were not in love. If Colin Powell had been the Republican nominee for president in 1996, instead of the very weak Bob Dole, there seems little doubt that Bill Clinton would have been in big trouble.

Other politicians also found the going rough. For example, incumbents quit in droves. In 1995, no less than thirty-two members of Congress left the House and twelve the Senate—among them some of the best and brightest including Pat Schroeder, Bill Bradley, William Cohen, Nancy Kassebaum, Sam Nunn, and Alan Simpson. The complaints were that our public discourse was too rude, the job too stressful and hostile to family life, the press too intrusive, and campaigns too expensive. Said Simpson on announcing his retirement after eighteen years as senator, "The job just isn't fun anymore."[26]

For a brief moment there was an exception to the general rule, one political leader who was able nearly single-handedly to transform the national debate. Moreover, Newt Gingrich did it from a position of authority not traditionally associated with creating change: He was Speaker of the House. Gingrich moved our political discourse to the right, and he forced federal officials finally to address the budget deficit. As *Time* put it when they named him 1995 Man of the Year, Gingrich had "killed the old order of American politics. No U.S. President, Democrat or Republican, is likely to propose spending more than the government earns, or expanding what it tries to do, for at least a generation."[27]

Of course, as in the case of Bill Clinton, questions about character soon haunted the speaker. Rebuked by the House for lying to its members and cheating on his taxes, by 1997 Gingrich was personally and politically humiliated. His popularity dropped like the proverbial stone and his dream of becoming president evaporated.

Withal, Speaker Newt Gingrich was able to demonstrate that political leadership in late twentieth-century America is possible. Moreover the Republican Revolution focused on five themes that years later continued to dominate the national discourse.

• Theme #1: *America is divided.*

Increasingly, everyone seems pitted against everyone else. While the positive side of diversity in America has come to be called, rather too prettily, multiculturalism, the truth is that, for reasons real and imagined, the 1990s have been characterized by persistent fractiousness.

Women still have a big gripe. (In 1996, they constituted only 3 percent of top management at the nation's largest one thousand firms.) Racism is alive and well. And class differences are becoming more pronounced. John Cassidy in the *New Yorker:* "America is no longer a middle class country."[28] Lester Thurow in the *New York Times Magazine:* "Among men working full time . . . inequalities in earnings between the top 20 percent of wage earners and the bottom 20 percent doubled in the [last] two and a half decades."[29] Joseph Spiers in *Fortune:* "The growing gap between the well-off and everyone else is the most troubling economic policy problem of our time."[30] Benjamin Schwarz in the *New York Times:* "The central economic fact of the past quarter century is that the very forces . . . that have enriched America's most educated and powerful have actually hurt nearly 45 percent of its citizens."[31]

• Theme #2: *Americans distrust Washington.*

Bashing the government is an old habit. But in the 1990s the level of hostility was ratcheted up. Three episodes stand out. Ruby Ridge (described by *Newsweek* as "one of the most shameful [events] in the history of American law enforcement")[32]; Waco, Texas; and Oklahoma City. Coupled with the widespread apathy of the American voter, violent incidents like these lend credence to the claim of a growing gap between the government and the people.

• Theme #3: *The government is inefficient.*

Why should we support a federal bureaucracy that is bloated and badly managed? Why should we pay taxes when the system itself is riddled with inequities? Why did things get so obviously out of hand that even "tax and spend" liberals called for "cutting back to basics" in government spending?

• Theme #4: *Polite civil discourse is dead.*

The language of politics has been debased and words themselves are politics as combat. During the 1996 presidential campaign Pat Buchanan said, "promiscuous homosexuals appear literally hellbent on Satanism and suicide"; and promised that if elected he would go to the National Endowment for the Arts to "padlock the place and fumigate it."[33] And this is how Speaker Gingrich explained the death of a three-year-old hit by a stray bullet: "For 30 years, we have liberated prisoners, tolerated drug dealers, put up with violence, accepted brutality, and done it all in the name of some kind of bleeding-heart liberalism which always had one more excuse, one more explanation, one more rationale."[34]

* Theme #5. *Values matter.*

As the century draws to a close, the signs are of a return to basics. Bad behavior is judged more harshly and good behavior deemed more than simply old-fashioned. At least some practices previously defended as merely modern—getting stoned, being single and having babies, getting divorced—are now condemned even by most mainstream politicians. In short, family values are back in style.[35]

What is less clear is why this attention to matters of moral fiber has not impacted on our elected officials. On the one hand we prattle on about values. But on the other, in 1996 we reelected a president who, for all his brains and drive, was manifestly not a paragon of virtue. In other words, as we approach the millennium there is in American political life a disconnect between our newfound concern for values in the abstract, and our willingness to tolerate a lack of personal probity in our political leaders.

To be sure, we have, in this last decade of the twentieth century, seen progress in some areas. The size of the federal bureaucracy is down and so is the nation's budget deficit. Moreover, there is a new professionalism in politics, which in some respects at least is heartening. Legislators in particular have access to vastly expanded computer facilities that enable them to receive and process more information; and our elected officials generally are an increasingly diverse lot—a decent development given the growing heterogeneity of the people they purport to represent.

But leadership at the highest level of government is still far short of what it ought to be. As we saw in the beginning of this chapter, leadership theorists have identified four basic problems with the contemporaneous practice of political leadership: the persistence of the industrial paradigm; the decline in democratic thought and practice; the leader-centric political culture; and the flawed nature of the leader-follower relationship. While there is ample evidence that some leaders in some places across America are addressing one or more of these concerns, it is also fair to say that by and large our leaders are stuck. Teaching old dogs new tricks has proved difficult, and with high officials in the executive and legislative branches of government skirting the law, and failing at the same time to be authentically innovative, our faith in what is supposedly America's top leadership cadre is being sorely tested. The literature on political leadership in America has generated some interesting ideas on how government leaders might change along with the times. But since the message has yet to get through to those in positions of highest authority, the American people, especially those in their twenties and thirties, are turning their attentions elsewhere.

BUSINESS LEADERSHIP

The ideas

The value that dominates the ideology of business leadership at the end of the twentieth century is equality. Materials targeted at leaders in the private sector now assume that in the postindustrial age those who lead depend absolutely on those who follow. As Joseph Rost put it,"Followers do not do followership, they do leadership. Both leaders and followers form one relationship that is leadership."[36]

Max DePree was chairman of the board of Herman Miller, Inc., which is a leading company in the furniture business. While in the 1990s Herman Miller's image as one of the most admired firms in the United States was tarnished by declining profits, DePree was nevertheless in the vanguard of those who believed the gap between leaders and followers—management and labor—should be narrowed. In his book *Leadership Jazz,* DePree insisted that followers (employees) have a right to ask many things of their leaders (employers) such as: What may I expect from you? Can I achieve my own goals by following you? Will I reach my potential by working with you? Can I entrust my future to you? Have you bothered to prepare yourself for leadership? Are you ready to be ruthlessly honest? Do you have the self-confidence and trust to let me do my job? What do you believe?[37] By the mid-1990s Depree's approach had metamorphosed into the norm. As organization theorist Bernard Bass put it, "Subordinates have the responsibility to exert upward influence on their bosses for their mutual benefit and the benefit of the organization as a whole."[38]

As indicated earlier, this elevation of the follower to the level of the leader reached its apotheosis in works such as Robert Kelley's *The Power of Followership*. Kelley not only endows followers with the power to decide whom they will follow, he nearly (but, as we shall see, not completely) dispenses with leaders altogether. Citing examples of citizens who acted on their own initiative in spite of no leadership or poor leadership, Kelley claims that, "We need not wait for leaders to lead, nor for society to bless followership. Too many societal institutions have a vested interest in keeping the spotlight on leadership. . . ."[39]

One consequence of the egalitarian ideas that permeate the end of the twentieth-century literature on leadership in business is the infatuation with teams. Indeed, any approach that hints at collaboration is definitely "in." (My use of words such as *infatuation* and *in* is not meant to denigrate the idea of collaboration. It is to indicate that in all change there is an element of fashion, and that changes in leadership theory are no exception.) Teams are groups of two or more individuals that interact with each other, are interdependent in some way over some period of time, and have a particular task to accomplish.[40] It was global economic competition in particular that triggered the need for collaboration. In turn, teamwork has been made much easier by communications technologies such as audio and video teleconferencing and electronic mail.

Teams can actually be quite large. Peter Senge writes they should include a range of players who have traditionally been excluded from the decision-making process, such as suppliers and customers. In any case, teams should certainly not be "led" in any conventional sense of the word. Decisions should be reached by consensus—think of how juries are supposed to function—and no designated leader should be necessary for the collaborative work to be done.

The team dream infuses organizations at the highest levels. Over the past fifteen years, as interest in collaboration grew, even high-level executives have changed the way they work. This new kind of leadership cadre is sometimes formalized, as in the "Office of the President." But even when the team is an informal one, the image of the lone man at the top of the organizational pyramid is clearly outdated. Writes Senge, "We see a group of people with shared responsibilities and clear accountabilities strategizing together, reaching decisions by consensus, coordinating implementation and generally performing many, if not all, the functions previously performed by a chief operating officer."[41]

Another reason business and industry have warmed to the idea of a growing parity between leaders and followers is because of increased pressures to appear politically correct. Rigid organizational hierarchies are simply not acceptable any longer, especially not those that would exclude from the upper ranks women and blacks. This is not to say that the private sector has become a model of diversity in the workplace. Rather it is to suggest that the ideology of business leadership can no longer afford to appear socially, politically, or economically exclusive.

Of course, as we have already seen, there remains in regard to diversity a glaring gap between what is preached and what is practiced. In theory, women's interactive leadership style should be particularly well suited to organizations that intone flattened hierarchies and collective decision making; to technologies that increase the frequency of interpersonal communication; and to a global economy that puts a premium on speed and flexibility. Yet, as Judy Rosener observes, "Despite the new appreciation for the interactive leadership style and the increasing emphasis on the importance of human resource utilization, the paradox of gender prevents organizations from seeing the huge untapped pool of women leaders that is in plain sight." [42]

Now that a line has been drawn between leadership and management, the imbalance is especially striking. For by every measure what at the end of the twentieth century is considered management is in keeping with how men typically behave, and what at the end of the twentieth century is considered leadership is in keeping with how women typically behave.

In fact, the distinctions between leadership and management constitute a major shift in our thinking about how the private sector should be organized. A mere four decades ago, leadership was a conception business and industry generally chose to ignore. But now the best and brightest agree that leadership belongs in the private sector as much as it does in the public one. The only question is how exactly leadership and management should be defined.

Robert House distinguishes between management, supervisory leadership, and general leadership. Managers are in positions of formal authority and they get other people to do what they are "supposed" to do. Supervisory leaders provide guidance, support, and feedback. Leaders have the highest calling. They are charged with giving organizations meaning and purpose; with forging consensus by appealing to shared values; and with getting everyone on board to pursue common goals.[43] John Kotter went so far as to devote a whole book to the question of "How Leadership Differs From Management." According to him, these are some of the differences:

- Creating an agenda. Leaders establish direction, have a vision of the future, and develop strategies for producing change. Managers, on the other hand, plan and budget, provide necessary steps and timetables, and allocate appropriate resources.
- Developing a network. Leaders communicate with those whose cooperation is required. Managers, meanwhile, organize, staff, and establish a structure for implementation.
- Execution. Leaders motivate and inspire. Managers are more pedestrian. They coordinate, control, problem solve, and monitor results.
- Outcomes. Leaders create change. Managers, in contrast, supply predictability and order.[44]

The relatively new and now ubiquitous distinction between leadership and management is perhaps the single best explicator of why leadership—the study of leadership and leadership education and training—has become a big business. Quite simply, the boss's role has changed. Whereas once it sufficed to manage well and to exert authority with competence and aplomb, the demands on CEOs and other upper level executives are much greater now, and the tasks themselves more variegated and difficult to perform.

Moreover, there is a moral imperative to leadership as currently conceived that is hard to realize in a world in which the reality is less good and plenty and more mean and lean. There is, in other words, a palpable tension between what leaders are told they ought to be and what they actually are, in a domain that is in the end defined by the bottom line.

Finally—and this returns us to a point made earlier—if there is any validity at all to the research on differences in leadership style between men and women, men are not naturally as gifted at, or disposed toward, leadership as women. The interaction now considered the essence of leadership—encouraging participation, sharing power and information, energizing others—is not part of the stereotypical male repertoire.

Given the postindustrial emphasis on followers and teamwork, it may seem that leaders have become less important. Our increasingly sophisticated understanding of the importance of context further fuels the perception. For years we have understood that it is not the leader per se, but the confluence between the leader, the followers, and the situation that determines the dynamic. In fact, there has recently been a further elaboration of what exactly "situation" consists of. In particular, the shrinking of the planet has obliged us to consider the impact of national culture on how leadership is exercised. For example, psychologist Harry Triandis has argued that although national cultures differ in many ways, one particularly salient variable is the balance they strike between individualism and collectivism.[45] Japan places a higher value on the collective than on the individual; in the United States the reverse holds true. It follows that in Japan the ideal leader has been paternalistic and controlling; while in the United States the ideal leader is supposed to respect, admire, and even encourage the autonomy of his or her constituents. (Of course, organizational cultures also have an impact on how leadership is exercised. Effective leaders take account of institutional traditions, values, rules, and meanings.)

Does all this mean that leaders are products of their situations rather than the other way around? Are followers now so important that leaders matter less? Has the balance of power shifted away from the once all-powerful hero-leader?

Yes, and no. Any fool can tell that in the late twentieth century leaders routinely have been pushed around—both by others and by circumstances beyond their control. But to assume, therefore, that those who study leadership have left leaders behind is to assume incorrectly. Even the most ardent advocates of the rights of followers, and the most fervent proponents of the importance of context, do not in the end diminish the leader.

It is one of the ironies of the contemporary literature on leadership in business that for all our greater understanding of how incredibly complex the leadership process is, the stories inevitably end where they began: with the figure of authority. For whatever deep-seated reasons—and here we come to fields tilled by both Freud and Jung—tales of how some come to exercise more control than others continue to enthrall.

Leaders, and authority figures, have a way of dominating the discussion even as their importance is downplayed. Robert Kelley's focus is on followers, but he also writes about how important it is for them to find "a worthy leader."[46] In Joseph Rost's postindustrial paradigm both leaders and followers do leadership, but the relationship between them is "inherently unequal because the influence patterns are unequal."[47] Ronald Heifetz concludes that, "habitually seeking solutions from people in authority is maladaptive,"[48] but his book focuses on how those with and without authority can create change. And when Peter Senge and his colleagues instruct on how to create dialogue, they acknowledge that someone—a "facilitator"—has to take responsibility for "evoking and retaining the team's collective attention, intervening in complex social systems, and actively inquiring into defensive routines."[49]

Moreover, those who were enamoured of leaders in the first place are still smitten. Bass, for example, has published extensively on the importance of the "transformational" leader—a leader who, among other things, evokes strong feelings, generates excitement, heightens expectations, and cultivates intense one-on-one relationships. Similarly, in his book *Charisma and Leadership in Organizations,* Alan Bryman restores some dignity to a word that in recent decades had become nearly meaningless. Bryman argues that for all their systems and structures, organizations are not immune to the pull of charismatic leaders with a vision, the capacity to communicate, and the ability ultimately to create significant change.

But, tellingly, the new charisma is not like the old charisma. In its original incarnation, charisma was a term used to connote leaders so personally powerful as to be nearly overwhelming. The new charisma speaks of followers as well as leaders, and manages somehow to make them sound equally important. Writes Bryman, sounding properly egalitarian, "The emphasis upon charismatic leadership has given followers . . . a much more prominent role than they traditionally enjoy. . . . However, it has been argued that . . . we could and should go [even] further in making followers central."[50]

The idea of followers in partnership with charismatic leaders would strike earlier leadership theorists—particularly, of course,

Max Weber—as something of a joke. Once again, this is not to imply that the current work is wrongheaded, or trapped inappropriately in the vise of political correctness. In fact, it almost certainly brings to our understanding of charismatic leadership a needed corrective. However, like everyone else, leadership theorists work in a context, and in the context of the late twentieth century, the egalitarian values that permeate the literature on private-sector leadership are strikingly similar to those that have long permeated the literature on public-sector leadership.

The reality

When Time Warner's flamboyant, legendary CEO, Steve Ross, died in 1993, his wife Courtney prepared for the funeral by completely renovating the art gallery of the Guild Hall in East Hampton, Long Island. The room in which the funeral was held was repainted. A carpet was run up the center aisle. A stage was built. The lighting was adjusted. And on the back wall, facing the room, Courtney Ross hung a huge de Kooning painting, one of her husband's favorites. When the service was nearly over, the so-called master of ceremonies turned toward Ross's giant visage and declared, "You are still with us, you'll always be with us, and you were truly one of a kind."[51]

He was. Ross was the epitome of a charismatic business leader who, during his decades at the top, transformed the character of the American entertainment industry. For those who needed proof that charisma and corporations were not mutually exclusive, Ross provided the evidence.

But for all his subsequent achievements, Ross's heyday was in the sixties and seventies. The question here is whether his death in the early nineties (and, arguably, his decline in the eighties) signalled the end of an era. Are there on the cusp of the twenty-first century other captains of industry with Ross's capacity for both panache and performance?

While the offhand answer may be no, the fact of the matter is that less dashing change agents, such as the singular Bill Gates, who has now metamorphosed from wunderkind to "Emperor Bill," are also the stuff of myth. Gates has amassed a personal fortune (on paper) of something over $40 billion (at late 1997 prices). But he is, of course, much more than merely the world's richest man. "He has become the Edison and Ford of our era," says *Time.* "A technologist turned entrepreneur, he embodies our digital era."[52] Gates is a genius and a leader. His face graces the cover of magazines and his personality ("an awesome and, at times, frightening blend of brilliance, drive, competitiveness and personal intensity," breathes *Time*) is the stuff of celebrity profiles. We know a lot about his personal history, about his company, and by now we even know a lot about the house Gates built. (On a bluff fronting Lake Washington, it consists of three connected glass pavilions, has a thirty-car garage carved into the hillsides, and cost Gates a cool $40 million.)[53]

In other words, a few captains of business and industry still manage to grab our attention, and even in the late twentieth century, and even after flamboyant types like Ross are largely gone from the scene, some corporate leaders seem larger than life. Michael Eisner and Disney have become virtually synonymous. Jack Welch made General Electric the most profitable company ever. Under the late Roberto Goizueta Coca-Cola's stockmarket value rose from $4 billion to some $150 billion. And there is Tom Peters's list of legends: Percy Barnevik (Asea Brown Boveri), "who abhors bureaucracy"; Anita Roddick (The Body Shop), "who believes joy has a place in business"; Mike Walsh (Union Pacific Railroad), "who has a lot of nerve"; and Ted Turner (CNN), "who's nuts."[54]

Of course, most business leaders are more retiring. Initially, people were skeptical of Louis Gerstner, who took over at ailing IBM in 1993. "Is He Too Cautious To Save IBM?" asked *Fortune* early on.[55] But one year later the man was, according to *Business Week,* "a hero of monumental proportions."[56] By 1995 Gerstner was gold: IBM was listed as one of ten companies that posted the biggest gains over the previous year, and the price of company stock had more than doubled. Nevertheless, throughout the 1990s Gerstner chose to remain in the background. Despite his now enormous wealth, the man who remade IBM stayed behind the scenes, content to be the religious, dedicated family man he was presumed to be all along.

Sometimes, of course, like their political counterparts, business leaders lose. Remember who sat next to Hillary Rodham Clinton during her husband's first State of the Union speech? It was John Sculley, at the time the proud head of Apple Computer. Unfortunately for Sculley, only a few months later he was out and another man, Michael Spindler, was in. "Can New CEO Michael Spindler Bring Back The Glory Days?" *Business Week* asked.[57] Apparently the answer was no. By February 1996, less than three years after he took over at Apple, Spindler too was gone, replaced by the former chairman and CEO of National Semiconductor, Gilbert Amelio. (As things turned out, Amelio's tenure at Apple was even shorter—less than eighteen months!)

Spindler's forced departure was instructive—especially, perhaps, to other business leaders still operating on the now clearly mistaken assumption that they were exempt from the public accounting their political brethren inevitably had to endure. Elected officials have always been subject to public scrutiny. In contrast, until recently, corporate leaders were spared public humiliation. Instead, their fates were in the hands of the board members to whom they were directly responsible (and who were often close colleagues), and the dramas, such as they were, were played out behind closed doors.

Now this has changed. Spindler was forced out not only because Apple was in trouble (it lost millions during his tenure at the top), but also because CEOs are no longer protected by the title they hold. Employees at Apple had rebelled openly, complaining to the press, taking calls from headhunters, and telling nasty jokes. ("What's the difference between Apple and a kindergarten? A kindergarten has adult supervision.") Shareholders also demanded to be heard. There was an explosion of opposition at Apple's annual meeting, with several major shareholders calling loudly for Spindler's resignation. "It's time to go, Mr. Spindler," announced an investment banker from New York. Moreover in the days following the meeting, there was a continuing stream of phone calls and e-mail messages from impatient institutional investors to board members, demanding that Spindler be replaced.

In late January Spindler still hoped to stop the bloodletting. He sent out a memo to Apple employees, urging them "not to believe media reports. . . . Their intent is disruption." But the damage had been done. The feeding frenzy of previous weeks had shaken the board's confidence in Apple's CEO to the breaking point.[58]

The case of Michael Spindler points to significant shifts of power. The CEO has ceded some of his clout to the board, and the board in turn has surrendered some of its control to shareholders. In theory, of course, boards of directors have always been responsible for hiring, monitoring, and firing chief executives. The practice, however, was different. As the *New York Times* noted in 1995: "They rarely fired them, hardly monitored them and usually left the job of naming a chief executive to his predecessor." [59] Now the game has changed. The pay and the perks for high-level executives may be lavish, but the leash is short and getting shorter.

Boards are themselves more closely monitored than they used to be. Institutional shareholders in particular "have become increasingly impatient over the years with poorly performing companies and they are not reluctant to express their opinions in no uncertain terms to corporate boards."[60] Indeed, since the 1980s, shareholders have been emboldened by their successes. They have gained a far bigger voice in how companies are run, and since 1992 their legal standing has been enhanced by a Securities and Exchange Commission ruling allowing large shareholders to take collective action against corporations without violating proxy rules.

General Motors, Sears, IBM, and Kodak are just a few of the companies that in the early 1990s experienced management shake-ups previously considered unthinkable. Moreover, investors are not limiting themselves to intervening only when there is trouble. In some cases they push a company that is doing well to do even better. In 1995 the Teachers Insurance and Annuity Association/College Retirement Equity Fund (TIAA-CREF), the world's largest pension fund, took on the board of W.R. Grace and effected a shakeup that was a watershed in the annals of corporate governance. While in general TIAA-CREF had been satisfied with its investment in Grace, and while in the past it had preferred private diplomacy to a public fight, by openly taking on Grace's board, John Biggs, TIAA-CREF's chairman and CEO, signalled a new era in which investors set increasingly high standards for company performance.[61]

The entertainment and communications industries provide as good an example as any of the increasingly insecure position of CEOs. While the high rate of turnover in these businesses is not typical, the sight of so many corporate corpses is nevertheless sobering. As Ken Auletta noted in February 1996, Frank Biondi, who had been with Viacom for nine years, was merely the latest in a long line of industry executives who in recent years had been forced out. They included Warner Music's chairman, Robert Morgado; HBO's chairman, Michael Fuchs; Disney Studios' chief, Jeffrey Katzenberg; Sony Corporation's American president, Michael Schulhof, and the Sony studio head, Peter Guber; Simon and Schuster's Richard Snyder; Paramount Communications' president, Stanley Jaffe; CNBC's president, Roger Ailes; Hearst Magazines' chief, Claeys Bahrenburg; and Fox's Barry Diller.[62] The list is striking not only because of its length, but also because most of those who are on it were, in fact, successful performers.

Of course, late-twentieth-century captains of business and industry have some extraordinarily difficult issues with which to contend. The twin challenges of technology and globalization are the most obvious examples, but there is also the difficult legacy of the recent past. Great companies such as IBM, Sears, and General Motors, had for years dominated their respective industries, suffered badly in the 1980s when times changed. For example, in 1992, GM reported a $23.5 billion loss, by far the largest ocean of red ink that had ever engulfed a Fortune 500 company. (Tellingly, when Roger Smith, GM's CEO from 1981 to 1990, was asked what had gone wrong, he replied, "I don't know. It's a mysterious thing.")[63]

Those who succeeded Smith and his failed contemporaries fought back. But there was a price to be paid. By the mid-1990s many of those at the top were burned out. "As corporations restructure, they are forcing managers through one of the most harrowing stress tests in business history. . . . Most painful of all, managers who were trained to build are now being paid to tear down. They don't hire; they fire."[64] No one knows for sure how many executives suffered from what has been called "survivor sickness," but a striking increase in the number of disability claims for mental illness may have been an indicator. UNUM Life Insurance, which writes more private disability policies than any other U.S. insurer, reported that the number of such claims processed rose from 7.8 percent of its total in 1989 to 10.2 percent of its total in 1993. The anecdotal evidence seems to corroborate that nothing is as difficult for upper- and middle-level managers as firing employees. As *Fortune* put it, "Like nothing else in a manager's repertoire, [firing] smells of defeat and retreat." What it was really like for AT&T's chairman, Robert Allen, to announce that he planned to cut AT&T's payroll by 40,000 jobs, is not recorded. For public consumption he said, "The way I get myself mentally over the tough bridge of what happens to 40,000 people is my responsibility for 300,000 people."[65]

Of course, it's been harder for employees than employers. We know full well that workers across America work more than they did before in order to keep up, and they are more worried than before that the opportunity to work will be taken from them. While in any given case the fear of being fired may be exaggerated, in fact wholesale dismissals are still a fact of American life. In late 1997 Levi Strauss gave pink slips to more than 6,000 employees and Kodak bid farewell to no fewer than 10,000.

Again, women and minorities continue to be especially hard hit. Victimized by being the last hired and first fired, their access to power also continues to be far more limited than that of white males. Harvard economist Clair Golden reported in the mid 1990s that just one middle-aged, college-educated woman in six could claim career success—even when "success" was defined only modestly.[66]

The news is bad in medicine, especially academic medicine. Despite the increasing representation of women on medical school faculties, relatively few have achieved senior academic ranks or leadership positions.[67] The news is bad in law. A report by the American Bar Association confirms that despite surging numbers of female lawyers, bias against women in the profession remains entrenched. The result: steep inequities of pay, promotion, and opportunity.[68] Finally, the news is bad in business. The federal government's first comprehensive study of barriers to promotion made it clear that while white women have poured into the workforce, women stumble, or they are tripped, as they near the top. According to the 1995 government report, "The glass ceiling exists because of the perception of many white males that as a group they are losing—losing the corporate game, losing control and losing opportunity." [69]

Minorities have fared no better. To be sure, they have made some progress in some areas—for example, the percentages of African American purchasing and personnel managers increased somewhat between 1983 and 1993, and by 1997 37 percent of Fortune 500 boards included black directors. But if many companies do try to hire qualified minority applicants, the problems begin after they are hired. The support systems that exist for white men are not generally available to black men (or women), and mentors are few and far between. In other words, protestations of good intentions notwithstanding, for blacks progress in the corporate world has been painfully slow.[70] (When a scandal involving racism hit Texaco in 1996, we learned that fewer than 1 percent of those earning more than $106,000 a year at the company were black.)

Even in the entertainment industry, in which African Americans have historically played a disproportionately prominent role, they are held back. *Newsweek* put it this way: "Despite a growing impact on the creative side of showbiz, few African Americans have managed to gain, or hold on to, much of a stake in the valuable assets they help produce. . . . African Americans haven't cracked the ranks of studio heads, network programmers and other powerful execs who run showbiz day to day—jobs that often lead to ownership positions."[71]

For all the ills that still plague business and industry in the last decade of the twentieth century, the remedies administered do not generally include the elegant and empowering ones promulgated by the contemporary leadership literature. Because the mantra of the decade has been "lean and mean," and because downsizing continues to play so large a part in the life of corporate America, the niceties touted by leadership theorists have remained largely unrealized. In fact, if truth be told, as the century draws to a close, America is still focusing its attention not on employees, supposedly the key followers, but on figures of authority, on the men (almost always) who hold the title of chief executive officer. Case in point? The *New York Times,* which in November 1997 described James Barksdale, CEO of Netscape Communications, as follows: "The person principally responsible for charting a course that enables Netscape to survive, even thrive, in the shadow of Microsoft is . . . James Barksdale [who] by all accounts deserves much of the credit for Netscape's resilience to date. He has brought strategic direction and management discipline to the young company . . . and he has proved to be a skillful salesman who can persuade button-down corporate America to buy from an Internet pioneer."[72]

By and large, so far as employee-followers are concerned, the new solutions do not eliminate the old problems. For example, in the 1990s many companies operated on the assumption that the new and different would work better than the tried and true and so they deliberately brought leaders in from the outside. When CEO Kay Whitmore was ousted by the board at Kodak, it was made clear right away that he would be replaced by someone new to the company.

And so it was: Whitmore was replaced by a man from Motorola; and the CEO at General Motors was replaced by a man from Proctor & Gamble; and the CEO at Tenneco was replaced by a man from Union Pacific; and the CEO at IBM was replaced by a man from RJR Nabisco; and the CEO at AlliedSignal was replaced by a man from General Electric; and the CEO at Goodyear was replaced by a man from Rubbermaid; and the CEO at AT&T was replaced by a man from Hughes Electronics; and so on.

The reasons for this restlessness are not hard to fathom. In times of uncertainty and tough competition, business, like politics—recall Ross Perot, Steve Forbes, and Colin Powell—is seized by the apparent virtues of a fresh approach. Not so incidentally, restive shareholders are generally quick to agree. When outsiders are brought in, stockholders benefit from what is usually a rise in the price of company stock, and they relish what they interpret as the board's commitment to strategic change.

Another supposed solution to the problems of corporate America was a hot new management tool known to those in the know as "reengineering." But for all the attention, there were at least three big problems. 1) It was difficult to define what exactly reengineering was; 2) It was in any case difficult to implement; 3) And instead of fostering collaboration and teamwork, it often put the fear of God into employees who tended to see it as little more than a euphemism for layoffs and increased workloads.

This is not to say that reengineering never worked. *Fortune* cited Liberty Mutual as an example of a company in which reengineering made a positive difference precisely because management got everyone involved in the change process.[73] But what happened at Liberty Mutual was the exception and not the rule. For by and large chief executive officers have learned to talk the talk, but they do not walk the walk. We have seen that the literature on leadership in the private sector is full of good intentions. It speaks eloquently about empowerment in the workplace, about collaboration between leaders and managers on the one hand and subordinates on the other, and about teams. It testifies to the virtues of diversity. It makes distinctions between managers and leaders that suggest that it is up to the latter to engage, motivate, and inspire all those charged with creating change. Finally, the literature makes clear that leaders are supposed to be moral agents, that is, they are supposed to take into account the wants and needs of their followers.

But, as already indicated, by now we know that in the real world things don't quite work that way. When AT&T announced one of the largest corporate work-force reductions ever, it wore kid gloves. The *New York Times* reported that "there were carefully scripted 'roundtable' meetings, moderated by neutral observers, or 'facilitators,' that decided who stays and who goes. Along the way there were lawyers, job counselors, psychological counselors and an army of management consultants."[74] But the upshot was the same. The niceties of "collaboration" notwithstanding, employees by the tens of thousands found that at work they had little or even no control.

The distinction we now make between leadership and management contributes to the feeling of inauthenticity. For most employees, job security is the biggest concern. But this is the one thing those at the top will not—some would argue cannot—guarantee those further down. Thus the notion that leaders, unlike managers as traditionally conceived of, authentically engage and inspire their followers is, to use Joanne Ciulla's word, bogus.[75]

Finally, the literature speaks of an ethical imperative. By definition, leaders are supposed to take followers into account. Let us, however, go back to the case of AT&T. Clearly, one can make a case for the dismissal of tens of thousands of employees. It's good for business. But how about the issue of fairness? Was it fair for workers to be dismissed en masse while AT&T's CEO, the now departed Robert Allen (he finally left in late 1997), made an extra pile of money because of what the company had wrought? Executive compensation is often pegged to the price of company stock. Since the price of company stock generally goes up when the payroll goes down, it came as no surprise that when the massive layoffs were announced, $6 billion was added to AT&T's stock market value. Overnight, this increased the (paper) value of Allen's stockholdings and options by more than $5 million. "Did I make the decision [in order] to increase my personal wealth?" Mr. Allen was asked by a reporter. "Hell no," he replied. "Increasing shareowner value is the right incentive for me to have at AT&T."[76] What Mr. Allen did not add was that in this case his personal wealth and shareholder value were one and the same.

In the introduction to this book, I made my thesis clear: that by the end of the twentieth century the contexts within which both public and private sector leaders were embedded had converged. I claimed further that as a result of this convergence, the notion that government leaders and business leaders are entirely different was simply outdated. This chapter has testified that as the 1990s draw to a close, theories of business leadership are nearly indistinguishable from theories of political leadership, and that leaders in both domains are required to perform similar tasks in similar ways.

• The ideology that now underlies both leadership in government and leadership in business calls for collaboration between leaders and followers, and considers that authentic leadership implies active, participatory followership.

• Political leaders are expected to provide meaning and purpose, to appeal to shared values, and to pursue common goals. And so are business leaders.

• Political leaders are embedded in the international as well as the national environment. And so are business leaders.

• Political leaders must be familiar now with the global marketplace. And business leaders must be familiar now with foreign as well as domestic policy.

• Political leaders are pushed around more than ever before. And so are business leaders. Like their political counterparts, corporate executives are now subject to public and media scrutiny, and they are increasingly vulnerable to campaigns against them by an array of interested groups.

• Political leaders are expected now to be good managers. Nowhere has this been evidenced more clearly than in the effort to "reinvent government" led by Vice President Al Gore. The American people are now called "customers," and the Clinton administration boasts of a "federal workforce that is the smallest in thirty years."[77] A particular premium is put on fiscal responsibility. In early 1997, President Clinton noted with great pride that during his tenure in the White House, the federal deficit had been cut by 60 percent. In turn, business leaders are expected to be good communicators and skilled political operators. Like their political counterparts, business leaders must now be able to use the media to their advantage—top executives appear regularly on CNBC—and act in a manner that is both personable and persuasive.

• Government leaders and corporate leaders face similar challenges. They include: increasingly restive and demanding constituencies; print and electronic media far more intrusive and aggressive than in the past; more demanding and more public performance reviews; increasingly diverse constituencies; diminished respect for authority; the still-growing power of money; the accelerated pace of change; and the two hard nuts—the information revolution and globalization.

• In both politics and business there is a yawning gap between what is preached and what is practiced. Most Americans do not experience a government that is by the people and for the people. Nor does today's cadre of political leaders evoke a high degree of public trust. Similarly, in an era still characterized by widespread downsizing, employees remain properly suspicious of employers' promises to empower them, collaborate with them, and integrate them into the decision-making process.

• Finally, political leaders and business leaders behave in more or less the same ways. In particular, the pieties of leadership theory notwithstanding, both usually fall far short of the moral model typically espoused.

Parts I and II of this book have demonstrated the ways in which, during the last half-century, leadership in government and leadership in business have converged. The question that remains is, how has this convergence affected what actually happens? It is to this issue that we now turn.

Part III

JOINED AT THE HIP

7
Impaired Learning

In the 1950s and 1960s, Americans assumed that leadership and excellence were one and the same. They generally believed that men who made a career of public service—especially executives and legislators in the upper echelons of American government—were decent and smart. And they presumed that captains of business and industry reached the pinnacle of success because they were in the most important ways better than their counterparts.

In those days the rhetoric of political leadership bore scant resemblance to the rhetoric of corporate leadership (managership). Whereas the first spoke of pluralism, participation, and persuasion (especially after the 1960s), the second conveyed command and control. Still, in one important way leaders in both domains were virtually identical: men high on the greasy pole were seen as, in the best sense, a breed apart.

By the late 1960s this had started to change, and by the 1970s America's political leaders in particular were vulnerable to a degree unthinkable merely a decade earlier. The "greening of America" was in full flower. A president had resigned in disgrace. And groups at the back of the bus, such as women and blacks, were demanding to move to the front. For the first time since the Depression, those in positions of political authority were being questioned at every turn.

Corporate America had also started to change. Business and industry were increasingly permeated by the notion that at least some attention should be paid to "subordinates." Bosses were expected to display at least modest interpersonal skills. And the rigid stratification that had long characterized organizational hierarchies started to give way.

But unlike political America, which was in turmoil during the early 1970s, corporate America was rather quiet. Business and industry were not faced as quickly and directly by the Civil Rights movement, or the women's movement, or the urban unrest, or the war in Southeast Asia. In other words, there was during the 1970s no particular crisis in the private sector and so, despite the changing rhetoric, it was not motivated to undertake major change.

During the 1980s government and business reversed roles. In what can only be described as an ironic turn, it was a decade during which the American polity was relatively quiescent, while American business was faced with a crisis of confidence.

The 1980s will be remembered forevermore as the decade of Ronald Reagan. To be sure, President Reagan wore the mantle of power lightly, and in fact it could reasonably be argued that this is precisely why it was bestowed on him for so long. In any case, eight years of the "great communicator" provided persuasive evidence that political leadership was not dead in America, and that it was possible to create change and remain popular at the same time.

Business and industry, in contrast, were plagued by an unfamiliar sentiment—self-doubt. For the private sector, the 1980s were generally a time of trouble. Faced with a revolution in information technology, stiff competition from corners of the globe heretofore remote, and foreign management techniques (especially Japanese) that seemed in many cases to work better than the home-grown kind, business leaders were, quite simply, caught off guard. For too long they had denied change and remained in place; by the time it dawned on them that something was seriously amiss it was in significant ways late in the game.

As the decade drew to a close there was an emerging consensus: The old ways of doing business were no longer good enough. Organizations would have to change. More precisely, hierarchies would have to be flattened; power more widely shared; decision making more freely delegated; and information more broadly distributed. This is not to say that leaders in business and industry were diminished. On the contrary, issues of leadership and management were more intensely debated than ever and leading men were still center stage.

By the late 1980s and early 1990s it had become clear that for both political and business leaders the domestic and global environments were changing in ways that could no longer be ignored. As we have seen, these changes were political, economic, technical, corporate, organizational, and cultural. In other words, they permeated virtually every aspect of late-twentieth-century life—which meant those in positions of authority who ignored them did so at their peril.

What to do? How to play a game in which the rules had changed so much and so fast? The rhetoric was certainly new and different. Business leaders were sounding more like government leaders—and vice versa. Above all, there was in the realm of ideas about leadership a commitment to greater equality and diversity in the nation generally, and in the workplace in particular. Teams and collaborations, leaders and followers, women and African Americans, flattened hierarchies and strong democracy—all spoke to morning in America.

The problem was, is, the gap—in particular the gap between what is being promised and what is being delivered. In other words, for all the newfangled rhetoric, and in spite of the '90s booming economy, there remains in the land a nagging sense of disappointment. By nearly every measure most Americans believe those in charge neither want to nor know how to fix what's broke. To take but one poignant example, on the eve of President Clinton's second inauguration, a mere 18 percent of Americans believed that when his term was over fewer Americans would be living in poverty.[1]

Men and women in positions of authority are generally not dumb, and so, in response both to the challenge of change and to the demand for improved performance, at least some of the old dogs decided to learn new tricks. In particular, we have seen the astonishing growth of what has been called the "leadership industry."

It should be noted at least in passing that even at the undergraduate level leadership education has in recent years proliferated. For adults, particularly those who have already spent some time in the workplace, leadership education and training programs are generally targeted at four different audiences: government leaders, business leaders, not for profit or independent sector leaders, and military leaders. By a margin so wide that the word *overwhelming* fails to capture it, most such initiatives are designed for men and women in positions of authority in business and industry. In fact, it is the corporate leader's most obvious counterpart, the political leader, who in this regard is largely ignored.

Why business leaders (and managers) get all the attention is clear: It is the widespread expectation that leader learning will improve leader performance. And if the leader's performance improves so, it is presumed, will the bottom line. In other words, corporate America is willing to invest in executive education because by and large it has come to believe the investment will pay off.

But what about political leaders? Why are they given short shrift? Does virtually no one think they would benefit from learning about leadership? Are elected officials—presidents, governors, mayors and legislators—considered impervious to the benefits of lifetime learning? Or is there simply a reluctance to invest in educating political leaders because the benefits are unclear and/or uncertain? In any case, there appears to be a widespread assumption that once politicians (and bureaucrats) hold positions of authority, they will somehow know what to do. Like parenting, it is assumed that learning on the job, in effect by osmosis, will be adequate.

What follows is an overview of leader learning in late-twentieth-century America. First, we will look at what is available to political leaders; then we will sample what is being marketed to private and independent sector leaders; and finally we will consider what is happening in the American military (the first bastion of leadership education in America). The exercise is designed to answer four basic questions: Is the market responding to customer demand? Does it adequately address change on the eve of the twenty-first century? Does it take account of the growing convergence between political leaders and business leaders? And does it instruct public- and private-sector leaders on the virtues of collaboration and on how it might be accomplished?

FOR PUBLIC-SECTOR LEADERS

One of the few programs targeted directly at politicians and bureaucrats is the Leadership Education Project at the John F. Kennedy

School of Government at Harvard University. Originally the conception of psychiatrist Ronald Heifetz, the program has grown from small sideshow to prominent part of the Kennedy School curriculum. Leadership courses now enlist recent college graduates who are enrolled in two-year master's programs, mid-career students (usually in their thirties, forties, and fifties) who are getting their master's degree in one year, and senior officials who register for brief periods in "executive programs."

As his book *Leadership Without Easy Answers* suggests, the curriculum Heifetz developed has had one primary objective: to help those in positions of authority in the public sector to be effective leaders.[2] For example, a course titled "Exercising Leadership: Mobilizing Group Resources" is portrayed in part as follows: "The aim of this course is to give students a fundamental and practical understanding of leadership . . . . The purpose is to increase one's capacity to sustain the demands of leadership and to develop further one's ability to exercise both leadership and authority." The course requires students to study leadership, to analyze their own successes and failures, and to participate in small groups in which the process itself becomes an object of study.

The Leadership Education Project also offers five-day seminars for senior bureaucrats and elected officials. The seminars are based on two basic assumptions: first, that "as we approach the end of the second millennium, political, social and familial traditions of authority are in the midst of crisis"; and second, that being a part of the Leadership Education Project is likely to "expand [students'] leadership capacity." (It should be noted that some of Harvard's courses and seminars mix men and women from the private sector with those from the public one.)

Arguably the most ambitious institutional investment in the education and training of political leaders, as well as in the promotion of leadership research, is being made at the James MacGregor Burns Academy of Leadership based at the University of Maryland. (Burns is widely considered the dean of leadership scholars and his life is an exemplar of social and political engagement.) Its earlier incarnation, the Center for Political Leadership and Participation, was established to foster future generations of political leaders through education, service, and research. Described as "the first academically sanctioned program in the country to support emerging leaders seeking elective office," the Academy made a great leap forward in 1996 when its founder and director, Dr. Georgia Sorenson, secured from the W. K. Kellogg Foundation a $5 million grant. The money is being used to raise additional funds with the intention of making the Academy the premier educational resource for political leaders (and scholars of political leadership) worldwide.

Academy programs are targeted at a wide range of political players including community activists, government bureaucrats, and elected officials. Moreover, faculty and staff are involved in research on leadership, the global distribution of information about leadership, the establishment of leadership networks in schools at both the secondary and post-secondary levels, and curriculum development. The Academy is dedicated to facilitating political change both at home and abroad, and it has already established ties to political leaders in other countries including Ireland, Estonia, Eritrea, Hungary, and South Africa. (At this writing I serve as director of the Academy's Center for the Advanced Study of Leadership.)

What else is there for political leaders? Not much. There are, to be fair, numerous community leadership development programs around the country, and some institutions of higher education make their leadership courses available to a wide audience. The United States Office of Personnel Management also operates the Federal Executive Institute, which has symposia and seminars for senior executive branch officials. But, in general, there is a glaring paucity of education and training programs for leaders in the public sector. For example, the Hubert H. Humphrey Institute of Public Affairs at the University of Minnesota has as its mission to "educate the next generation of leaders." To this end it offers three different master's programs—all of which are clearly designed to prepare students for diverse careers in public affairs. But although educating leaders is the ultimate goal, and although courses are offered on various public policy issues, the Humphrey Institute has for years not offered a single course in Leadership Studies per se. Unlike the Kennedy School, which in the last decade has acknowledged that leadership is in and of itself worthy of study, the Humphrey Institute, by virtue of what it does not offer, makes no such admission.

In other words, while there are some programs around the country that offer courses to leaders and managers in the public sector, such programs are few in number, small in size and, usually, narrowly focused (such as those targeted at, for example, school administrators). In short, the sum total of what is available to those in positions of political authority who want to learn more about what they can and should do is puny.

In addition, advice or guidance in this area—specifically on how political leaders might hone their skills and improve their capacity to create change—is equally spare. We have seen that there is a substantial body of scholarly work on political leadership. But hard-nosed, pragmatic instruction is hard to come by. For whatever reasons, even those who know a thing or two about political leadership have by and large not packaged their wares for use in the real world.

FOR PRIVATE-SECTOR LEADERS

Training

What a contrast! Unlike political leaders, business leaders have available to them a rich palette of programs—programs about their inner selves and relations with others; short-term tasks and long-term goals; traits and skills and tactics and strategies; organizations and communities; constituents and competitors; peers and followers; risks and rewards. Even the most casual observer might reasonably conclude that while political leaders are attention-deprived, corporate leaders are suffering from information overload.

Lessons begin in the equivalent of first grade. By now, many of the nation's business schools have integrated courses on leadership into their curricula, which means that many business school graduates are already acquainted with the fundamentals of leadership learning. Schools of business have also learned to capitalize on the hunger for leadership education among those already in positions of authority. Many of them offer "short courses," or "leadership weeks," or "executive seminars," designed to capture those long since in the world of work.

But, as Jay Conger's 1992 book *Learning to Lead* testifies, the search for wisdom does not by any means stop in school: "As part of their desperate search for improved competitiveness, corporations are pouring millions of dollars into some form or other of leadership training."[3] It should be noted, though, that Conger remains sceptical. He concludes that although short courses of a week or less can have a positive short-term impact on leadership performance, their long-term benefits are less clear.[4]

Most leadership programs are designed to appeal to those with a general interest in the subject. Typically, they are offered by free-standing enterprises, of which the Center for Creative Leadership in Greensboro, North Carolina, is the outstanding example. The Center has been a remarkably successful undertaking. For three decades it has trained nearly 30,000 would-be leaders, thriving on the clearly accurate assumption that corporate America is willing to shell out big bucks for leader learning.

Most of the Center's eighteen different programs are open to any "qualified" participant. Moreover the list of offerings is so long that virtually anyone who even thinks of applying is likely to find something of interest. The Center also markets and sells a variety of instruments and simulations designed to help leaders "select the right tools to meet [their] organizational assessment or leadership development goals." For example, "Benchmarks" is for individuals: It is a "comprehensive 360-degree leadership instrument that assesses strengths and development needs, encourages and guides change, and provides strategic insight for executives and managers." "EdgeWork," in contrast, is for groups: It is "an action learning partnership built around a new organizational simulation."[5]

Of course, the Center for Creative Leadership is by no means the only game in town. In fact, because corporate America has developed such a large appetite for leadership programs, narrow markets are now the rage.

• *Leader Training for a Particular Purpose.* For instance, the American Institute for Managing Diversity, based at Morehouse College, helps leaders and managers understand how cultural differences affect the way people work. The head of the Institute, Dr. Roosevelt Thomas, argues that diversity training must be an "across-the-board operation," from the CEO on down; and that diversity training should be made widely available—if only because by the twenty-first century most new hires will be women and minorities.[6]

• *Leader Training in a Particular Domain.* For instance, the Healthcare Forum Leadership Center is dedicated to the proposition that to transform the healthcare industry, healthcare leaders must themselves be transformed. A report titled "Bridging the Leadership Gap in Healthcare" concludes that six transformational competencies will be critical for leading twenty-first-century healthcare organizations: 1) mastering change; 2) developing systems thinking; 3) fostering a shared vision; 4) inspiring quality improvement; 5) redefining healthcare ("to focus on healing, changing lifestyles, and the holistic interplay of mind, body, spirit"); and 6) serving the public/community.[7]

• *Leader Training for Changing Organizations.* For instance, Development Dimensions International (a human resource development and consulting firm) and The Leadership Research Institute (a nonprofit research organization) worked together on "high-involvement leadership." Since many of the recent approaches to change, such as total quality management, reengineering, and teams, depend on empowering employees, the question was, How can leaders adapt to the new demands and give others what they need? Some of the conclusions were that by and large high involvement leadership had yet to be realized; that leaders often stumbled in implementing high involvement; and that training in empowering leadership had a positive effect on leader performance.[8]

• *Leader Training for Special Situations.* Example: Leading teams. When General Electric's medical systems division introduced team management several years ago, planning was inadequate. The different teams did not report to a single individual who had clout inside the company, nor did enough members of enough teams have the opportunity to interact.[9] GE's experience was typical—so typical, in fact, that training team leaders became a subset of training leaders more generally.[10]

Example: Leading "wired" companies. Computer networking has been called "the most important development in the management of organizations since Du Pont, General Motors, and others invented the modern corporation . . . before World War II."[11] The question is, How does this development impact on how leaders should lead? Some answers: Eliminate obsolescent hierarchies. Use tools such as e-mail, teleconferencing, and groupware to eliminate fixed department and corporate boundaries. Create multidisciplinary teams and develop interpersonal skills.[12]

Example: Leading in hard times. As we have seen, in early 1996 there was an uproar when AT&T announced it planned to fire tens of thousands. In the past, corporate leaders were generally able to slash and burn without much fear of a political backlash. (Between 1990 and 1995 Du Pont prepared for a recession by eliminating 37,000 jobs, shuttering or divesting fifty-eight plants and businesses, and cutting funds for new plants and equipment as well as research and development.) By the mid-1990s, however, the climate had changed. Executives determined to downsize had to be more circumspect to survive downturns.

Example: Leading the revolution. In the early 1990s, Jack Welch of General Electric, Lawrence Bossidy of AlliedSignal, Bill Weiss of Ameritech, and Mike Walsh of Tenneco all believed that their companies' futures could be secured only through radical change. Noel Tichy, a professor of Management at the University of Michigan who was in fact hired by Welsh to consult at GE, argued that corporate revolutions entail three phases: 1) awakening (making the organization aware of the need for change), 2) envisioning (clarifying the purpose of the revolution), and 3) re-architecting (redesigning and rebuilding the organization).[13]

Example: Leading within particular organizations. Increasingly, companies such as Hewlett-Packard, McKinsey, and Pepsico are developing their own in-house leader learning programs. In 1992 Shearson Lehman Brothers' National Training and Development Department offered branch managers courses to enable them to "increase productivity and create a branch environment which empowers, motivates and enhances the effort to provide clients with unparalleled advice and service." Clearly, Shearson Lehman believed leadership education paid off. Just as clearly it was motivated by this belief to invest in what it called "training and development."[14]

GE is another example of a company willing to put its money where its mouth is. It spends more than $500 million annually on leadership development and CEO Jack Welch makes it a point to get directly involved. Starting each January, 80,000 employees and their bosses fill out one-page "internal resume" forms that provide information on their skills, career goals, and development needs. Then, between March and May, Welch and a few other senior executives visit each of GE's twelve operating units to conduct one-day personnel reviews. In the end, about 500 of GE's top executives have been monitored, evaluated, and placed in slots deemed a perfect fit.[15]

• *Leader Self-Help*. Corporate America is willing to support all kinds of leader learning, including that which comes from introspection and analysis. By the 1990s, no respectable leadership education program was without a component designed to provide leaders with information on who they were, and feedback on how they were perceived by others. At one end of the spectrum is a program offered by the Menninger Clinic called "Professionals in Crisis." Part of the Menninger Leadership Center, it was created in 1991 for leaders who felt they were losing control at work and at home. It includes a complete medical and psychiatric exam, individual counseling, and group psychotherapy. Stays range from days to weeks and cost more than $1,000 a day. Executives apparently welcome the opportunity to talk openly about their hopes and fears. Says a senior associate at the Leadership Center: "Here they have the luxury of complete honesty."[16]

Clearly, so far as the private sector is concerned, leadership is "in." Business schools from coast to coast have integrated courses on leadership into their curricula (although, ironically, whether or not it can successfully be taught is still a matter of debate). And corporate America is intent on providing top executives with programs, courses, seminars and symposia designed to satisfy virtually their every need. Leadership education is required now to remain on the cutting edge, and CEOs are similarly expected to "go beyond the typical MBA-type training" in order to learn how to lead change.[17] In other words, as far as corporate America is concerned, individual and organizational development have been joined.

Reading

The countless programs available to corporate leaders are apparently inadequate. Private sector leaders and managers also consume a neverending supply of books, journals, magazines, and videos dedicated to their self-improvement. How-to lessons—how to organize, how to argue and win, how to compete, how to negotiate, how to persuade, how to navigate the information superhighway, how to reengineer, how to be highly effective, how to utilize women as a management strategy, how to "survive and thrive" in today's world—are considered necessary supplements to more formal leadership education and development.

Books range from those that are clearly scholarly; to those that contain some references to theory but are addressed nevertheless to practitioners; to those that say, in effect, to would-be leaders and managers, "Let me take you by the hand and show you what to do." A book that falls into the first category is *The Challenge of Organizational Change: How Companies Experience It and Leaders Guide It*.[18] With Rosabeth Moss Kanter—professor at the Harvard Business School and former editor of the *Harvard Business Review*—as lead author, it comes as no surprise that this volume, while advertised as "required reading for any leader," is not exactly easy going. Long and densely written, it is nevertheless supposed to be not only for analysts of change, but for change agents themselves.

Tom Peters's book, *Liberation Management: Necessary Disorganization for the Nanosecond Nineties,* falls into the second category.[19] The length of this book is even more daunting than Kanter's (834 pages), but its forty-seven snappy chapters were intended for real-world leaders and managers with a short attention span.

Finally, there are the various "how-to" books, some of which were written by top experts on leadership in corporate America. For example, Warren Bennis teamed up with Joan Goldsmith to produce "a workbook on becoming a leader." The workbook starts with a general introduction to leadership "for the 1990s and beyond"; goes on to a discussion about "knowing yourself"; and concludes by elaborating on how to communicate a vision, maintain trust, and reach goals. The book is full of graphics and exercises of all kinds. It is, in other words, what it was designed to be—user friendly.

Most striking about workbooks such as these is the total confidence with which they assume that leadership can be taught. As indicated earlier, in some circles at least, the question of whether men and women can learn to lead remains open. Bennis and Goldsmith register no such doubts: "We have designed this course of study to enable you to become . . . a leader . . . . Learning to lead is a lot easier than most of us think it is, because each of us possesses the capacity for leadership."[20]

Peter Senge, author of the widely praised book on learning organizations, *The Fifth Discipline*, has also (along with four MIT colleagues) produced a leadership manual: *The Fifth Discipline*

Fieldbook.[21] Senge's book is targeted at those already in positions of authority, and it intends to teach. Readers are asked to "Mark up the pages. Write answers to the exercises in the margins. Draw. Scribble. Daydream." This playful note notwithstanding, the book's overarching aims are of course entirely serious: superior performance, improved quality, better service, competitive advantage, an energized and committed workforce, and the effective management of change. In fact, Senge's five "learning disciplines" are tantamount to no less than a lifelong commitment to the study and practice of leadership.

In addition to the many books on management and leadership in corporate America—some of which are written in a popular style and have sold in the many millions—two familiar and widely circulated periodicals (as well as others of more modest renown) are also targeted at captains of business and industry. The more scholarly of the pair is, of course, the *Harvard Business Review* (HBR), which can reasonably be viewed as something of a bi-monthly business bible. In addition to interviews with CEOs of companies like Xerox, Silicon Graphics, Stride Rite, Whirlpool, and AlliedSignal (not to mention conversations with the likes of football coach Bill Walsh), by the early 1990s articles on the theory and practice of leadership had become a regular part of HBR's heady mix.

A sampling:

• In 1992 there were leadership lessons by "Oriental masters who taught the wisdom of life through parables." The parables demonstrated the "essential qualities of leadership and the acts that define a leader: the ability to hear what is left unspoken, humility, commitment, the value of looking at reality from many vantage points, the ability to create an organization that draws out the unique strengths of every member." [22]

• In 1994 HBR published an article critical of "flavor-of-the-month managing." A chart detailing the enormous growth of the "management industry" revealed that between 1982 and 1992 the number of MBAs awarded grew 33 percent; total consulting revenues shot up 334 percent; total expenditures on corporate training climbed 350 percent; and the sales of business books rose 118 percent. In spite of this growth, the authors concluded that executive performance fell short of expectations. "Given that managerial innovations disappoint with such regularity, we are surprised that companies continue to adopt them with such abandon. . . . Managers find themselves adrift in a sea of competing ideas, increasingly insecure about whether the right approach will ever be found."[23]

• One year later, a more positive note was struck. An article in HBR listed eight things leaders could do to transform their organizations: 1) Establish a sense of urgency; 2) Form a powerful guiding coalition; 3) Create a vision; 4) Communicate the vision; 5) Empower others to act on the vision; 6) Plan for and create short-term wins; 7) Consolidate improvements and produce still more change; 8) Institutionalize the new approaches.[24]

For leaders disinclined to anything too scholarly, and of course for leadership junkies, there is also *Fortune*. It provides a neverending supply of articles on leadership and management in corporate America.

Random samples from the 1990s:

• "The Information Wars: What You Don't Know Will Hurt You" advised those in charge to innovate lest they get left behind; to learn everything they can about the other guy's business; and to become indispensable.[25]

• "Think for Yourself, Boss" discussed a book by Eileen Shapiro titled *Fad Surfing in the Boardroom*.[26] The piece argued that in their quest for instant success, and because downsized companies "shed managerial brain cells as well as bureaucratic fat cells," executives had become unduly susceptible to "fad floggers."[27]

• "Trying to Grasp the Intangible" urged managers to value their organization's intellectual capital and, for that matter, any other asset defined as "intangible." (Such assets do not appear on the company's balance sheet, but cost money if they have to be recreated from scratch.)[28]

• "Don't be an Ugly American Manager" claimed that 25 percent of American managers were likely to fail in their overseas assignments. Leaders were urged to get their managers to think globally, and to demonstrate "the capacity to appreciate the beliefs, values, behaviors and business practices of individuals and organizations from a variety of regions and cultures."[29]

- "Wanted: Company Change Agents" focused on the importance of "midlevel change leaders" who are "determined, willing to break rules, and great at motivating their troops." The problem: Such leaders are in short supply. The solution: Teach CEOs to recognize change agents, and then place them in key positions.[30]
- "The Nine Dilemmas Leaders Face" discussed apparently contradictory goals such as independence vs. interdependence, creativity vs. discipline, trust vs. change, and people vs. productivity.[31]
- "What Women Can Learn from Machiavelli" reviews a book that seeks to provoke women into using and expanding the power they already have. Women, it is argued, should take their cues from *The Prince* and break the glass ceiling they themselves helped erect.[32]

Clearly the amount of information and advice available to those in positions of corporate authority is enormous. But for all the ideas on how leaders and managers might improve their performances, virtually no attention is paid to anything outside the domains for which they are directly responsible. Executives are urged to think big, but so far as the still expanding and highly profitable leadership industry is concerned, thinking big does not include anything beyond the corporate world that is of immediate concern.

FOR INDEPENDENT-SECTOR LEADERS

This book has not yet addressed the nonprofit or independent sector. But because this sector is of considerable size and consequence, and because there is an expanding market for programs and materials that cover the governance of nonprofit organizations, this third domain merits at least brief discussion.

Nonprofit institutions are actually older than either government bureaucracies or modern corporations. But only in the last fifteen years or so has the question of how nonprofits should be led and managed received much attention. Now there are more than three dozen university-based centers focusing on various aspects of independent-sector life, including nonprofit economics, public policy, and leadership and management. Many MBA and MPA programs include courses in governing nonprofit organizations, and a few institutions, such as Case Western Reserve University, offer degree programs that focus exclusively on this area.

High time. No fewer than 900,000 exempt organizations are registered with the Internal Revenue Service, and this number does not even include religious congregations or the local affiliates of many national organizations such as the Boy Scouts and the American Cancer Society. Brian O'Connell, former president of Independent Sector (a national coalition that supports nonprofit initiatives), estimates the real number of nonprofit organizations is something over two million. He points out that nonprofit organizations include neighborhood improvement societies, Catholic Charities, overseas relief organizations, private schools and colleges, United Way, corporate foundations and public service programs, the United Negro College Fund, fraternal benevolent societies, conservation and preservation groups, the Council of Jewish Women, community foundations, and National Public Radio.[33]

By definition, the newfound attention to the leading and managing of nonprofit organizations assumes that they are in important ways different from their private and public-sector counterparts. The key questions include, what do we know about leadership and management that pertains to all three sectors? What are the differences? Do personnel in nonprofit organizations have motivations and aspirations different from those working in government and business? What skills are required to keep nonprofit organizations solvent? Are the management skills needed for small nonprofits, such as soup kitchens, different from those needed for large nonprofits, such as hospitals and universities?[34]

Even a cursory review of the work on leadership and management in nonprofit organizations reveals that by and large it resembles the work on leadership and management in for-profit organizations. The key tasks are the same: creating a vision, communicating the vision, enlisting and empowering others, planning strategically and tactically, and implementing.

Consider this essay titled "Leadership in Human Services: Key Challenges and Competencies." (A human service agency is defined as a nonprofit organization that provides services to the community in areas such as health, welfare, arts, and recreation.) On the basis of interviews and survey results, the following twelve items were listed as the "core leadership challenges faced by human service administrators": 1) Utilizing resources and building support for change; 2) Directing and motivating staff; 3) Building outside support and understanding; 4) Improving the agency's performance; 5) Time pressures; 6) Lack of a supportive working environment; 7) Clashes with the board; 8) Problems with clients and external groups; 9) Responding to competing demands; 10) Uncertain or limited resources; 11) Generating volunteer involvement; 12) Lack of knowledge or experience.[35]

Moreover, the following leadership "competencies" were considered most important: flexibility, resourcefulness, leading subordinates, integrity, setting a developmental climate, hiring talented staff, team orientation, building and mending relationships, doing whatever it takes, balancing personal life and work, compassion and sensitivity, self-awareness, putting people at ease, decisiveness, being a quick study, and confronting problem subordinates.

With the exception of item 11 every one of the nonprofit sector leadership "challenges," and each of the leadership "competencies," has a distinctly familiar ring. In other words, what is perhaps most striking about the work on nonprofit-sector leadership is its strong resemblance to the work on private-sector leadership.

However, as indicated earlier, this is not to argue that nonprofit organizations are mere clones of their corporate counterparts. There are in fact at least three important differences. The first is the role of values. To paraphrase Thomas Jeavons: If the work of business revolves around wealth (and the work of government revolves around power), then the work of nonprofit organizations revolves around values. Jeavons points out that the independent sector has its roots in religion, and that many schools, hospitals, and service agencies were started by religious organizations.[36]

The second key distinction between the nonprofit and private sectors is the role played in the former by volunteers. Most nonprofit institutions get by with a relatively small paid staff and a relatively large cadre of volunteers critical to the overall effort. Volunteers enlist to help others and they serve without pay. Since money motivates most people to work for private-sector organizations, a key question for leaders of nonprofit organizations is, What rewards other than a salary do I have to bestow? (Such rewards include knowledge, professional enhancement, social contacts, increased self-esteem, feelings of virtue, and the joy of giving.)[37]

Finally, independent-sector leaders confront different fiscal issues. In particular, fund-raising efforts are crucial. Should they fail, the organization is likely to fold. Here too, the ways in which nonprofit leaders motivate others to do what they want them to do involve rewards other than the usual ones. Obviously in this case those who give money do so not because they receive something material in return, but rather because they believe donating will do good.

What seems clear is that while the similarities among private-, nonprofit-, and even public-sector leadership outweigh the differences, in order to be successful, nonprofit leaders must be particularly skilled at exercising interpersonal influence. How else can they get others to go along?

John Whitehead was co-chair of Goldman Sachs from 1976 to 1984, and he also served as Deputy Secretary of State. In what he has called the third stage of his life, Whitehead went on to preside over several nonprofit institutions, including Harvard University's Board of Overseers, the Brookings Institution, the Trustees Council of the National Gallery of Art, and the Greater New York Councils/Boy Scouts of America. As a result of these experiences, Whitehead was persuaded that the leadership and management of nonprofit organizations left much to be desired. In 1995, he gave $10 million to the Harvard Business School to endow the John C. Whitehead Fund for Not-for-Profit Management. His goals: to encourage research in nonprofit management techniques, to expand the teaching of these techniques, and to put greater emphasis on training business school students to be leaders and managers of nonprofit groups. Said Whitehead: "I became fascinated by nonprofits. Their reach is much bigger than I realized. One out of every ten workers in the United States works for a nonprofit, and if you add in the volunteer time, it's even greater. But I came to realize that while people who run nonprofits are fully committed, they are not very good managers, and nonprofits are not very well run."[38]

FOR MILITARY LEADERS

It is simply impossible to talk about leader learning in America without making at least brief reference to the armed services. (To be sure, the military is in fact a government agency and in fact civilian public employees have had limited access to some of its training programs.) Long before leadership education was a growth industry targeted primarily at business and industry, leadership development was a component of military schooling.

In the last decade or so, leader learning in the armed forces has been thoroughly updated. Like business leadership, military leadership was once tantamount to command and control. But just as corporate leaders and managers have been obliged to change their approach, so military leaders have had to adapt as well. This is not to say that it is expected now that decisions made in the heat of battle will be reached by consensus. It is to say that the military has not been exempt from the social, political, and technological shifts that have changed the way organizations work.

A 1990 Department of the Army manual provides a good illustration of what we might call "new age" military leadership. The basic requisites are predictable: tactical and technical competence, a mastery of fundamental soldiering, and the maintenance of discipline. But along with these traditional skills are a few others with a distinctly contemporary ring. They include: 1) Teach subordinates ("Our leaders must take the time to share with subordinates the benefits of experience and expertise"); 2) Be a good listener ("We must listen with equal attention to our superiors and our subordinates"); 3) Treat soldiers with dignity and respect ("Leaders must show genuine concern and compassion for the soldiers they lead").

Moreover, the army expects its leaders to be self-aware and self-critical ("Am I reliable? Do I lead by example? Am I a decision maker or a 'decision ducker'?"); and to carry out their "ethical responsibilities" ("Ethics are principles or standards that guide professionals to do the moral or right thing—what ought to be done").[39]

In 1994, *Fortune* put its stamp of approval on the U.S. Army by declaring it a learning organization superior to "business in retraining senior managers and keeping the chief's attention fixed on the future." No longer rigid and hierarchical, the army was now touted as "everything the modern organization is supposed to be—adaptive, flexible, a learning enterprise." Army Chief of Staff General Gordon Sullivan was given credit for recognizing that the army had to move rapidly into the information age and for instilling in the ranks a level of egalitarianism that was heretofore unthinkable.

The army also instituted procedures that revolutionized the way officers are judged. At the National Training Center in California officers engage in simulated warfare. When the exercise is over their performances are evaluated not only by superiors, but by peers and subordinates as well. Said Sullivan, "There was a lot of resistance. But we do it because in high-performance organizations the parts are supposed to talk to one another." Concluded *Fortune:*" "No other army is so egalitarian. Nor are there many corporations in which senior executives sit down with those who will eventually succeed them and explain how under pressure they overlooked some vital information that blew the deal."[40]

To be sure, the army is hardly perfect. In 1997, after the largest investigation ever of sexual misconduct in its ranks, it was forced to concede that sexual harassment exists throughout the organization, and that it crosses gender, rank, and racial lines. Moreover, the report by the panel of investigators stated that the army's leadership was to blame.

Nevertheless, for most of the decade it has been widely presumed that military leaders have a thing or two to teach business leaders. In fact, the *Harvard Business Review* regularly reviews books that make just this point. In his piece on Colonel Larry R. Donnithorne's *The West Point Way of Leadership,* Alan Webber writes: "The West Point model of leadership is a fascinating and insightful one. . . . With its emphasis on moral guidance, values, and appreciation of the feelings and emotional growth of subordinates . . . it constitutes an important departure from the conventional wisdom."[41]

HBR also features articles written by military leaders such as Lieutenant General William Pagonis. Pagonis led the 40,000 men and women who fed, clothed, sheltered, and armed more than 550,000 people during the Gulf War. He wrote about the importance of empathy as well as expertise, and argued that leaders should take an active role in shaping their environments: "The work of leadership, therefore, is both personal and organizational. The bad news is that this means hard work—lots of it. The good news is that leaders are made, not born."[42]

For further evidence of the widespread belief that military leaders can teach us wisely and well, consider Persian Gulf War heroes Generals H. Norman Schwartzkopf and Colin Powell. Both men wrote autobiographies. Both books became immediate best-sellers.

Schwartzkopf told us he enjoyed being a leader, even at West Point. In his senior year he was made cadet captain and company commander: "It was my first taste of leadership and I found I was good at it."[43] Later, when Schwartzkopf was made division commander, he apparently proved equally skilled at asserting his authority and getting the job done. His leadership code was developed during this period: "Long after the house had fallen quiet and my family was asleep, I lay awake wondering, 'What does a division commander do?'" In time he developed five core goals, all of which, he assures us, were in place during his Gulf War command: 1) Make sure the division was combat ready; 2) Take care of the soldiers; 3) Take care of the soldiers' families; 4) Encourage camaraderie and cohesion; and 5) Teach subordinates.[44]

Powell was modest about his capacity for leadership. He never addressed the subject directly, although at the end of his long (612 pages) book, in a postscript of sorts, he provided us with "Colin Powell's Rules." These rules tell us a good deal about how Powell conceived of his leadership role:

1. It ain't as bad as you think. It will look better in the morning.
2. Get mad. Then get over it.
3. Avoid having your ego so close to your position that when your position falls, your ego goes with it.
4. It can be done!
5. Be careful what you choose. You may get it.
6. Don't let adverse facts stand in the way of a good decision.
7. You can't make someone else's choices. You shouldn't let someone else make yours.
8. Check small things.
9. Share credit.
10. Remain calm. Be kind.
11. Have a vision. Be demanding.
12. Don't take counsel of your fears or naysayers.
13. Perpetual optimism is a force multiplier.[45]

Given the assignments the military is now being asked to carry out, it is changing just in time. Of the mission in Bosnia, Rick Atkinson of the *Washington Post* wrote, "These are warriors without a war, and, for many, the soldiering business has never been more difficult or more removed from their orthodox notions of command. Yet Bosnia is recognized as a likely paradigm for future military actions: a multinational peacekeeping deployment to a place that is neither benign nor wholly hostile, under circumstances in which vital American interests are peripheral at best." Concurred one old-timer, Major General William Nash, who was the commander of U.S. forces in Bosnia, "I've trained for 30 years to read a battle-field. Now you're asking me to read a peace field. It doesn't come easy. It ain't natural; it ain't intuitive."[46]

This chapter began with four basic questions: Does leadership education in late-twentieth-century America respond to customer demand? And to change on the cusp of the new millennium? And to the growing convergence between political and business leaders? And does it instruct all leaders on the virtues of collaboration and on how it might be accomplished?

As we have seen, as far as political leaders are concerned, the questions are nearly irrelevant. Only a few programs address the issue of how leaders and managers in the public sector might mobilize others to create change.

Without taking the position that more public leadership programs would fix what's broke, the fact of the matter is that, overwhelmingly, "customers" are dissatisfied. Only 25 percent of the American people believe the federal government does the right thing "just about always/most of the time." This figure is down from 75 percent three decades ago. Moreover, there is an erosion of trust in virtually every federal institution: in the presidency, in Congress, in the Supreme Court, and in the military. The message is clear: Americans do not believe their political leaders are capable of making things much better. In fact, when asked whether specific policy problems such as those relating to entitlements and education are likely to be addressed, the average American is a skeptic at best.[47]

In fact, Americans are so alienated from their government they hardly pay attention. The overwhelming majority do not know the names of their elected representatives, do not know the name of the Senate majority leader, and do not know that the U.S. government spends far more on Medicare than it does on foreign aid. Moreover fully half think the Democratic Party is more conservative politically than the Republican Party—or don't feel they know enough even to hazard a guess.[48]

As we have seen, in the private sector the picture is different. It boasts what can only be described as an overabundance of programs and materials on how to exercise corporate leadership. The question is, How well do they work?

If "customers" are defined as stockholders, and if we do not insist on proof of a link between the abundance of leadership education programs and corporate performance, then we can say simply on the basis of the public record they work very well. As the great bull market that began in the early 1980s testifies, top management has done something right—assuming "right" is defined as strengthening the bottom line. To take but one shining example, in the five-year period between 1992 and 1997, under the leadership of CEO Larry Bossidy, AlliedSignal's stock went up nearly 400 percent!

Of course others—employees, for example—have been treated less well. As the impetus to downsize grew, so did the pool of laid-off workers who felt victimized by management's unrelenting focus on organizational performance. In addition, in spite of an economy that has been very strong, and to which corporate America has clearly contributed, in business as well as in government there is a nagging sense that something is not working as well as it should. As James O'Toole put it in his book *Leading Change,* "Nearly everywhere, the requisite for change is being addressed by one or more of a variety of powerful techniques: reengineering, restructuring, downsizing. . . . [But] it is increasingly clear to executives that while these techniques are absolutely necessary, they are not sufficient. . . . Something is missing."[49] Adds James Bolt, a leading consultant in the field of leadership development, "Worldwide, corporations approach the twenty-first century with a severe deficit of business leaders equipped to deal with the complexities, volatility, and new rules of the global marketplace."[50]

Which brings us to question number two. Is leadership education in America preparing us for the twenty-first century? I have argued that as a society we are failing to address precisely those problems that are neither fully public sector, nor fully private or independent sector—for example, poverty and education. It is at this macro level that leader learning falls woefully short. Put another way, with regard to the second question, the answer is clearly no.

The few exceptions notwithstanding, leadership education as currently conceived does not in any comprehensive way address the complex political, economic, technical, corporate, organizational, social, and cultural challenges that lie ahead. Nor does it even begin to prepare leaders for the trans-sectoral work—for the work that cannot be done within one sector only—that is necessary even now.

Fairness is one example of a growing problem that remains largely ignored. On the one hand, top executives sit pretty, even when they fail.[51] When Michael Ovitz was pushed out of Disney after little more than a year, he received a severance package totalling a cool $90 million. On the other hand, the gap between Americans at the top and those at the bottom has widened sharply. Moreover, opportunities to move up, from one economic class to the next, have been sharply reduced. Facts like these are disquieting in and of themselves; more ominous, perhaps, is the growing belief that such inequities are permanent and likely to grow more severe.[52]

Moreover, problems of fairness inevitably become problems of race. As William Julius Wilson makes clear, however bad a situation in white America, in black America it is likely to be worse. Wilson points out that in many inner-city neighborhoods most adults do not work. More than half of all African American men between the ages of twenty-five and thirty-four are either unemployed or do not earn enough to support a family of four above the poverty level. Moreover, in 1994, nearly one in three black males in his twenties was in prison, out on parole, or in some other way under the supervision of the justice system.[53]

Are problems such as these political or economic? Clearly the answer is both. Can they be solved either by government or business—or, for that matter, nonprofits—acting alone? Clearly the answer is no. But because leadership education in America is largely sector-specific (public or private), it does not teach leaders and managers how to address precisely those problems that are the most chronic and complex. It does not teach the tactics of transcendence, nor does it convey to those who in fact have a vested interest in hearing it Wilson's warning, "If we don't stem the tide now, the jobless percentage I'm talking about will seem mild. And there is no serious planning going on for this. There will come a day when ignoring the poor is not an option."[54]

Thus, despite all the evidence that political and business leader-ship now look alike, and despite the obvious fact that both civic and corporate America stand to benefit from collaborative work, leader learning has generally remained stuck. Until political leadership is more widely taught, and until leadership in both government and business is more broadly conceived, leadership education itself will be behind the times. So much for the answers to questions three and four.

8
Fault Lines

On the one hand, I have argued throughout this book that political and business leadership have converged, and that those late-twentieth-century problems that are the most chronic and complex require collaboration between (among) the sectors. On the other hand, I have maintained that at the national level such collaborations are few and far between, and that leadership education, which should be on the cutting edge, is itself failing to recognize the importance of joint efforts.

At the micro level, the legacy of this failure to work in concert is a host of problems that appear irremediable. As we saw in chapter 4 they include, but are not limited to, inadequate health care, poor schools, urban decay, deteriorating infrastructure, pollution, and a decline in civic consciousness.

This chapter will provide an overview of what the failure to collaborate has wrought at the macro level. In particular, I am suggesting that the fault line between political and business leaders has allowed other fissures to widen. To cite just one obvious example, the fact that poor schools persist, especially in low-income areas, fuels the divide between black Americans and white Americans. There is, in other words, a connection between the failure to address micro-level problems and the macro-level divisions that continue to bedevil us.

Still, top leaders in government and business remain by and large impervious to the challenge of change. They are stuck—stuck in the sectors where they work and stuck in a time when successfully leading one particular group to one particular place was the definition of success.

Note that I do not argue that leaders are failing altogether.

Within the sectors they have come to know and love, many perform very well indeed. For example, I have no quarrel with *Fortune*'s claim that Campbell's CEO David Johnson is "making America's no. 1 soupmaker grow again"; or with the proposition that his "showmanship, combined with a laserlike focus on financial rigor, has paid off, imbuing the 127-year-old Campbell with renewed vigor."[1] Rather, what I am saying is that in the twenty-first century, leaders who can reinvent themselves in keeping with the times will have the skill and will to move from one side of the divide to the other—and then back again.

In fact, what I am advocating is more than consultation and collaboration. The problem with such gestures is that all too often they are short-lived. That is, when the immediate issue has been addressed, those in positions of authority return to home base and to the circumscribed role that was initially theirs. What I would really like to see is more than a series of ad hoc responses to nasty situations. We should be establishing permanent systems and structures that will facilitate cooperation both consistent and widespread.

I am a pragmatist. I have no illusions about the capacity of all leaders to make the leaps to which I refer, nor about our ability fully to repair fault lines that run deep and wide. But I am claiming that unless political and business leaders develop a more vigorous working relationship, we will be doomed to repeat and perpetuate the mistakes of the past. (In the interest of economy, I do not refer to nonprofit leaders in the discussion. But the point pertains.)

Whether our ills are more resistant to conventional cures than they used to be is an open question. Maybe it just seems as if we are condemned, as the Chinese proverb would have it, to live in interesting times. In any case, the list of our political, economic, and social problems would seem to confirm that none of those generally considered "intractable" can be solved by either political or business leaders acting alone. In fact, it can reasonably be argued that they have proven intractable precisely because we do not have in place the collaborative arrangements properly to address them.

To be fair, change is in the air. We have already observed that leaders in government are now expected to perform with at least a modicum of efficiency. We have also seen that business leaders are, like their political counterparts, increasingly held accountable—to employees, stockholders, boards, and customers. In addition there has been more talk about blurred lines.

• Political scientist James Q. Wilson expressed doubts that we can have a government that is, simultaneously, big and well managed. He was nevertheless intrigued by the fact that Vice President Al Gore's National Performance Review called for a government that "works better and costs less."[2]

• The book *Reinventing Government,* which inspired the vice president's initiative, has already been cited in this book. Once more: "Most people have been taught that the public and private sectors occupy distinct worlds; that government should not interfere with business, and that business should have no truck with government. . . . But the world has changed too much to allow an outdated mind-set to stifle us in this way."[3]

• Charles Handy tells us that the "newly emerging language of organizations is very different." He writes that this is a language "of politics, not of engineering, of leadership, not of management," and that soon we will see political theory take "its rightful place as a core course in our business schools."[4]

• Sally Helgesen predicts that in the future organizations will look to those "on the front lines for leadership." She believes that in this respect the private sector will emulate the public one: "This has already begun to happen in the political arena, where citizens are finding ways to use power more directly."[5]

• Rosabeth Moss Kanter warns that "leaders of the future can no longer afford to maintain insularity." They will need to become more "cosmopolitan." "Cosmopolitan leaders of the future must be integrators who can look beyond obvious differences among organizations, sectors, disciplines, functions, or cultures."[6]

But despite the fact that on occasion the words "government" and "business" are actually uttered in the same breath, the push to change generally ends there. Moreover, because the most visible of our political and corporate leaders—our so-called role models—have failed to do something new and different, the probability that any of the rest of us will make a big move is diminished. Put another way, who is teaching us the most important leadership lessons? If leadership educators lag behind, and if leading leaders do not themselves collaborate, who will?

The overarching fault lines to which I referred earlier may be said to fall into five categories. These are not meant to be all-inclusive; they merely indicate some of the areas of conflict that, under other circumstances, could at least be ameliorated.

DIVIDED BY GROUP

Race

To a degree at least, America at the turn of the century is characterized by large groups pitted against other large groups. The most obvious schism is between white Americans and black Americans.[7] (This is not to minimize the importance of other rifts—for example between Asians and Hispanics.) Studies indicate that African Americans still experience life very differently from their white counterparts, and that these differences exacerbate relations between the races. Nor is the black middle class exempt from this general pattern; in fact, it views white America with a more jaundiced eye than does the black lower class.[8]

Despite the fault line between the races, one that the O. J. Simpson criminal trial revealed to be far deeper and wider than was generally supposed, there has been since Martin Luther King no leader, black or white, who has effectively bridged the divide. Among African Americans, Jesse Jackson was for a time thought of as King's successor. But his "Rainbow Coalition" ultimately fizzled, and his reference to New York City as "Hymietown" (a derogatory reference to New York Jews) ultimately made it impossible for him to pick up where King left off.

The black community also boasts the gifted orator and architect of the remarkable "Million Man March," Louis Farrakhan. But for all his talents, Farrakhan remains a divisive figure. He has insulted non-blacks in general (his predecessor as head of the Nation of Islam, Elijah Muhammed, regularly referred to whites as "blue-eyed devils"), and Jews in particular. Moreover anyone who believes, as Farrakhan apparently does, that a cabal of Jews secretly controls the world, is not exactly a candidate for bridge-builder. (Henry Louis

Gates Jr. makes the interesting point that in this regard Farrakhan's views resemble Pat Robertson's.)[9]

Colin Powell might have been the exception. He might have been the one African American capable of being heard, simultaneously, by black and white Americans. Indeed, for a moment (late 1995) many of us thought Powell might run for president. But in the end he pulled back, leaving some prominent African Americans angry and disappointed. Wrote Juan Williams in the *Washington Post,* "If Powell does not answer the call and remains secluded as an honored speaking guest among corporate elites and in his castle in McLean, history will not forgive him. He will suffer the awful damnation visited on those who had the rare chance to create a better future for their country—and especially for those who squander the chance to break the bonds of racial divisions."[10]

In 1996 Eldridge Cleaver was quoted as saying that, "We have the worst leadership in the black community since slavery." Gates makes a similar point, noting that Farrakhan's success "owes much to a vacuum of radical black leadership."[11] Although Gates is referring in this quote to "radical" black leadership in particular, the message is clear: There is no outstanding late-twentieth-century African American leader creating change for the benefit of the whole.

Among white Americans there are, of course, any number of political and business leaders who make nice to blacks. But since Lyndon Johnson, no top white leader has made improving black lives, improving race relations, a priority. (Bill Clinton's effort in this regard was late in the day and, therefore, not nearly as effective as it might have been.) As what historian George Fredrickson calls the "growing conviction that the United States faces a crisis in black-white relations" testifies, by and large white Americans have failed to persuade black Americans that we are all in this together.[12]

Gender

In politics, the gender gap endures. Women vote differently from men. (In the 1996 presidential election they favored Bill Clinton over Bob Dole by a margin of 16 percent.) Women have a different level of representation than men. (As I write, only nine of one hundred senators are women.) And they have a much harder time getting to the top than men. (Twenty-five states have no women at all in Congress.)

In business the gender gap also endures. Women continue to suffer the slings and arrows of sexual harassment. They continue to be vastly overrepresented in staff jobs (like human resources and planning) which offer few chances at top positions; and vastly underrepresented (about 15 percent) in career-building areas such as operations, general management, sales, and marketing. They have a hard time getting to the top because of persistent "male stereotyping and preconceptions of women."[13] And female enrollment at the Harvard Business School remains (as of 1997) under 30 percent.

Since the 1960s and early 1970s, women have also lacked a visible, credible, and effective cadre of leaders at the national level. This is not to say that there are no women out there fighting the good fight or, for that matter, that there are no men out there who are scrupulously fair. Rather, it is to say that because women remain subordinate to men in both civic and corporate America, fundamental feminist goals do in fact remain on the national agenda. The fault line between men and women is not as pernicious as that between blacks and whites, but it persists nevertheless.

Class

For the first time since the Great Depression, discourse in America is riddled with references to class—the growing underclass and the vanishing middle class. This terminology is the result of several factors, including the displacement of millions of workers who once thought they had it made, and the growing gap between those who have a lot of money and those who have very little.

Some, of course, quarrel with the statistics and how they are used to score political points. For example, Robert Samuelson and H. Erich Heinemann have argued that even the "serious" press, particularly the *New York Times,* which ran a seven-part series on "The Downsizing of America," was guilty of "wild distortions" by editors and reporters who were "prisoners of prevailing intellectual or economic fashion."[14]

But theirs is the minority view. The headlines tell the story:

— From the series in the *New York Times:* "On the Battlefields of Business, Millions of Casualties."[15]
— From the *New York Review of Books:* "The New, Ruthless Economy."[16]

— From the *New Yorker:* "Who Killed the Middle Class?"[17]
— From the *New York Times Magazine:* "Why Their World Might Crumble: How Much Inequality Can a Democracy Take?"[18]

Add to all this the fact that the median income, adjusted for inflation, actually fell in 1996 for the poorest 20 percent of families and you get the picture: While the fat cats got fatter the poor, even in a robust economy, remained mired at the bottom.

In the past, labor unions provided a ballast. But for the moment anyway, unions play only a modest role in American business and industry (in 1995 there were only thirty-two strikes involving about 1,000 workers); and so, for now, the escape valve is anger. As House Democratic leader Richard Gephardt put it in a 1997 speech to the Economic Policy Institute, the widening gap between working families and the well-off is America's "one unacceptable problem."[19]

DIVIDED BY TERRITORY

In America, the most obvious territorial divide is between the city and country. To many, the city is simply the "inner city"—a hotbed of poverty, crime, drugs, and other social ills ranging from poor schools to high unemployment. Even those more benignly disposed tend to see urban America as a nice place to work and visit, but not one in which to live or raise children.

The other side of the divide—the "country"—appeals to the still-growing numbers who want to reside in the small towns, suburbs, exurbs, semirural and rural locations presumed to be relatively free of the aforementioned ills, and of the blacks and Hispanics, most of them poor, typically associated with them.

Of course, the fault line between city and country is not merely one of geography. It is a metaphor for tensions among whites and blacks and Hispanics and Asians, and between rich and poor. As Bill Bradley has observed, "Race and the American city are inextricably bound together in fact and in the public perception. The people who live in America's cities are poorer, sicker, and less educated, and their circumstances are more violent than at any point in my lifetime."[20]

Demographers say the population shifts are producing racial

and ethnic polarizations in which a few states (mainly those along both coasts) are becoming more diverse, while the rest of the country remains overwhelmingly white. Says William Frey, "What this means in terms of Balkanization is that while there is increasing diversity, it is not happening all over America."[21]

Recent data reveal the strength of the trend. Made mobile in part by technologies such as fax machines, video conferencing, and the Internet, Americans are moving away from city centers, and toward what until recently was considered hinterland. After losing population for decades, rural areas are now adding people at three times their 1980s growth rate—a shift that comes on top of an even larger move into smaller metropolitan areas. For example, in the early 1990s, the populations of both Arizona and Idaho expanded at nearly three times the national average, and Nevada grew at nearly five times the national norm. Conversely, between 1990 and 1994, more than 850,000 people moved out of New York City.

Nor have corporations been immune from the "Valhalla syndrome." For a variety of reasons ranging from lower costs to executive preferences for a homogenous and well-educated work force, companies continue to move to places like Lancaster, Pa., and Huntsville, Ala., or to smaller cities such as Orlando, Austin, Nashville, and Salt Lake City.[22]

The tension between city and country is played out in the realm of public policy, such as the debate in recent years over whether or not to eliminate the Department of Housing and Urban Development. It is reflected in choices about where to live and work and play. And it is mirrored in our popular culture, which tends on the one hand to romanticize America's rural heritage, and on the other easily to exaggerate the evils of the big city.

I should add that territory also divides at the international level. Americans are torn between the familiar attractions of nationalism and the twenty-first century draw of globalism. That the planet is shrinking is by now a commonplace. At the same time, Americans, like most people around the world, retain a strong sense of national identity, and are in fact generally unwilling to sacrifice money and lives on behalf of some greater global good.

The tension between home and abroad is apparent in the heated debates over security and trade policies, and also in the fights over immigration. In the past, the United States was a relatively homogeneous country in which most people were of white European stock. Now men, women, and children move from one country to another, indeed from one continent to another, with an ease and speed unimaginable even a quarter of a century ago. In 1970, New York City's population was 62 percent white. By the year 2000, this number will drop to 34 percent. In other words, despite intermittent attempts to lock the gates and keep America looking as much as possible like it did when Beaver Cleaver reigned, the United States, like most countries (less than ten percent are now considered homogeneous), will inevitably become more diverse.

In fact, the territorial divisions imposed by the boundaries of nation-states are in many ways increasingly irrelevant. Problems pertaining to the globalization of markets as well as to a host of other matters—overpopulation, balkanization, deteriorating environment, nuclear proliferation, terrorism—can be addressed only by transnational cooperation. And so we are torn between Jihad on the one hand, and McWorld on the other.[23] On the one hand, we, the American people, want to be left alone. But on the other we recognize full well that the quality of our air will suffer if there is a gas-powered car in every Chinese garage. In other words, while some of America's problems can be addressed at the local, state, and federal levels, many others are not so simple. They require global cooperation.

What is remarkable in any case is that no late-twentieth-century public official—either in the United States or, for that matter, anywhere else—has tried in any sustained way to bridge the divide of place. For example, the Reverend Al Sharpton is a forceful spokesman for his own constituency, which consists, in the main, of African Americans in New York City. But his reach has not extended even to other residents of New York State, nor, obviously, to those who live, say, in Arizona or Nebraska. By the same token, we might reasonably ask how effectively Governor George Pataki, to stay for a moment in the Empire State, of Peekskill and Garrison, communicates with the people of Harlem, or Crown Heights, or, for that matter with residents of San Antonio, Texas.

Similarly, there have been in the late twentieth century few elected officials who in creative and significant ways have sought to move beyond the nation-state. (Helmut Kohl was one of the notable exceptions.) Given the magnitude of the concerns that transcend national boundaries, it seems remarkable that by and large we leave it to multinational corporations and international organizations to do the collaborative work. But in the case of the former, the interest is in profit rather than in the public good; and in the case of the latter, the demand far outstrips the supply. With the debatable exception of the United Nations, international organizations are generally inadequately structured, staffed, and equipped to meet the challenges that confront us even now. What is clear, in any case, is that, overwhelmingly, world leaders remain convinced that all politics is local.

DIVIDED BY TECHNOLOGY

In the summer of 1995, Louis Begley, the novelist and international lawyer, took four weeks of vacation. He looked forward with great anticipation to being in the country, spending time with his grandchildren, and finishing a novel that because of work on a legal case he had not touched for months.

Begley ended up doing it all: he continued to supervise the ongoing case; he spent time with his family; and he wrote. How was this accomplished? Begley made clear that it was through "superior organization and efficient use of technology." Each afternoon, he wrote, "my secretary would send by Express Mail all the documents received that day, and by fax a report on the day's events, telephone calls, and E-mail. . . . Then telephone calls, usually to voice-mail boxes. . . . Meanwhile the fax machine frothing at the mouth."[24] In other words, Begley was able to do what he did because of telephones, answering machines, fax machines, and computers.

The question is, How many Americans are similarly well endowed? About 98 percent have telephones, and 60 percent have answering machines. But only about 40 percent have personal computers, only about 34 percent computer printers, only about 19 percent modems, and a mere 8 percent have home fax machines.[25] In other words, most Americans still lack the technology that made Begley's "vacation" possible.

Concern about the divide between technology haves and have-nots is growing. The Telecommunications Act of 1996 directed the Federal Communications Commission and the fifty states to require telephone and cable television companies to provide "universal access" to a range of new information delivery services. And in Bill Clinton's second term he proposed to the Congress a budget that included funds for hooking up classrooms around the country to the Internet. Moreover, regulators are expected to mandate access and cut-rate services for schools and public libraries nationwide.

But the fact is that prophets such as Bill Gates, who speak in glowing terms about how cyberspace will bring us all together, are at odds not only with those who have no access to the new information technology, but also with those who view it as downright unhealthy. True believers insist that the information revolution will in positive ways restructure the political, economic, and social landscape.[26] Naysayers, on the other hand, continue to worry. Clifford Stoll writes that "computers and networks isolate us from one another."[27] Kirkpatrick Sale considers technology to be a harbinger of social disintegration.[28] And Vartan Gregorian, former head of Brown University and the New York Public Library, argues that "The popular prediction that electronic communication would create a global village has been shown to be wrong. What is being created is less like a village than an entity that reproduces the worst aspects of urban life."[29]

In other words, the technological divide has three separate components. Those who are computer literate have advantages over those who are not. Those who have more information are in a better position than those who have less. And those who see "the road ahead" (to use Gates's term) as full of promise are at odds with those who think it fraught with peril. (There is a technological divide at the international level as well. Joseph Nye Jr., and William Owen view this gap as an opportunity yet to be seized: "America has apparent strength in military power and economic production. Yet its more subtle comparative advantage is its ability to collect, process, act upon, and disseminate information. . . . This information advantage can help deter or defeat traditional military threats at relatively low cost.")[30]

Whatever the inequities generated by the new information technology, this generation of political and business leaders is ill equipped to respond. By and large, leaders in both the public and private sectors are in their forties, fifties, and sixties. In other words, compared to their offspring, most of them are technologically disadvantaged.

DIVIDED BY VALUES

In his memoir, Bill Bradley recalls his childhood home in Crystal City, Missouri, and describes his parents. His father, he writes, "had a clear sense of ethics and lived by a rigid code of conduct"; and his mother, a former schoolteacher and daughter of a devout Methodist, was "energetic, churchgoing, and civic-club attending."[31] "What happened," Bradley then asks, "to the common sense notion that two parents are better than one? What happened to making the effort and taking pride in a job well done? What happened to the widespread belief that volunteering . . . is one way not only of helping others, but of finding one's own self fulfillment? What happened to employer loyalty and employee conscientiousness?"[32]

This kind of fin de siècle nostalgia is not uncommon. Lines of thought include:

- A sense of loss. America is no longer what it once was. Many Americans miss their own (real or imagined) equivalent of Crystal City and everything small-town America used to imply—family, decency, neighborliness, and security.

- The lack of connection. Robert Putnam has decried what he calls the "strange disappearance of civic America." He blames shrinking networks and weakened norms for the decline in our communal and political engagement.[33]

- The decline of citizenship. In his book *Democracy's Discontent,* Michael Sandel insists, "Our public life is rife with discontent." He blames the lack of a "public philosophy"—the lack of a shared notion of citizenship that used to inform the national debate. American politics has lost its civic voice, Sandel maintains; thus, we must relearn how to debate questions "we have forgotten how to ask."[34]

At the most basic level, then, the fault line is between those who think national values in late-twentieth-century America have declined, badly, and those who do not. Of course, on another level, values divide us in very specific ways, for example on issues such as abortion, welfare, and gun control. Finally, there is the notion that values harden into coherent, and competing, belief systems that according to Mark Gerzon, for example, "struggle for America's soul": the religious state, the capitalist state, the disempowered state, the superstate, the transformation state, and the governing state.

- The core belief of the religious state is that faith in Jesus Christ as Lord and Savior should shape every aspect of American life.
- The core belief of the capitalist state is that economic growth enriches society and makes progress possible.
- The core belief of the disempowered state is that exploitation and oppression in American society must be resisted.
- The core belief of the superstate is that society is liberated from ignorance and parochialism through freedom of communication.
- The core belief of the transformation state is that social action based on higher consciousness will save the world.
- The core belief of the governing state is that government, as the agent of the people, should have final authority.[35]

The message that values matter has been heard in any case, particularly by Democrats, who in recent decades had ceded the so-called values issue to Republicans. In the mid-1990s, it was Democrat Bill Bradley who asked, "What happened to the common sense notion that two parents are better than one?" But in the early 1990s, it was Republican Dan Quayle who had the temerity to suggest that there might just be a better role model for American women than single mother "Murphy Brown."

DIVIDED BY POWER, AUTHORITY, AND INFLUENCE

The party line is that the distinctions between leaders and followers are being blurred. And indeed Americans who are not male, white, straight, young, and mentally and physically intact do have more of a voice than they did before. Similarly, in business and industry, the gap between those at the top and those at the bottom has in some ways narrowed. Why, then, do so many Americans feel so bad? Why do seven out of ten people believe that "most elected officials don't care what people like me think," and why is there such scant hope that things will improve?[36]

Because the party line is wrong. Because the fact of the matter is that the fault line between leaders and followers persists and will endure. For all the rhetoric about the power of followership, for all the insistence that we eschew the hero-leader and turn instead to ourselves to do what needs to be done, most of us feel we have no choice but to leave most of the decision making to others. This is an assertion most late-twentieth-century scholars of leadership find difficult to accept. In line with the fashion of our trade, we prefer to think the increasing talk of collaboration and consensus means closing the gap between leaders and followers.

But, as the great political theorist, Robert Michels, claimed nearly ninety years ago, eliminating those in authority is, at least in complex social systems, impossible. To be fair, when he developed the "iron law of oligarchy" (in 1911), Michels had in mind the public sector, not the private one. He was arguing against Rousseau's concept of direct popular democracy which, at the time, underlay socialist as well as traditional democratic theory. But, in fact, the point applies to the corporate realm as well as to the civic one. As Seymour Martin Lipset made clear in his introduction to Michels's classic, *Political Parties,* oligarchy, the control of a society or an organization by those at the top, "is an intrinsic part of [any] bureaucracy or large-scale organization." Thus the dilemma: We cannot have "large institutions such as nation states, trade unions, political parties, or churches, without turning over effective power to the few who are at the summit of these institutions."[37]

It is inconceivable that the age of the flattened organizational hierarchy would have dissuaded Michels from his view. In fact, history clearly confirms that it is simply not practical for followers to call most of the shots most of the time. A few will always do the work of the many. Is it possible nevertheless that the gap between them (those in positions of authority) and us will narrow?

Unfortunately for those who view parity as the ultimate goal, the answer is no. Collaboration and consensus are not irrelevant. They matter, but only when circumstances allow. When push comes to shove, when times get tough, the divide between those who are in charge and those who are not remains.

In recent years, this fact of life has been blatantly obvious in the private sector. The newfangled rhetoric notwithstanding, when executives are forced to chose between equity and efficiency, they almost always opt for the second over the first. It is no small irony that the push to downsize reached a critical mass just when the language of business leadership became nearly indistinguishable from the language of political leadership. Flattened hierarchies, teams, worker participation, empowerment—all speak to a workforce that enjoys democratic participation. But to the extent that corporate leaders feel obliged to fire large numbers of those in their employ, they undermine the very values they now claim to embrace: freedom and fairness in the workplace. This fault line, the one between what is said and what is done, is perhaps the most pernicious.

The distance between promise and performance has in recent years characterized the public sector as well as the private one. At a time when eight out of ten Americans believe "our leaders are more concerned with managing their images than with solving our nation's problems,"[38] the divide between the government and the people has widened to the point where it can best be described as a yawning gap.

9
Ties That Bind

I have chosen in this book not to focus on the constitutional and institutional contexts within which big government and big business necessarily operate. In fact, my basic argument, about the convergence between public- and private-sector leadership, might convey the impression that I consider the environments within which they are embedded of secondary importance. But let me be clear. I acknowledge the obvious: that presidents, for example, operate within the legal and political constraints of the office they hold; and that chief executive officers work within a capitalist system that supports the private ownership of property for the purpose of making a profit.

I have nevertheless argued that for a variety of reasons—with the information revolution and globalization being high on the list—the theories and practices of leadership in government and business have converged. This book, then, makes three basic arguments: first, that individual leaders remain important; second, that political and business leadership are converging; and third, that effectively to address problems that have otherwise proved intractable, leaders in different places should join forces. This final chapter will explore the real-world implications of the ties that bind.

POLITICAL AND BUSINESS LEADERS: SIMILAR PROFILES

As we have seen, in the past, political and business leaders were distinct. They were exposed to different theories and practices. They travelled in different circles. And they claimed followers that had different expectations and demands.

207

As we have also seen, on the cusp of the twenty-first century the differences between political and corporate leadership have been greatly diminished. The question now is, does it matter? What impact does the closing of the gap between government and business leaders have in the real world? And what conclusions can be drawn?

Conclusion # 1: Twenty-first century leaders will move from business into politics, and from politics into business, more easily and frequently.

During the two most recent presidential campaigns, businessman-candidates were plausible players. In 1992 Ross Perot made a strong showing against Bill Clinton and George Bush (receiving a full 19 percent of the vote), and in 1996 Steve Forbes made what initially at least was a big splash in the Republican primaries. Here is why in the new millennium businessman-candidates—many of whom in fact are already in politics—are likely to have a leg up.

1. The enormous importance of money in politics, the exponential growth of corporate interest groups, and the globalization of markets have compelled business leaders to become active participants in the political process.

2. Successful executives are likely to have the financial resources necessary to run political campaigns. In the past, personal wealth and access to money more generally were considered something of a political liability. Now they signal freedom from special interests.

3. The public sector now puts a premium on skills heretofore associated with the private sector—for example, fiscal responsibility and managerial competence.

4. The nature of foreign policy has changed. These changes, which relate primarily to globalization and privatization, equip business leaders with knowledge and experience every bit as relevant to foreign affairs as the more traditional security concerns.

5. Business leaders in their forties, fifties, and sixties are more likely than political leaders in the same age cohort to be familiar with information technology.

6. Policy areas such as welfare and education, which were viewed

until recently as being entirely in the public domain, are increasingly seen as necessitating corporate involvement. Conversely, civic virtues such as equality and diversity are now shaping the ideology, if not the practice, of corporate America.

7. Because the mantras of business leadership have changed, corporate executives are now viewed as capable of a far more sophisticated approach to followers than merely command and control.

8. In comparison with political leaders, corporate leaders are credited with having an independent, can-do attitude. Unfettered by a lifetime of compromise, businessman-candidates tend to see government as a business that needs nothing so much as to be well run.[1]

9. The demands on business leaders now mirror the demands on political leaders. They include providing followers with meaning and purpose; standing up to public scrutiny; dealing with the media; being accountable to various and demanding constituencies; and coping with diminished authority.

Does all this mean that in the future corporate leaders will move en masse into politics, or, for that matter, that large numbers of former mayors, governors, and senators will run businesses? Am I predicting that IBM's Louis Gerstner will become president of the United States or that Texas governor George W. Bush will take over as CEO of General Electric? Of course not. But what I am saying is that in the next century a man like Gerstner could, if he chose to, make a creditable bid for elective office, even at the highest level. I am also saying that even now, public officials routinely serve on corporate boards and therefore often participate actively in running a business. (To be sure, the transition from being a political leader to being a CEO will continue to be difficult. By and large, elected officials are seen as managerial novices.)

Of course, as we have also seen, the similarities between government and business transcend those pertaining only to leadership roles. The sectors themselves now converge in two ways in particular. First, we expect government to be more efficient. This is not to say that we believe government can, or necessarily should, be a model of managerial competence. As Henry Mintzberg put it in the *Harvard Business Review,* "I am not a mere customer of my government, thank you. I expect something more than arm's length trading and something less than the encouragement to consume."[2]

But charges made by experts such as Paul Light, who claimed that the "unwieldy, towering hierarchy" that constituted the federal government was responsible for sins ranging from inefficiency to a lack of accountability, hit hard and had an impact.[3] (Tellingly, Light cited corporate guru Tom Peters on the evils of "bloated staffs.")[4] And so did works like *Banishing Democracy,* in which authors David Osborne and Peter Plastrik claimed that Britain and New Zealand—not the U.S.— are the best models of government reform.[5]

To be sure, for all the good intentions, the task of reforming government is daunting and resistance to change remains great. While Bill Clinton and Al Gore have cut both the deficit and the bureaucracy, fiascos persist.

• "A close look at the quarter of all defense outlays that has gone into nuclear weapons suggests that a good portion was wasted," reported the *New York Times* in 1995. "Even the most useful nuclear weapons cost too much to build for the same reasons the Pentagon pays too much for toilet seats and canned ravioli."[6]
• "Stymied by Mismanagement," read a *Times* piece in 1996, "the Federal Aviation Administration has squandered 15 years and at least a half billion dollars on a new air traffic control system that is still years from completion and already obsolete."[7]
• "IRS Admits Lag in Modernization," reported the *Times* in 1997. The Internal Revenue Service conceded it had spent $4 billion developing modern computer systems that "do not work in the real world."[8]

Just as we expect government to be more efficient, so we expect business to be more democratic. This is not to say that we now believe CEOs should poll employees before deciding how the company should be run. It is to say that virtually all large companies are now expected to mouth the new conventional wisdom: that to be virtuous is to embrace flattened hierarchies and empowered workers.

But just as public-sector organizations remain vulnerable to the charge that because of their "long-standing cultures" they "accomplish very little" (see Osborne's quote below), so private-sector organizations are still accused of failing to move far enough fast enough.

- James O'Toole: "Organizations must decentralize, de-layer, and destroy bureaucracy in order to obtain the entrepreneurialism, autonomy, and innovation needed to serve customers effectively."[9]
- Gifford Pinchot: "The new organizations will be pluralistic to the core, preferring conflict between competing points of view to the illusory security of bureaucratic command and internal monopolies of function."[10]
- Peter Senge: "The basic assumption that only top management can cause significant change is deeply disempowering. Why, then, in the 'age of empowerment,' do we accept it so unquestioningly?"[11]

Thus, while there has been over the last five decades real convergence between political leaders and their corporate counterparts, and indeed between government and business more generally, the demand for change has not let up. Government is still expected to be more efficient and business is still expected to be more democratic—which is one of the main reasons why those who cling to the idea that political and business leaders are a breed apart make a mistake.

Conclusion #2: The "Leadership Industry" must develop a more integrated approach to leadership education.

America's anti-authority culture has always made the exercise of leadership in America difficult. Any national creed that values above all life, liberty, and the pursuit of happiness does not, by definition, worship authority. Put another way, Americans have always grappled with the tension between their wish for community and order on the one hand and their passion for individualism and independence on the other.

But since the late 1960s the exercise of political leadership in particular has become even more challenging. The assassination of John Kennedy, and campus radicals, and black power, and women's liberation, and Vietnam, and Watergate, and even change agents such as Greenpeace caused the old order to give way. Now, sources of authority are always being challenged, and "individuals are more willing than ever to ask what justifies particular social arrangements, configurations of power, or customs."[12]

Arguably, this "crisis of leadership"—which, of course, affects business as well as government—should be the most fundamental concern of leadership educators. But, as we have seen, leader learning in late-twentieth-century America is not, in general, very ambitious. The flaws include

1. The continuing segregation in the classroom between political and business (and nonprofit and military) leaders and managers—in spite of the obvious and important similarities among them.[13]
2. The dearth of leadership education programs for those in the public sector.
3. The continuing distinction between content targeted at political leaders and content targeted at business leaders.
4. The failure to address honestly the perennial gap between what is being promised (for example, empowerment) and what is being delivered (for example, downsizing).
5. The reluctance to tackle precisely those social, political, and economic problems that have proved most intractable.
6. The lack of attention to collaboration. There is too little instruction on how to cross the divides of sectors, groups, interests, and nations.
7. The failed focus on character.
8. The failure satisfactorily to explore how followers can be productively engaged.
9. The feeble response to diversity in America. The divide between white men on the one hand, and women and minorities on the other, persists.
10. The failure to ask how leaders can and should be judged. What are the criteria for good leadership? And if they are not met, how should followers respond?
11. The failure to distinguish clearly between short-term tasks and long-term goals. Whereas in general followers fare better when leaders (political and corporate) adopt a long-term perspective, self-interest typically precludes their doing so.
12. The failure to distinguish between nature and nurture. The

increasingly obvious importance of genetics to leadership and followership is almost entirely ignored.

13. The lack of dialogue between theoreticians and practitioners, particularly those involved in the public sector.
14. The inadequate investment in leadership education. We train men and women for many years to be doctors and lawyers. Why do we give such short shrift to educating leaders? What assumptions underlie what is, arguably at least, this neglect?

The time to overhaul leadership education in America is now. Granted, the argument for investing in leader learning is difficult to make because proving that it pays off has been notoriously difficult. Moreover, the fact that there are two different kinds of leadership education—learning about leadership (Leadership Studies) and learning how to be a good leader (Leadership Training or Development)—has tended to muddy the field. (Incidentally, in my view this distinction is generally artificial and unproductive.) But, if we are to have any kind of leader learning at all, this is as good a moment as any to create a new kind of leadership education, one that sheds many of the old assumptions and is willing simultaneously to take on the hard issues.

At a minimum, twenty-first-century leadership educators should bring leaders and managers from different places together; pay greater attention to public sector leadership; integrate content so that all leaders can profit from all of the materials; address the divide between promise and performance; meet head-on the challenges posed by the world's most intractable problems; teach collaboration; instruct more persuasively on the importance of character; clarify the nature of follower engagement and explore how it might more effectively be realized; develop criteria for good leadership; explore the question of how to use the results of assessment; and create institutions and procedures that make it possible for the relevant players to work together. (Relevant players include leaders and managers from different places, key constituents and, arguably, leadership experts.)

Conclusion #3: The character issue remains impenetrable.

Of all the problems that beset leadership in America at the end of the twentieth century, the so-called character issue is perhaps the most troubling. True, we hear more about the character flaws of political leaders than of business leaders. (The former are, of course, still much better known than the latter.) But, as the polls testify, leaders generally are considered morally deficient.

The political process clearly has been corrupted by what Gary Wills calls "the unholy trinity of polls, ads, and money."[14] Big money is necessary to win elections and politicians are selling themselves to the highest bidders. The distinction between the system and those who people it is critical here. Elected officials are fond of saying, in effect, "The system makes me do it." But, as Fred Wertheimer argues in an article on the 1996 presidential campaign pointedly titled "The Dirtiest Election Ever," it boils down to the men and women who themselves constitute the process. "Put simply, we've seen that the attitude of our national leaders when it comes to campaign laws is no different than that of tax evaders, deadbeat dads and welfare cheats. The most powerful people in the country have proved in the 1996 political season that they do not believe the law applies to them. The abuses involve the Democratic president and his Republican challenger; the Democratic and Republican national party committees; Democrats and Republicans running for Congress; labor unions, corporations, wealthy individuals and foreign based interests. Special mention must be made of the incumbent president who has led the way in setting the tone and unleashing an escalating money war that resembles the Cold War arms race."[15]

Bill Clinton has played a not inconsiderable role in creating the end-of-the-century impression that politics is dirty. To be sure, as Wertheimer points out, none of the major players are pure. But for whatever constellation of reasons, the impression remains: even in the Oval Office, the man remained "slick Willie." Whether or not Bill Clinton will ever be held in any way legally responsible for Whitewater, or Travelgate, or Filegate, or sexual misconduct, or the Democratic Party's campaign fundraising practices is almost beside the point. What matters is the constant drumbeat of impropriety, and what matters even more is that the American people are now so jaded that they—we—no longer seem to care. (In 1997 polls indicated that more than 60 percent of the American people disapproved of the way presidential and congressional campaigns are financed, and more than 60 percent of the American people said they had little hope that the president or the Congress will substantively change things.)

It should be noted that business leaders are not exempt from the general sense that those in positions of authority are not to be trusted. While as individuals they are generally still able to avoid the intense day-to-day scrutiny that besets their political counterparts, as a collective their integrity has come under public attack on at least two fronts. First, they are charged with individual and corporate greed. On the one hand they are held responsible for massive layoffs, and on the other they have manifestly profited from historic rises in the prices of company stock.

To be sure, by the end of the decade there was a growing awareness that firing people while simultaneously raking in record profits was somehow unseemly. Wrote the prolific Henry Mintzberg, again in the *Harvard Business Review,* "There is nothing wonderful about firing people. True, stock market analysts seem to love companies that fire frontline workers and middle managers (while increasing the salaries of senior executives) . . . [but] lean is mean. So why do we keep treating people in these ways?"[16] But let us not be misled. In general, business leaders will continue to do what they think they must in order to improve the bottom line. If that means letting workers go, so be it. The lesson learned is not to stop being hardnosed when necessary, but to be hardnosed in less obvious ways.

The second charge against corporate executives relates to the old saw about democracy in the workplace. Obviously, buzzwords like "empowerment" notwithstanding, notions of corporate loyalty are largely obsolete and people are less secure in their jobs than they used to be. Too little truth and too little trust—in spite of the fact that truth and trust are considered in virtually every document on the subject the sine qua non of great corporate leadership. A "characteristic of great management," writes Thomas Teal, "is integrity. . . . Integrity means being responsible, of course, but it also means communicating clearly and consistently, being an honest broker."[17]

I said earlier that of all the problems that plague leadership in America at the end of the twentieth century it is the character issue that is probably the most troubling. It disturbs not only because it is so obviously corrosive, but also because what should be done about it remains entirely unclear. The apparent lack of integrity that characterizes so many of those in positions of authority is not the consequence of inattention. Forests have been felled for paper on which to write about the ethics of leadership; and there isn't a leadership education program in the country that fails to address the virtues of being virtuous. But all too often, the pious intoning falls on deaf ears. Attention should be paid.

Conclusion #4: Our image of the ideal political leader has converged with our image of the ideal business leader.

Popular perceptions about the differences between them notwithstanding, leaders from different sectors are, so far as our fantasies about them are concerned, virtually interchangeable. Here, then, as drawn by both the public- and private-sector literatures, is the picture-perfect leader, the Reinvented Leader for all sectors and seasons.

THE REINVENTED LEADER

Traits/Attributes

Considerable Experience
Some Expertise
Good Education
Rather High Intelligence
High Level of Activity
Drive for Achievement
Rather Assertive
Independence
Extroversion
Well-adjusted
Tolerance for Stress, Delay,
 Uncertainty
Willingness and Ability to Exercise
 Authority and Influence
Empathy and Insight
Flexibility
Creativity
Good Character

Challenges

Mastering Information
Coping with Complexity
Understanding Technology
Managing Change
Managing Conflict
Making Decisions under Conditions
 of Uncertainty

Implementing
Extracting Efficiency
Developing Loyalties
Managing Crises
Creating Diversity
Creating Alliances
Addressing Resistance and
 Dissent
Making Time for Reflection
 and Analysis

Strategies

Envisioning
Agenda Setting
Communicating
Listening
Educating
Inspiring
Mobilizing
Coalition Building
Planning
Using Authority and Exercising
 Influence
Being Ingratiating
Adapting
Delegating
Collaborating
Empowering
Encouraging
Enabling
Questioning
Evaluating
Negotiating
Unifying

Values

Integrity
Self-Knowledge
Curiosity
Balance and Stability
Change (when change is in order)
Noncoercion
Bestowing respect
Inclusion
Mutuality of Purpose (with followers)

Now the question is whether this overlap, this composite picture of what ideal leaders look like, implies that there are no significant differences between leaders in government and business. The answer is obviously no. Clearly, men and women in politics have different interests from men and women in business. The business of politics is making public policy; and the business of business is making money. But the fact that the most obvious task of the political leader is different from that of the business leader does not, as we have by now come to see, negate or even overwhelm the commonalties.

In an interview that appeared in the *Harvard Business Review* David Osborne acknowledged that "Yes, government is different from business. Businesses typically exist in fiercely competitive markets; most public organizations don't. Businesses have clear bottom lines; governments don't. Businesses usually know who their customers are; most public organizations don't."[18] These major distinctions did not, however, stop Osborne from teaching corporate-sector lessons to "public managers." He advised them to strengthen relationships with "customers," to create consequences (positive and negative) for how people perform, to flatten organizational hierarchies, and to work to change the public-sector culture. "In the federal bureaucracy long-standing cultures have taught people to keep their heads down, stay out of trouble," he noted. "Unfortunately, they have accomplished little."[19]

Authors of books such as *Public Entrepreneurs* similarly exhort political leaders to act like their corporate counterparts, urging them to create change by becoming the "public-sector equivalent of private-sector entrepreneurs."[20] The commonalties, in short, are clear. Americans want their political and business leaders to be perfect in most of the same ways. What is not apparent in the model outlined above is that all leaders should also be ready, willing, and able to transcend their immediate concerns and domains. They should seek to make the transition from self-interest toward the public good. In fact, it is to this theme—of transcendence and integration—to which we finally turn. Put another way, the sine qua non of the Reinvented Leader is the capacity to create ties that bind between interests ordinarily considered competing. Reinvented Leaders conjure constituencies other than their own and conceive of interests other than only those preceded by the word "self."

POLITICAL LEADERS AND BUSINESS LEADERS:
COMMON INTERESTS

Not long ago, Harlan Cleveland (one of the most interesting leadership scholars) bemoaned the lack of "generalist" leaders. "The problems of a nation, of a city, of a village," he wrote, "are to be seen as interconnected and therefore to be tackled simultaneously and as a complex, not separately or sequentially. The community's future comprises economic, social, cultural and political as well as technical facets; these cannot be dealt with by the politician alone, or by the economist, the engineer, or the scientist in isolation." Cleveland went on to point out that although real-world problems are interdisciplinary, and solutions are interdepartmental, interprofessional, interdependent, and international, our institutions—particularly our institutions of higher education—start with a heavy bias against breadth.[21]

This section is based on Cleveland's simple assumption: that common interests demand common work. The questions are, How do these common interests manifest themselves? and How does common work get done?

Conclusion #5: Technology has tied government to business and changed the nature of leadership

We know the information revolution changed the way the private sector works. And we also know that it has finally started to change the way the public sector works. Said President Clinton in his February 1997 State of the Union message, "We have only begun to spread the benefits of a technology revolution that should be the modern birthright of every citizen."[22]

We understand less well how the information revolution is changing the relationship between the two.[23] What we can say is that at a minimum technology is fueling the convergence—bringing government and business closer together.

Of course, with each passing year technology matters more, if only because of the numbers. In the early 1990s, about one million people were wired. Since then, the number of Internet users worldwide has grown to an estimated fifty-seven million; by the end of the century, the number will reach 700 million. Even the telephone will still make a major difference. Early in the twenty-first century its use in previously isolated corners of the globe is expected to increase exponentially.

The sequence, then, goes something like this. Technologies change economies and economies, in turn, change politics. While in the developed world the impact of the information revolution is arguably not as dramatic as in the developing world, in fact some of the countries of Europe, and also Japan, have had problems making the economic, political, and social adjustments necessary to the nanosecond nineties. For example, in the last decade of the twentieth century, the Japanese were held back by the same patterns and practices that had only recently (in the 1970s and 1980s) built Japan Inc: groupism, conformity, and hierarchies. Indeed, the 1997 collapse of Asian financial markets testified to the domino effect. Technology made Asia's burgeoning economies possible; but when the "Asian flu" struck, national governments were forced to respond and, in one or another fashion, to change their ways.

However differently the drama is played out in different places, no leader, political or corporate, is immune to the effects of the information revolution. Above all leaders are learning (albeit in some cases, such as China, only with great difficulty) that the attempt to control information is destined to fail. Information expands as it is used. It is easily transportable. And it leaks.[24] In short, "when it comes to pure content regulation . . . government authorities have lost their grip completely."[25]

Of course, the hunger for information is driven by economic necessity. In the interest of growth, most governments—even most authoritarian ones—have shown themselves increasingly willing to assume the political risks of full disclosure.

China's recent history illustrates the dilemma. In 1978, Deng Xiaoping initiated a radical restructuring of China's economic system and a dramatic opening up to the outside world. But, as economic reforms gradually took hold, disruptive political values such as individualism, freedom of expression, and democracy made inevitable inroads into the still highly controlled society. By spring 1989, hundreds of thousands of students and other citizens were demonstrating on a regular basis in Tiananmen Square, demanding dialogue and democracy. The result was probably inevitable: On

June 4 the People's Liberation Army stormed into Beijing, killing and wounding thousands of unarmed protesters.

Even now some 3,000 people languish in Chinese prisons because of their political views. But China's development in recent decades is more complex than its record on political dissidents would seem to suggest. While China is not at all free for a very small number of people, it is in nearly every way far freer than it used to be for the large majority.

This brings us to another way in which the information revolution affects those in positions of authority: controlling others is more difficult. As Cleveland pointed out in his small book *Leadership and the Information Revolution,* the people, not their "leaders," are doing the leading. The peaceful revolutions that started with the collapse of the Soviet Union were sparked not by distant visions of Utopia, "but by rapidly spreading information about neighbors who were obviously getting more goods and services, more fairness in distributing them, and firmer guarantees of human rights."[26]

The impact of this link between technology, economics, and politics is not, of course, confined to domestic affairs. Even as political leaders nurture high-tech growth for their citizens, they face the challenge of defending national security in the age of interconnectivity. In 1997 the Pentagon's Defense Science Board urged the federal government to invest $3 billion into protection against information warfare. Why? Because the most computer-dependent nation in world, the United States, is also the most vulnerable to "cyber attack." Explains strategic analyst Ariel Sobelman, "The more dependent you are on information technology, the more you are also increasing your vulnerability not just to bombs, as in the Gulf War, but to computer viruses and worms."[27]

The information revolution has changed not only the definition of national security, but also the relevance of geography and territory in fashioning political arrangements. National leaders in particular will have to contend with the fact that the modern state is getting weaker. As Cleveland describes it, the state is "leaking power in three directions at once."[28] It leaks from the bottom, as information and communications enable individual citizens and local authorities to take governance into their own hands. It leaks from the sides, as transnational businesses and nongovernment organizations play increasingly important roles in international affairs. And it leaks from the top, as states have to pool their sovereignty in order not to lose it altogether.

Clearly technology has changed the way public- and private-sector leaders do their work. Increasingly, all leaders must be versed in the ways of both politics and business and, increasingly, all leaders must understand the ways in which technology complicates the task of creating change. The information revolution is one of the main reasons why the gap between the public sector and the private one has narrowed, and why leaders in different places find themselves wrestling with many of the same problems in many of the same ways.

Conclusion #6: The New Foreign Policy demands increased collaboration between government and business.

The fact that commercial interests play a role in American foreign policy is nothing new. But, as Jeffrey Garten has pointed out in an important 1997 article that appeared in *Foreign Affairs,* during the next few decades "the interaction between them will become more intense, more important, more difficult to manage, and more complicated for the American public to understand."[29]

Garten maintains that because government and business have been slow to respond, now there is no time to waste: they must get their "collective act" together. "Their objective should be a new partnership based on two realities of the changing global marketplace. The first is that the federal government's ability to conduct foreign policy in a world preoccupied with economic stability and progress is dwindling. . . . The second is that even though business has the money, technology, and management that make today's world spin, it needs Uncle Sam's help more than ever, particularly in a world where governments are awarding big contracts abroad and companies are becoming ensnared in issues such as human rights, labor practices, environmental protection, and corruption."[30]

Garten does not believe the interests of the country and the business community intersect at every turn. He nevertheless advocates the development of a framework that would enable the public and private sectors to "work together for their mutual benefit." Above all, the administration and the foreign policy establishment must reach consensus about the centrality of commercial interests in foreign policy.

The New Foreign Policy, one in which economic and traditional security interests coexist, is a hybrid that has by now become the norm. The evidence is everywhere.

• November 1996: At a meeting in Manila attended by President Clinton and leaders of seventeen other Pacific Rim nations, Commerce Secretary Mickey Kantor spoke of the emergence of a "Clinton Doctrine." What is the Clinton Doctrine? It is "not mutually assured destruction and a policy of containment, but mutually assured prosperity and a policy of engagement."[31]

• December 1996: Thomas Friedman noted in the *New York Times* that for too long the American business community in China has behaved as if human rights and business rights were two different things. "Wrong. Human rights and business rights are just flip sides of the same coin . . . and the coin is called the rule of law." As Friedman goes on to point out, we have leverage with the Chinese. "They crave Big Macs, Macintosh, Microsoft and Mickey Mouse."[32]

• January 1997: Jessica Mathews wrote in the *Washington Post* that while Clinton's second-term foreign policy team faced an array of familiar challenges (NATO expansion, China, Middle East peace), new kinds of issues were also on the agenda, for example, global warming. This issue is "weighted with national and private interests, highly technical, and explosively controversial."[33] Mathews argues that complex problems such as greenhouse warming must be considered within the purview of American foreign policy and must, therefore, be addressed with the same passion and persistence the American government used to expend on, for example, mutual deterrence.

A foreign policy shaped to a considerable degree by the imperatives of the global marketplace also has domestic implications. Donors to Clinton's 1996 campaign included the Lippo Group, based in Indonesia, and the Chaoren Pokaphand Group, based in Thailand. Both consortiums made huge investments in China, are controlled by ethnic Chinese families, and operate in countries dominated by Chinese minorities. By helping to fill Clinton's campaign coffers they sought to ensure that the United States would not constrain China's export-driven economic expansion.[34]

There is another much larger question that neither governments nor businesses have yet come to grips with: Is the uncontrolled integration of information, trade, and finance an economic threat to the have-nots in the short term and, therefore, a political threat to the haves in the longer term? Critics like Ethan Kapstein have argued that in order to protect workers from the negative consequences of globalization (for example, growing job insecurity), and to protect democracies from the unrest that such dislocations would inevitably generate, governments will be forced to provide programs such as education, training, and unemployment insurance. Kapstein puts it bluntly: "The welfare state is the cornerstone of the global economy."[35]

What, precisely, are the implications of the New Foreign Policy for political and corporate leaders? At least three are obvious. First, the politicians and bureaucrats who constitute America's official foreign policy cadre should be as familiar with international economics as they are with international politics. Unfortunately, whatever their other merits, neither of President Clinton's two Secretaries of State, Warren Christopher and Madeleine Albright, fit the bill in this regard. Both are of a generation whose view was shaped by World War II and the Cold War that followed it. And both have been far more worried about how to expand NATO than about how to cope with global warming (clearly more of a twenty-first-century threat than Russia's now-decimated military or, for that matter, nuclear proliferation) or economic instability.

Second, U.S. foreign policy institutions and systems should be restructured to reflect the new global reality. Moreover coordination among the various economic, diplomatic, and military initiatives that now constitute American foreign policy should be accelerated and strengthened.

Finally, the business community should be brought in a more systematic way into the American foreign policy process. Inevitably, if unofficially, business leaders already have a profound impact on the conduct of foreign affairs. The question that remains is how to integrate their growing involvement into the work done by the traditional foreign policy establishment. For the time being the nation-state will survive the globalization of the economy and the information revolution that preceded it. But, as Peter Drucker has pointed out, "it will be a greatly changed nation-state, especially in domestic fiscal and monetary policies, foreign economic policies, control of international business, and, perhaps, in its conduct of war."[36]

Conclusion #7: To create change twenty-first century leaders will have to join forces.

When Bill Clinton became president, he declared healthcare reform his number one priority. Moreover, 70 percent of the American people agreed with the two basic principles underlying his plan: that all American families should have health insurance and that all employers should contribute to paying for employee premiums.

What went wrong? Why was it that for all the good intentions and for all the popular support Clinton's attempt at health care reform was a political disaster? Here I will name only one of several reasons for the fiasco: the administration's failure to understand that leadership initiatives of this magnitude require extensive collaboration over an extended period of time. What we got were covert conversations and secret plans; what we got was a proposal owned by the administration and disowned by nearly everyone else. In particular, Bill and Hillary Clinton's failure to engage private-sector participation in their public-sector planning was a major mistake.[37]

The lesson was learned. From that point on President Clinton made it a point to involve business and industry in virtually every significant federal initiative. Listen to Clinton on the subject of welfare reform in his 1997 State of the Union speech. "Here is my plan. Provide tax credits and other incentives to businesses that hire people off welfare. . . . And I say especially to every employer in this country who has ever criticized the old welfare system: You cannot blame that old system anymore. We have torn it down. Now do your part. Give someone on welfare the chance to work. Tonight I am pleased to announce that five major corporations—Sprint, Monsanto, UPS, Burger King and United Airlines—will be the first to join in a new national effort to marshal America's businesses, large and small, to create jobs so people on welfare can move to work."[38]

While big government and big business have been slow to act, at the state and local levels there is a growing body of evidence in support of the proposition that joining forces—bringing the public, private, and also the nonprofit sectors together—is the most effective way to create change.

• In Connecticut, Tom Ritter, Speaker of the State House of Representatives, and Wick Sloan, a business executive, assembled a group of legislators, bankers, city and state officials, and neighborhood activists to develop legislation that would eliminate discriminatory mortgage lending practices. Their proposal was quickly passed by both houses of the state legislature.[39]

• In Harlem, a confluence of city, federal, and private money rebuilt West 140th Street, by all accounts one of New York City's most ravaged blocks. The specifics of the initiative were worked out by the mayor's office. But the cornerstone of the program was a federal tax credit that entices corporations and wealthy individuals to contribute money for buildings and upkeep in poor neighborhoods.[40]

• In Colorado, the State Department of Health convened a group to develop a plan for the prevention of AIDS. Gay activists, state health officials, doctors, healthcare providers, educators and representatives of conservative political and religious groups were included. Through a carefully designed collaborative process, the group was able to agree on a comprehensive plan for controlling the spread of AIDS.[41]

• In Baltimore, a coalition that included community activists, business interests, school administrators, and government officials brought an integrated and ultimately successful approach to previously fragmented efforts to keep students in school.[42]

• In Missoula, under the leadership of Mayor Dan Kemmis, collaborative work addressed the challenges of growth. The tensions of development were familiar: suburban sprawl and industrial development vs. the desire for a more livable community, private property rights vs. broader community values, and new job creation vs. environmental amenities. But rather than succumbing to conflicting interests, Kemmis helped the city develop common goals and shared strategies. Various stakeholders were involved, including leaders in government, business, nonprofit organizations, interest groups, and academia. Public forums were created to develop alternative futures, identify policy recommendations and tools, establish a credible and open process, address difficult and divisive issues, and create a broad base of support for implementation.[43] To be sure, creating change was not easy. But over the years Missoula became a model of what a community can do to promote the public good. As Kemmis observed (and outsiders concurred), "In Missoula we went against the trend—and we have been rewarded with a tremendous strengthening in our civic culture and a heightened respect for public service."[44]

As indicated, it would be a mistake to downplay the difficulties involved in sustaining collaboration over a period of time. For example, the evidence suggests that business leaders in particular have a low level of tolerance for long and frequent meetings with community leaders.[45] But there are ways of overcoming obstacles such as these, and there is ample evidence to suggest the hard work pays off in the end.

Indeed, this evidence is starting to accumulate. Case studies of cities and regions across the land describe "how diverse segments and sectors of the community are working together in new patterns of collaboration and partnership."[46] Consider Cleveland, one of the "Rustbelt" cities hardest hit in the 1960s and 1970s by the decline in local manufacturing. The population of the city declined precipitously, unemployment shot up, crime rates rose, poverty increased, racial tensions flared, and in 1969 the heavily polluted Cuyahoga River caught fire, fixing in the nation's mind a disastrous image of what Cleveland had become. In 1978 Cleveland hit bottom: It declared bankruptcy, thereby becoming became the first American city to default on its debts since the Depression.

How to explain the urban "comeback kid"? What accounts for Cleveland's remarkable recovery in recent years—one symbolized since 1995 by the internationally famous and architecturally stunning Rock and Roll Hall of Fame? Obviously, the reasons are many and complex, but if one stands out it is the development in recent decades of scores of local organizations that initiate and then sustain multi-sector collaboration. "Cleveland has perhaps the strongest network of civic, community, religious and nonprofit organizations anywhere in the country."[47] They include

- Cleveland Community Foundation;
- George Gund Foundation (convenes civic players to deal with community challenges);
- Cleveland Tomorrow (a business group formed in the early 1980s that by now has expanded its reach beyond the downtown area to local neighborhoods);
- Greater Cleveland Roundtable (focuses on human relations);
- Cleveland Community Building Initiative and Neighborhood Progress, Inc. (both attack poverty in depressed neighborhoods);
- Cleveland Initiative for Education (a vehicle for coordinating business and foundation support for Cleveland's public schools).

Each of these organizations testifies to the efficacy of public/private/nonprofit partnerships. In fact, these partnerships are how the city does its work. And they have created through the years networks of individual leaders who contributed to the various institutional collaborations. During the 1980s Cleveland's leaders included Mayor George Voinovich, City Council President George Forbes, tax lawyer Carlton Schnell, business executive William Seelbach, and corporate leader George Dively (who hired McKinsey and Company to help determine how to turn Cleveland around). As the president of the Gund Foundation put it, the secrets of Cleveland's success are the people who build "constellations of trusting relationships" and "serve as the glue between the business and government communities."[48]

None of this is to suggest that Cleveland's work is complete. In fact, if anything at all has been learned by regional and local leaders across the country, it is that the joined efforts must be ongoing. It is, however, to say that by all accounts Cleveland's collaborations have been remarkably fruitful ones and that "a foundation for hope has been laid."[49]

We have already seen that at the national level government and business leaders are learning only now that the common interest demands work done in common. What then can we expect at the international level? Is there any evidence that even a small number of public- and private-sector leaders understand the virtues of joining forces? Obviously it is easier to get leaders to collaborate at the state and local levels than it is at the federal one. Just as obviously it is easier to get them to collaborate at the national level than at the international one. But, as suggested throughout this book, if a transnational problem—deforestation, for example, or volatile currencies—is to be effectively addressed, big government and big business must be involved both at home and abroad.

Perhaps the biggest obstacle to collaboration on this large a scale is the near-total absence of institutions designed first to generate and then to support international, cross-sectoral work. The world is full of associations of all kinds designed to address problems of all kinds. But these groups and organizations are nearly always limited in their memberships and limited therefore in what they are able to accomplish. There are public affiliations and private ones, and there are regional affiliations and global ones. But we have no instrument whose mission it is to enable political and business leaders from different places to work together in the common interest.

Arguably, there is one exception to this general rule: the World Economic Forum—known to those in the know simply as Davos. In the early 1970s, Klaus Schwab, a Swiss professor of business administration, began to gather in Davos, a world famous ski resort, European CEOs for annual conversations about the emerging challenges of the global marketplace. A decade later these meetings had been transformed. They were now attracting political and business leaders from around the world.

By the late 1990s, the World Economic Forum was billing itself as "the foremost international membership organization integrating leaders from business, government and academia into a partnership committed to improving the state of the world."[50] Moreover, it was able to claim several achievements of no mean consequence. They included the first joint appearance outside South Africa of F. W. de Klerk, Nelson Mandela, and Chief Buthelezi (in 1992), and the draft agreement between PLO Chairman Yasser Arafat and Prime Minister Shimon Peres on Gaza and Jericho (in 1994).

But it is the global economy that is front and center in Davos. For example, President Carlos Salinas of Mexico is said to have conceived of the North American Free Trade Agreement in Davos (1990). And, in collaboration with the Council on Foreign Relations, the World Economic Forum convened Middle East–North Africa Economic Summits in 1994 and 1996. Moreover, at its regional summits the Forum has panels and discussions that specifically include government representatives and regulators as well as corporate executives.

Although the World Economic Forum is "committed to improving the state of the world," in fact it is, by its own proud testimony, an organization in which membership is severely restricted: "The Forum is a club, providing its members with networking opportunities at very high level throughout the world. In an informal atmosphere, Forum members meet business and government leaders to exchange first-hand information and share experiences in a given region or on a given subject. Experts from academia, the sciences and the media are integrated into these exchanges."

Who belongs? In principle, club membership is made up of the "1000 foremost global enterprises." But the success of the Forum is explained not by its formal membership roster, but rather by the remarkable assortment of players who in fact attend the various functions. Put another way, Schwab's genius is that he transformed what was originally a regional association of business leaders into an international association of leaders from different sectors. (In 1998 the net was cast even wider. John Sweeney, president of the AFL-CIO, was in Davos—the first union official ever to come from the United States in the Forum's twenty-seven years.)

The written report on the Forum's 1996 South Africa Economic Summit observed that there is in the region a "gulf between government imperatives and those of businessmen and investors who can pick their investment targets from the entire world." The report concluded, "The challenges facing Southern Africa cannot be resolved without creating a close partnership between the public and private sectors on a regional scale." To Schwab's enduring credit, it is this logic—the logic of transectoral collaboration—that he is attempting to market worldwide.

While on paper those who gather annually at Davos are committed to "improving the state of the world," in fact, they are, of course, looking out for number one. Moreover there is a growing awareness that the globalized markets so enshrined in the Forum's world view have a downside that both political and corporate leaders have yet fully to acknowledge. Finally, there are the inevitable questions about what all the high power and hot air at Davos actually accomplishes. Richard Holbrooke calls the annual meeting "the world's greatest Ponzi scheme," and Euan Baird, the head of Schlumberger Ltd. decided in 1997 not to attend, presumably on the assumption that it was not worth his time.[51]

Still, there is about the meetings in Davos an air of excitement and energy that is singular. In 1997, Nelson Mandela, Jack Welch, Yasir Arafat, Bill Gates, Vaclav Klaus, Kofi Annan, Benjamin Netanyahu, Javier Solana Madariaga, Newt Gingrich, Andrew Grove, and Malcolm Rifkind were only a few of those who made up the heady mix. Why did they bother to go to Davos? Because it is the only place in the world that provides them with the opportunity to meet their various counterparts. Thus, while it can hardly be claimed that the World Economic Forum is perfect, it is the only institution of its kind. It is transsectoral and transnational, and it is sweeping in its ambition. As *Forbes* put it, the Forum is a business, but it is a business built on a high-minded premise: "that a continuing dialogue between businessmen and government leaders will help produce more rational decisions on both sides. At the Forum the two sides meet not as antagonists but as *confrères*."[52]

In the new millennium it will be even clearer than it is now that leaders in government and business are much more similar than they are different. There will also be a paradigm shift. Whereas in the past leaders were specialists—for example, political leaders, or business leaders, or military leaders—in the future they will be generalists. Reinvented Leaders will be leaders without borders. They will have the capacity to forge integrated strategies, make connections between individuals and institutions that have long been at odds, and conjure constituencies other than their own.[53] If we are to avoid "applying to the present the habits of the past," there is no alternative.

NOTES

Introduction: Reinventing Leadership

1. For more on the American Creed, see Samuel Huntington, *American Politics: The Promise of Disharmony* (Cambridge: Harvard University Press, 1981), chapters 2 and 3.

2. James Q. Wilson, "Reinventing Public Administration," *PS: Political Science and Politics* 27 (December 1994): 669.

3. David Osborne and Ted Gaebler, *Reinventing Government: How the Entrepreneurial Spirit is Transforming the Public Sector* (Reading, Mass.: Addison-Wesley, 1992), p. 324.

4. Vaclav Havel, "The New Measure of Man," *New York Times*, 8 July 1994, p. A17.

5. Eric Hobsbawm, *The Age of Extremes: A History of the World, 1914–1991* (Pantheon, 1995). Quoted by Tony Judt in *New York Review of Books,* 25 May 1995, p. 20.

Chapter 1. The 1950s and 1960s: Different Worlds

1. Adam Yarmolinsky, "The Explicit Recognition of Excellence," *Daedelus* 90 (Fall 1961): 725.

2. Robert Dahl, *Who Governs?* (New Haven: Yale University Press, 1961), p. 86.

3. Ibid., p. 316.

4. James MacGregor Burns, *The Deadlock of Democracy* (Englewood Cliffs, N.J.: Prentice-Hall, 1963), p. 324.

5. Ibid., p. 328.

6. Betty Friedan, *The Feminine Mystique* (New York: Norton, 1963), p. 27.

7. Ibid., p. 361.

8. Clinton Rossiter, *The American Presidency* (New York: Harcourt, Brace, Jovanovich, 1956), p. 68.

9. Donald Matthews, *U.S. Senators and Their World* (New York: Norton, 1960), p. 126.

10. Ibid., p. 127.

11. Richard Neustadt, *Presidential Power* (New York: John Wiley, 1960). See chapter 3.

12. Fred Greenstein, *The Hidden-Hand Presidency: Eisenhower as Leader* (New York: Basic, 1982).

13. Fred Greenstein, "Dwight D. Eisenhower: Leadership Theorists in the White House," in *Leadership in the Modern Presidency,* ed. Fred Greenstein (Cambridge: Harvard University Press, 1988), pp. 105, 106.

14. G. William Domhoff, *The Higher Circles: The Governing Class in America* (New York: Random House, 1970), p. 106.

15. "A War for Peace," *Time,* 11 July 1955, p. 15.

16. "Carl Albert: Nose-Counter from Big Tussle," *Time,* 12 January 1962, p. 13.

17. Carl Brauer, "John F. Kennedy: The Endurance of Inspirational Leadership," in *Leadership in the Modern Presidency,* ed. Greenstein, p. 109.

18. Quoted in Doris Kearns, *Lyndon Johnson and the American Dream* (New York: Harper & Row, 1976), p. 209.

19. Ibid., p. 317.

20. Bundy is quoted in Larry Berman, *Lyndon Johnson's War* (New York: Norton, 1989), p. 194.

21. Bernard Bass, *Stogdill's Handbook of Leadership* (New York: Free Press, 1981), pp. 276–282.

22. William H. Whyte, *The Organization Man* (New York: Simon and Schuster, 1923.

23. Ibid., p. 129.

24. Philip Selznick, *Leadership in Administration: A Sociological Interpretation* (Berkeley: University of California Press, 1957). See chapters 1 and 5 for Selznick's discussion of leadership.

25. Ibid., p. 27.

26. Douglas McGregor, *The Human Side of Enterprise* (New York: McGraw Hill, 1960).

27. Ibid., p. 48.

28. Ibid. For managerial strategy based on Theory Y, see chapter 5, pp. 61–76.

29. *Harvard Business Review* 45 (January–February 1967).

30. Fred Lesiur and Eldridge Puckett, "The Scanlon Plan Has Proved Itself," *Harvard Business Review* 47 (September–October 1969).

31. McGregor, *Human Side.* For full discussion of Scanlon Plan, see chapter 8, pp. 110–123.

32. "The Scanlon Plan," p. 118.

33. "How Businessmen Make Decisions," *Fortune,* August 1955, p. 87.

34. "How Top Executives Live," *Fortune,* July 1955, p. 78.

35. W. Lloyd Warner and James Abeggien, "Successful Wives," *Harvard Business Review* 34 (March–April 1956): 65.

36. "Brown-Forman's Big-Time Bourbons," *Fortune,* November 1955, pp. 123–24.

37. "The Transformation of U.S. Steel," *Fortune*, January 1956, p. 90.

38. "How Harlow Curtice Earns His $750,000," *Fortune*, February 1956, p. 133.

39. Renis Likert, "Motivational Approach to Management Development," *Harvard Business Review* 37 (July–August 1959): 75.

40. "T-Groups," *Harvard Business Review* 42 (March–April 1964): 61.

41. "Democracy is Inevitable," *Harvard Business Review* 42 (March–April 1964): 51

42. "The Egghead Millionaires," *Fortune*, September 1960, p. 173.

43. "The Prime Movers," *Fortune*, February 1960, p. 99.

44. "George T. Baker's Feud with the World," *Fortune*, March 1960, p. 154.

45. "Is Bill Lear Taking Off Again?" *Fortune*, July 1965, pp. 38–40.

46. "Businessmen in the News: Roche of G.M." *Fortune*, July 1965, p. 43.

47. "A Fellow Can Be Civilized Though Executive," *Fortune*, 1 September 1968, p. 972.

2. The 1970s: Different Drummers

1. David Broder, *The Party's Over: The Failure of Politics in America* (New York: Harper & Row, 1971).

2. Hunter Thompson, *Fear and Loathing on the Campaign Trail '72* (New York: Popular Library, 1973).

3. Theodore White, *Breach of Faith: The Fall of Richard Nixon* (New York: Dell, 1975).

4. J. Anthony Lukas, *Nightmare: The Underside of the Nixon Years* (New York: Viking, 1976).

5. Christopher Lasch, *The Culture of Narcissism: American Life in the Age of Diminishing Expectations* (New York: Norton, 1979).

6. Center for Strategic Studies, University of Michigan.

7. Gerald Ford, *A Time to Heal* (New York: Harper & Row, 1979).

8. White, *Breach of Faith*, p. 411.

9. Thompson, *Fear and Loathing*, p. 416.

10. Broder, *The Party's Over*, p. xi.

11. Lasch, *Culture of Narcissism*, pp. 29, 30.

12. Frank Parkin, *Class Inequality and Political Order* (New York: Praeger, 1976).

13. Richard Sennett and Jonathan Cobb, *The Hidden Injuries of Class* (New York: Vintage, 1972), p. 17.

14. Jo Freeman, *The Politics of Women's Liberation* (New York: Longman, 1995), p. 122.

15. Jimmy Carter, *Keeping Faith: Memoirs of a President* (New York: Bantam, 1982).

16. Glenn Paige, *The Scientific Study of Political Leadership* (New York: Free Press, 1977).

17. James MacGregor Burns, *Leadership* (New York: Harper & Row, 1978).

18. Ibid. See pp. 12–17 for discussion on power.

19. Edwin Hollander, *Leadership Dynamics: A Practical Guide to Effective Relationships* (New York: Free Press, 1978), p. 7.

20. Saul Alinisky's most important books are *Reveille for Radicals* (New York: Vintage, 1969) originally published in 1946, and *Rules for Radicals* (New York: Vintage, 1971).

21. Paulo Freire, *The Pedagogy of the Oppressed* (Harmondsworth: Penguin, 1972). For a brilliant exploration of how Freire might play out on American soil, see John Gaventa, *Power and Powerlessness: Quiescence and Rebellion in an Appalachian Valley* (Urbana: University of Illinois, 1980).

22. Fred Emery, *Watergate: The Corruption of American Politics and the Fall of Richard Nixon* (New York: Times, 1994), p. xi.

23. Hedrick Smith, *The Power Game: How Washington Works* (New York: Random House, 1988), p. 20.

24. Sidney Blumenthal, *The Permanent Campaign: Inside the World of Elite Political Operatives* (Boston: Beacon, 1980), p. 1.

25. Ibid., p. 6.

26. F. Christopher Arterton, "Campaign Organizations Confront the Media-Political Environment," in *Race for the Presidency,* ed. James David Barber (Englewood Cliffs, N.J.: Prentice-Hall, 1978), p. 3.

27. Roger Porter, "Gerald R. Ford: A Healing Presidency," in *Leadership in the Modern Presidency*, ed. Greenstein, p. 197.

28. James David Barber, *The Presidential Character* (Englewood Cliffs, N.J.: Prentice-Hall, 1985), p. 441.

29. Robert Peabody, *Leadership in Congress: Stability, Succession, and Change* (Boston: Little, Brown, 1976), p. 6.

30. Harry Boyte, *The Backyard Revolution* (Philadelphia: Temple University Press, 1980), pp. 64, 65.

31. Peabody, *Leadership in Congress*. See especially pp. 472–475.

32. Robert Townsend, *Up the Organization* (New York: Knopf, 1970), p. 43 and passim.

33. David Ewing, "Who Wants Corporate Democracy?" *Harvard Business Review* 49 (September–October 1971): 12.

34. Mark Honan, "Make Way for the New Organization Man," *Harvard Business Review* 49 (July–August 1971): 133.

35. Chris Argyris, *Increasing Leadership Effectiveness* (New York: Wiley, 1976).

36. Peter Drucker, *Management: Tasks, Responsibilities, and Practices* (New York: Harper & Row, 1973).

37. Ibid., p. ix.

38. Robert McMurray, "Power and the Ambitious Executive," *Harvard Business Review* 51 (November–December, 1973): 140.

39. Ibid., p. 140.

40. John Kotter, "Power, Dependence and Effective Management," *Harvard Business Review* 55 (July–August, 1977): 125.

41. Ibid., pp. 135–136.

42. M. Barbara Boyle, "Equal Opportunity for Women is Smart Business," *Harvard Business Review* 51 (May–June 1973): 85.

43. Rosabeth Moss Kanter, *Men and Women of the Corporation* (New York: Basic, 1977).

44. Ibid., p. xi.

45. Ibid., p. 166.

46. Abraham Zaleznik, "Managers and Leaders: Are They Different?" *Harvard Business Review* 55 (May–June, 1977): 67–84.

47. Chris Argyris, "The CEO's Behavior: Key to Organizational Development," *Harvard Business Review* 51 (March–April 1973): 63.

48. Neil Churchill and John Shank, "Affirmative Action and Guilt-Edged Goals," *Harvard Business Review* 54 (March–April 1976): 111

49."Women MBA's: How They're Doing: Harvard 1973," *Fortune*, 28 August 1978, p. 52.

50. "Black Executives in a Nearly All-White World," *Fortune*, September 1972, p. 140.

51. Ibid.

52. Edward W. Jones Jr., "What It's Like to Be a Black Manager," *Harvard Business Review* 51 (July–August, 1973): 108.

53. "The Rapid Rise of Your Good Friend, Dave Mahony," *Fortune*, November 1972, p. 97.

54. "How a Hotelman Got the Red out of United Airlines," *Fortune*, March 1972, p. 73.

55. "Ford: The Road Ahead," *Fortune*, 11 September 1975, p. 37.

56. "Irving Shapiro Takes Charge at Dupont," *Fortune*, January 1974, p. 79.

57. "How the Boss Stays in Touch with the Troops," *Fortune*, June 1975, p. 173.

58. "The American Kind of Worker Participation," *Fortune*, October 1976, p. 174.

59. "The Japanese Are Coming—With Their Own Style of Management," *Fortune*, March 1975, p. 118.

3. The 1980s: Narrowing the Differences

1. Barbara Kellerman, ed., *Leadership: Multidisciplinary Perspectives* (Englewood Cliffs, N.J.: Prentice-Hall, 1984).

2. Barbara Kellerman, *The Political Presidency: Practice of Leadership* (New York: Oxford University Press, 1984).

3. James David Barber and Barbara Kellerman,, eds., *Women Leaders in American Politics* (Englewood Cliffs, N.J.: Prentice-Hall, 1986).

4. Barbara Kellerman, ed., *Political Leadership: A Source Book* (Pittsburgh: University of Pittsburgh Press, 1986).

5. Barbara Kellerman and Jeffrey Rubin, eds., *Leadership and Negotiation in the Middle East* (New York: Praeger, 1988).

6. Joseph Rost, *Leadership for the Twenty-First Century* (New York: Praeger, 1991), p. 69.

7. Ibid., pp. 70–88.

8. Robert C. Tucker, *Politics as Leadership* (Columbia: University of Missouri Press, 1981).

9. Robert C. Tucker, "The Dictator and Totalitarianism," *World Politics* 17 (July 1965): pp. 555–83.

10. Valerie Bunce, *Do New Leaders Make a Difference?—Executive Succession and Public Policy under Capitalism and Socialism* (Princeton: Princeton University Press, 1981). See pp. 133–35 for discussion of advantages of "honeymoon" period.

11. Eugene Lewis, *Public Entrepreneurship: Toward a Theory of Bureaucratic Power* (Bloomington: Indiana University Press, 1980), p. 9.

12. Jameson Doig and Erwin Hargrove, eds., *Leadership and Innovation: A Biographical Perspective on Entrepreneurs in Government* (Baltimore: Johns Hopkins University Press, 1987), p. 5.

13. Ibid., p. 2.

14. Ann Ruth Willner, *The Spellbinders: Charismatic Political Leadership* (New Haven: Yale University Press, 1964).

15. For a good discussion of Reagan's "rhetoric of human liberty," see William Muir Jr., "Ronald Reagan: The Primacy of Rhetoric," in *Leadership in the Modern Presidency,* ed. Greenstein (Cambridge: Harvard University Press, 1988), pp. 262–82.

16. Lou Cannon, *President Reagan: The Role of a Lifetime* (New York: Simon and Schuster, 1991), p. 793.

17. Ibid., p. 90.

18. Ibid., p. 836.

19. Aaron Wildavsky, "President Reagan as a Political Strategist," in *The Reagan Legacy: Promise and Performance*, ed. Charles O. Jones (Chatham, N.J.: Chatham House, 1988), p. 295.

20. Fred Greenstein, ed., *The Reagan Presidency: An Early Assessment* (Baltimore: Johns Hopkins University Press, 1983), p. 6.

21. Fred Greenstein, "In Search of a Modern Presidency," in *Leadership in the Modern Presidency*, ed. Greenstein, p. 345.

22. Wildavsky, *President Reagan*, p. 304.

23. Jean Blondel, *Political Leadership* (London: Sage, 1987), p. 203.

24. David Broder, *Changing of the Guard* (New York: Simon and Schuster, 1980), p. 11.

25. Ibid. For section on Newt Gingrich, see pp. 459–63.

26. Hedrick Smith, *The Power Game* (New York: Random House, 1988), p. 142.

27. Roderick Hart, *The Sound of Leadership* (Chicago: University of Chicago Press, 1987), p. 148.

28. Cannon, *President Reagan*. For a description and discussion of Reagan at Normandy, see pp. 483–92.

29. Hart, *Sound of Leadership*, p. 39.

30. Kellerman, *Political Presidency*, pp. 244–53.

31. Paul Light, *The President's Agenda: Domestic Policy Choice from Kennedy to Carter—with Notes on Ronald Reagan* (Baltimore: Johns Hopkins University Press, 1983).

32. James Pfiffner, *The Strategic Presidency* (Pacific Grove, Cal.: Brooks/Cole, 1988).

33. Erwin Hargrove and Michael Nelson, *Presidents, Politics and Policy* (Baltimore: Johns Hopkins University Press, 1984).

34. Ibid., p. 272.

35. Ross Baker, *Friend and Foe in the U.S. Senate* (New York: Free Press, 1980), p. 194.

36. Ibid.

37. Jane Mansbridge, *Why We Lost the ERA* (Chicago: University of Chicago Press, 1986).

38. Robert Bellah et al., *Habits of the Heart: Individualism and Community in American Life* (New York: Harper & Row, 1985), p. 208.

39. "Wanted: Corporate Leaders," *Fortune*, 30 May 1983, p. 135.

40. Rosabeth Moss Kanter, *The Change Masters: Innovation and Entrepreneurship in the American Corporation* (New York: Simon and Schuster, 1983), pp. 17, 18.

41. John Kotter, *The Leadership Factor* (New York: Free Press, 1988), p. 6.

42. Warren Bennis and Bert Nanus, *Leaders: The Strategies for Taking Charge* (New York: Harper & Row, 1985), p. 6.

43. Thomas Peters and Robert Waterman Jr., *In Search of Excellence: Lessons from America's Best-Run Companies* (New York: Harper & Row, 1982), p. xviii.

44. Ibid., p. xx.

45. Ibid., p. xxiii.

46. Ibid., p. 82.

47. Rost, *Leadership*, p. 90.

48. Bennis and Nanus, *Leaders*, pp. 26–68.

49. Kanter, *Change Masters*, pp. 221–228.

50. Kotter, *Leadership Factor*, p. 18.

51. Gary Yukl, *Leadership in Organizations* (Englewood Cliffs, N.J.: Prentice-Hall, 1989), p. 12.

52. Warren Bennis, *On Becoming a Leader* (Reading, Mass.: Addison-Wesley, 1989), pp. 53–71.

53. Ibid., p. 71.

54. Jay Conger, *Learning to Lead* (San Francisco: Jossey-Bass, 1992), p. 45.

55. Ibid., p. 50.

56. Perry Smith, *Taking Charge: Making the Right Choice* (Garden City Park: Avery, 1989). See chapters 12 and 13.

57. "Hard Times Catch Up With Executives," *Fortune*, 20 September 1982, p. 50

58. John De Lorean's Long Ride Downhill," *Fortune*, 15 November 1982, p. 61.

59. "Arrow Electronics Strikes Back," *Fortune*, 30 April 1984, pp. 79–98.

60. "The Trouble with Managing Japanese Style," *Fortune*, 2 April 1984, pp. 50–56.

61. Ibid., p. 51.

62. "The Revolt Against Working Smarter," *Fortune*, 21 July 1986, p. 59.

63. "Why Women Aren't Getting to the Top," *Fortune*, 16 April 1984, p. 40.

64. "Microsoft's Drive to Dominate Software," *Fortune*, 23 January 1984, p. 82.

65. "America's Most Successful Entrepreneur," *Fortune*, 27 October 1986, p. 24.

66. "At Corning, A Vision of Quality," *Fortune*, 24 October 1988, p. 64.

67. *Iacocca: An Autobiography* (New York: Random House, 1984).

Chapter 4. The Winds of Change: Politics, Economics, and Technologies

1. Richard Pipes, "Misinterpreting the Cold War," *Foreign Affairs* 74 (January/February 1995): 159.

2. John Reilly, *American Public Opinion and U.S. Foreign Policy* (Chicago: Council on Foreign Relations, 1995), p. 10.

3. Zbigniew Brzezinski, *Out of Control: Global Turmoil on the Eve of the Twenty-first Century* (New York: Scribner, 1993), p. 53.

4. Samuel Huntington, "The Clash of Civilizations." *Foreign Affairs* 72 (Summer 1993): 22–49. Also see idem, *The Clash of Civilizations and the Remaking of World Order* (New York: Simon and Schuster, 1996).

5. Paul Kennedy, *Preparing for the Twenty-First Century* (New York: Random House, 1993), p. 129.

6. Leslie Gelb, "Quelling the Teacup Wars," *Foreign Affairs* 73 (November/December, 1994): 3–6.

7. Thomas Friedman, "The G-Who?" *New York Times*, 28 May 1995, p. E11.

8. Paul Brace and Barbara Hinckley, *Follow the Leader: Opinion Polls and the Modern Presidency* (New York: Basic, 1992), p. 3

9. Elizabeth Drew, *On the Edge: The Clinton Presidency* (New York: Simon and Schuster, 1994), p. 124.

10. Woodrow Wilson, "Leaders of Men," in *Political Leadership: A Source Book*, ed. Barbara Kellerman (Pittsburgh: University of Pittsburgh Press, 1986), p. 437.

11. Michael Lind, *The Next American Nation: The New Nationalism and the Fourth American Revolution* (New York: Free Press, 1995), p. 259.

12. Robert Reich is quoted in "Productivity is All, But It Doesn't Pay Well," *New York Times*, 25 June 1995, p. E 4.

13. Brzezinski, *Out of Control*, pp. 102 ff.

14. Kennedy, *Preparing for the Twenty-first Century*, p. 290.

15. Ibid., pp. 290–325.

16. Peter Drucker, *Post-Capitalist Society* (New York: Harper-Collins, 1993), pp. 7–8.

17. Ibid., p. 182.

18. Drew, *On the Edge*, p. 57.

19. Paul Krugman, "Competitiveness: A Dangerous Obsession," *Foreign Affairs* 73 (March/April 1994): 71.

20. Ira Magaziner and Robert Reich, *Minding America's Business: The Decline and Rise of the American Economy* (New York: Harcourt Brace Jovanovich, 1982,), p. 4.

21. Lester Thurow, "Microchips, Not Potato Chips," *Foreign Affairs* 73 (July/August 1994): 191.

22. See, for example, *Foreign Affairs* 73 (March/April 1994).

23. F. A. Hayek quoted in Tom Peters, *Liberation Management: Necessary Disorganization for the Nanosecond Nineties* (New York: Knopf, 1992), p. 499.

24. Ibid., p. 501.

25. "Die, Computer, Die!" *New York*, 24 July 1995, p. 24.

26. Neil Postman appeared on McNeil/Lehrer Newshour on 25 July 1995.

27. Steven Lubar, *Infoculture* (Boston: Houghton Mifflin, 1993). Steven Levy is quoted on p. 346.

28. "Technomania: The Hype and the Hope," *Newsweek*, 27 February 1995, p. 3.

29. Nicholas Negroponte, *Being Digital* (New York: Knopf, 1995), p. 4.

30. Ibid., p. 165.

31. "Want Ads," *New York Times*, 10 November 1996, p. D13.

Chapter 5. The Winds of Change: Business, Organizations and Culture

1. "Crystal Ball," *Fortune*, 17 May 1993, p. 39.

2. "Technophobia," *Newsweek*, 27 February 1995, p. 53.

3. "Surviving Information Overload," *Fortune*, 11 July 1994, p. 60.

4. "Robodocs and Mousecalls," *Newsweek*, 27 February 1995, p. 66.

5. "P & G Viewed China as a National Market and is Conquering It," *Wall Street Journal*, 12 September 1995, p. 1.

6. " Commerce Official to Head Yale Management School," *New York Times*, 29 September 1995, p. D2.

7. Charles Handy, "Balancing Corporate Power," *Harvard Business Review* 70 (November–December, 1992): 60.

8. Ibid., p. 60.

9. "Harvard B-School: An American Institution in Need of Reform," *Business Week*, 19 July 1993, p. 60.

10. "Reengineering the MBA," *Fortune*, 24 January 1994, pp. 38–39.

11. "How We Will Work in the Year 2000," *Fortune*, 17 May 1993, p. 39.

12. Richard J. Barnet, "Lords of the Global Economy," *Nation*, 19 December 1994, p. 754. This piece predated all the subsequent attention to the same issue.

13. "Threat of Privatization is Robbing Public Employees of Clout," *New York Times*, 4 September 1995, p. 24.

14. Barnet, "Lords of the Global Economy," p. 756.

15. Daniel Yankelovich quoted in "The New Ideal," *Fortune*, 23 June 1994, p. 44.

16. "The End of the Job," *Fortune*, 19 September 1994, p. 62.

17. Alan Webber, "Surviving in the New Economy," *Harvard Business Review* 76 (September–October, 1994): p. 76.

18. "New Paths to Success," *Fortune*, 12 June 1995, p. 90; and "Planning a Career in a World Without Managers," 20 March 1995, p. 72.

19. "New Secret of Success: Getting off the Ladder," *New York Times*, 19 March 1995, p. C14.

20. Quoted in *1994 Information Please Business Almanac and Desk Reference* (Boston: Houghton Mifflin, 1993), pp. 380, 381.

21. "It's Time to Trim Hefty Paychecks," *New York Times*, 3 December 1993, p. F13.

22. "A Quiet Boardroom Revolution: Power Shifts to Outside Directors," *New York Times*, 25 May 1995, p. D1.

23. "Managing in a Wired Company," *Fortune*, 11 July 1994, p. 44.

24. Peters, *Liberation Management*, pp. 4, 10, 50, 60, 110, 143.

25. "For Stay-at-Home Workers, Speedbumps on the Telecommute," *New York Times*, 17 August 1997, p. F14.

26. Rosabeth Moss Kanter, Barry A. Stein, and Todd D. Jick, *The Challenge of Organizational Change* (New York: Free Press, 1992), pp. 15, 16.

27. David Osborne and Ted Gaebler, *Reinventing Government,* p. 12.

28. "Family Decay Global, Study Says," *New York Times*, 30 May 1995, p. A5.

29. Ibid.

30. "Many Seek Security in Private Communities," *New York Times*, 3 September 1995, p. A22.

31. "The Pat Solution," *Time*, 6 November 1995, p. 28.

32. "Atmosphere in the House Becomes Personal and Mean and Nasty," *New York Times*, 19 November 1995, p. A20.

33. John Cassidy, "The Return of Karl Marx," *New Yorker*, 20 October 1997, p. 254.

34. Ibid., p. 114

35. "Present Shock," *New York Times Magazine*, 11 June 1995, p. 48.

36. "The Return of Shame," *Newsweek*, 6 February 1995, p. 21.

37. William Bennett, *The Book of Virtues: A Treasury of the World's Great Moral Stories* (New York: Simon and Schuster: 1993) and idem, *The Moral Compass: Stories for Life's Journeys* (New York: Simon and Schuster, 1995); and Francis Fukuyama, *Trust: The Social Virtues and the Creation of Prosperity* (New York: Free Press, 1995); and Ben Wattenberg, *Values Matter Most: How Republicans or Democrats or a Third Party Can Win and Renew the American Way of Life* (New York: Free Press, 1995).

38. Wattenberg, *Values Matter Most,* p. 16.

39. Alan Wolfe, *One Nation, After All* (New York: Viking, 1998).

Chapter 6. The 1990s: Side by Side

1. Rost, *Leadership*, p. 100.

2. Osborne and Gaebler, *Reinventing Government.*

3. Paul Light, *Thickening Government: Federal Hierarchy and the Diffusion of Accountability* (Washington: Brookings, 1995), p. 1.

4. Bruce Miroff, *Icons of Democracy: American Leaders as Heroes, Aristocrats, Dissenters, and Democrats* (New York: Basic, 1993), p. 349.

5. Benjamin Barber, *Strong Democracy* (Berkeley: University of California, 1984).

6. Ronald Heifetz, *Leadership Without Easy Answers* (Cambridge: Harvard University Press, 1994), p. 72.

7. Stephen Skowronek, *The Politics Presidents Make: Leadership from John Adams to George Bush* (Cambridge: Harvard University Press, 1994), p. 8.

8. Charles O. Jones, *The Presidency in a Separated System* (Washington, D.C.: Brookings, 1994), p. xiii.

9. Woodrow Wilson, "Leaders of Men," in Kellerman, *Political Leadership: A Source Book.* "Leaders of Men" is an address delivered by Wilson on 17 June 1890.

10. Brace and Hinckley, *Follow the Leader: Opinion Polls and the Modern Presidents.*

11. Gary Wills, *Certain Trumpets: The Call of Leaders* (New York: Simon and Schuster, 1994), p. 13.

12. Bruce Mazlish, *The Leader, The Led, and the Psyche* (Hanover, N.H: University Press of New England, 1990), p. 252.

13. Robert Kelley, *The Power of Followership* (New York: Doubleday, 1992), p. 229.

14. Rost, *Leadership*, p. 109.

15. Robert Putnam, "Bowling Alone," *Journal of Democracy*, January 1995.

16. David Chrislip and Carl Larson, *Collaborative Leadership: How Citizens and Civic Leaders Can Make a Difference* (San Francisco: Jossey-Bass, 1994).

17. Thomas Baylis, *Governing by Committee: Collegial Leadership in Advanced Societies* (Albany: State University of New York Press, 1989).

18. Harlan Cleveland, "The Management of Peace," *The GAO Journal*, Winter 1990/91.

19. Eugene Lewis, *Public Entrepreneurship: Toward a Theory of Bureaucratic Political Power* (Bloomington: Indiana University Press, 1980).

20. Osborne and Gaebler, *Reinventing Leadership,* p. 27.

21. Heifetz, *Leadership,* chapter 4.

22. Richard Morin quoted by Walter Dean Burnham, "The Legacy of George Bush," in *The Election of 1992,* ed. Gerald Pomper. (Chatham, N.J.: Chatham House, 1993), p. 30.

23. Ibid., p. 32.

24. Ross Baker, "Sorting Out and Suiting Up: The Presidential Nominations," in *The Election of 1992*, ed. Pomper, p. 68.

25. Wattenberg, *Values Matter Most*.

26. Joe Klein, "The Year Everyone You Liked Quit," *Newsweek*, 25 December 1995/1 January 1996, p. 119.

27. "Master of the House," *Time*, 25 December 1995/1 January 1996, p. 54.

28, John Cassidy, "Who Killed the Middle Class?" *New Yorker*, 25 October 1995, p. 114.

29. Lester Thurow "Why Their World Might Crumble: How Much Inequality Can a Democracy Take?" *New York Times Magazine*, 19 November 1995, pp. 78–79.

30. Joseph Spiers, "Why the Income Gap Won't Go Away," *Fortune*, 11 December 1995, p. 65.

31. Benjamin Schwarz, "American Inequality: Its History and Scary Future," *New York Times*, 19 December 1995, p. A25.

32. "The Echoes of Ruby Ridge," *Newsweek*, 28 August 1995, p. 25.

33. "The Pat Solution," *Time*, 26 November 1995, pp. 29–30.

34. "Scholars of Political Speech Are Giving Gingrich Some Very Mixed Grades," *New York Times*, 17 December 1995, p. A34.

35. Wattenberg, *Values*, p. 396.

36. Rost, *Leadership*, p. 109.

37. Max De Pree, *Leadership Jazz* (New York: Doubleday, 1992), p. 24.

38. Bass, *Stogdill's Handbook of Leadership*.

39. Kelley, *Followership*, p. 235.

40. Daniel Ilgen et al., "Team Research in the 1990s," in *Leadership Theory and Research*, ed. Martin Chemers and Roya Ayman (New York: Academic Press, 1993), pp. 245–70.

41. Peter Senge et al., *The Fifth Discipline Field Book* (New York: Doubleday, 1994), p. 436.

42. Judy Rosener, *America's Competitive Secret: Utilizing Women as a Management Strategy* (New York: Oxford University Press, 1995), pp. 10–13.

43. Robert House, "Leadership in the Twenty-First Century," in *The Changing Nature of Work*, ed. Ann Howard (San Francisco: Jossey-Bass, 1995).

44. John Kotter, *A Force for Change: How Leadership Differs from Management* (New York: Free Press, 1990), p. 6.

45. Harry Triandis, "The Contingency Model in Cross-Cultural Perspective," in Chemers and Ayman, *Leadership Theory*, pp. 167–88.

46. Kelley, *Followership*, p. 232.

47. Rost, *Leadership*, p. 112.

48. Heifetz, *Leadership*, p. 73.

49. Senge, *Fifth Discipline*, p. 376.

50. Alan Bryman, *Charisma and Leadership in Organizations* (Thousand Oaks, Cal.: Sage, 1992), p. 176.

51. Connie Bruck, "A Mogul's Farewell," *New Yorker*, 18 October 1993, pp. 70, 93.

52. "In Search of the Real Bill Gates," *Time,* 13 January 1997, p. 32.

53. Also see John Seabrook, "E-Mail from Bill," *New Yorker,* 11 January 1994.

54. Tom Peters, *Liberation Management,* p. v.

55. "Is He Too Cautious to Save IBM?" *Fortune,* 3 October 1994, p. 78.

56. "IBM Reboots—Bit by Bit," *Business Week,* 17 January 1994, pp. 82–83. For recent profile of Gerstner see "He's Smart, He's Not Nice, He's Saving Big Blue," *Fortune,* 14 April 1997, pp. 68–81.

57. "Apple's Future: Can New CEO Michael Spindler Bring Back the Glory Days?" *Business Week,* 5 July 1993, pp. 22–28.

58. "Changing Guard at Apple: The Board Says 'Enough,'" *New York Times,* 4 February 1996, pp. A 1, 28; "Apple Ousts Spindler as its Chief, Puts National Semi CEO at Helm," *Wall Street Journal,* 2 February 1996, pp. A3–A4; "Apple Says Goodbye to 'The Diesel,'" *Newsweek,* 12 February 1996, p. 44.

59. " The Right Choice for the Job," *New York Times,* 7 September 1995, p. D1. Also see the following articles on shareholder activism: "Shareholders Exercise New Power with Nation's Biggest Companies," *New York Times,* 1 February 1993, p. D1; and "Have Shareholder Activists Lost Their Edge?" *New York Times,* 30 January, 1994, p. F7.

60. "Leashes Get Shorter for Executives," *New York Times,* 18 July 1997, p. D1.

61. "Big Investor Talked, Grace Listened," *New York Times,* 10 April 1995, pp. D1–D2.

62. Ken Auletta, "That's Entertainment," *New Yorker,* 12 February 1996, p. 30.

63. " Dinosaurs?" *Fortune,* 3 May 1993, p. 41.

64. "Burned-Out Bosses," *Fortune,* 25 July 1994, p. 44.

65. "For Whom Bell Tolls," *Newsweek,* 15 January 1996, p. 44.

66. "Economic Scene," *New York Times,* 7 September 1995, p. D2.

67. "Promotion of Women Physicians in Academic Medicine," *Journal of the American Medical Association* 27 (5 April 1995): 1022.

68. "Equal Opportunity Recedes for Most Female Lawyers," *New York Times,* 8 January 1996, p. A9.

69. "Women and Minorities Still Face Glass Ceiling," *New York Times,* 16 March 1995, p. A22.

70. "Some Action, Little Talk," *New York Times,* 20 April 1995, p. D4.

71. "A Piece of the Action," *Newsweek,* 18 December 1995, p. 48.

72. "Defying the Juggernaut," *New York Times,* 10 November 1997, p. D10.

73. "Beating the Risks of Reengineering," *Fortune,* 15 May 1995, pp. 106–108.

74. "Don't Go Away MAD, Just Go Away," *New York Times,* 13 February 1996, p. D1.

75. Joanne B. Ciulla, "Leadership and the Problem of Bogus Empowerment," Ethics and Leadership Papers, Kellogg Leadership Studies Project (unpublished), pp. 43–67.

76. "For Whom Bell Tolls," *Newsweek,* 15 January 1996, p. 45.

77. *Blair House Papers,* National Performance Review, President Bill Clinton, Vice President Al Gore, January 1997.

Chapter 7. Impaired Learning

1. "Americans Foresee Harmony in Capital," *New York Times,* 20 January 1997, p. A1.

2. Ronald Heifetz, *Leadership Without Easy Answers* (Cambridge: Harvard University Press, 1994).

3. Jay Conger, *Learning to Lead.* p. xi.

4. Ibid., p. 188.

5. The information on the Center for Creative Leadership is available from the Center. Further on down the legitimacy ladder is an enterprise like The Covey Leadership Center in Provo, Utah. It employs seven hundred people (up from fifty a decade ago) and sells audiotapes and CD-ROMs, and presents workshops based on the wisdom of Stephen Covey, the author of *The Seven Habits of Highly Effective People.*

6. "Diversity Training: Now More Comprehensive," *New York Times,* 12 November 1995, p. 6 WF. Also see "Making Diversity Pay," *Fortune,* 9 September 1996, pp. 177–80.

7. "Bridging the Leadership Gap in Healthcare," The Healthcare Forum, San Francisco, 1992, p. 6.

8. Ann Howard and Richard Wellins, "High Investment Leadership: Changing Roles for Changing Times," Development Dimensions International and Leadership Research Institute, Tenafly, N.J., 1994.

9. "Managing by Team is Not Always as Easy as it Looks," *New York Times,* 18 July 1993, p. F5.

10. "What Team Leaders Need to Know," *Fortune,* 20 February 1995, p. 94.

11. "Managing in a Wired Company," *Fortune,* 11 July 1994, p. 44.

12. Ibid., p. 56.

13. "Revolutionize Your Company," *Fortune,* 13 December 1993. p. 118.

14. Shearson Lehman, *Branch Manager Training Program Manual 1992,* pp. 7, 8.

15. "How Tomorrow's Best Leaders are Learning their Stuff," *Fortune,* 27 November 1995, pp. 93–94.

16. "Time Out," *Wall Street Journal,* 26 February 1996, p. R5.

17. James Bolt, "Achieving the CEO's Agenda: Education for Executives," *Management Review,* May 1993, p. 44.

18. Kanter et al., *The Challenge of Organizational Change.*

19. Peters, *Liberation Management.*

20. Warren Bennis and Joan Goldsmith, *Learning to Lead: A Workbook on Becoming a Leader* (Reading, Mass.: Addison-Wesley, 1994).

21. Peter Senge et al., *The Fifth Discipline Fieldbook* (New York: Doubleday, 1994).

22. W. Chan Kim and Renee Mauborgne, "Parables of Leadership," *Harvard Business Review* 70 (July–August 1992): 124.

23. Nitin Nohria and James Berkley, "Whatever Happened to the Take Charge Manager?" *Harvard Business Review* 72 (January–February 1994): 130.

24. John Kotter, "Leading Change: Why Transformation Efforts Fail," *Harvard Business Review* 61 (March–April 1995): 61.

25. 12 June 1995, p. 121.

26. *Fad Surfing in the Boardroom: Reclaiming the Courage to Manage in the Age of Instant Answers* (Reading, Mass.: Addison-Wesley, 1995).

27. "Think for Yourself, Boss," *Fortune,* 2 October 1995, p. 162.

28. "Trying to Grasp the Intangible," *Fortune,* 2 October 1995, p. 157.

29. "Don't Be an Ugly American Manager," *Fortune,* 16 October 1995, p. 225.

30. "Wanted: Company Change Agents," *Fortune,* 11 December 1995, p. 197.

31. "The Nine Dilemmas Leaders Face," *Fortune,* 18 March 1996, pp. 112–13.

32. "What Women Can Learn from Machiavelli," *Fortune,* 14 April 1997, p. 163.

33. Brian O'Connell, *People Power: Service, Advocacy, Empowerment* (New York: The Foundation Center, 1994), p. 2.

34. Dennis Young, Robert Hollister, Virginia Hodgkinson, eds., *Governing, Leading, and Managing Nonprofit Organizations* (San Francisco: Jossey-Bass, 1993), p. xvi.

35. Cynthia McCauley and Martha Hughes, "Leadership in Human Services: Key Challenges and Competencies," in *Governing, Leading, and Managing Nonprofit Organizations,* Young, Hollister, and Hodgkinson, eds., pp. 158–60.

36. Thomas Jeavons, "The Role of Values: Management in Religous Organizations," in in *Governing, Leading, and Managing Nonprofit Organizations,* Young, Hollister, and Hodgkinson, eds., p. 56.

37. E. Gil Clary and Mark Snyder, "Persuasive Communications Strategies for Recruiting Volunteers," in in *Governing, Leading, and Managing Nonprofit Organizations,* Young, Hollister, and Hodgkinson, eds., p. 125.

38. "How to Succeeed in Non-profits By Really Trying," *New York Times,* 1 October 1995, p. F8.

39. "Military Leadership," Field Manual No. 22-100, Headquarters, Department of the Army, Washington D.C., July 1990, pp. 1, 2, 30, 38.

40. "New Ideas from the Army (Really)," *Fortune,* 19 September 1994, p. 204.

41. Alan Webber, "Surviving in the New Economy," *Harvard Business Review* 72 (September–October 1994): 82.

42. William Pagonis, "The Work of the Leader," *Harvard Business Review* 70 (November–December 1992): 118.

43. H. Norman Schwartzkopf, *The Autobiography: It Doesn't Take a Hero* (New York: Bantam, 1992), p. 67.

44. Ibid., p. 237.

45. Colin Powell, *My American Journey* (New York: Random House, 1995), p. 613.

46. "What West Point Doesn't Teach," *Washington Post National Weekly Edition,* 22–28 April 1996, p. 12.

47. "Americans Foresee Harmony in Capital," *New York Times,* 20 January 1997, p. l.

48. "Americans Losing Trust in Each Other and Institutions," *Washington Post,* 28 January 1996, p. A1.

49. James O'Toole, *Leading Change: Overcoming the Ideology of Conflict and the Tyranny of Custom* (San Francisco: Jossey-Bass, 1995), p. xiv.

50. James Bolt, "Developing Three Dimensional Leaders," in *The Leader of the Future,* ed. Frances Hesselbein et al. (San Francisco: Jossey-Bass, 1996), p. 163.

51. "Getting What They Deserve?" *New York Times,* 22 February 1996, p. D1.

52. "Economic Scene," *New York Times,* 28 March 1996, p. D2.

53. David Remnick, "Dr. Wilson's Neighborhood," *New Yorker,* 29 April and 6 May 1996, p. 106.

54. Ibid., p. 107.

Chapter 8. Fault Lines

1. "Stirring It Up at Campbell," *Fortune,* 13 May 1996, p. 80.

2. James Q. Wilson, "Reinventing Public Administration," *PS: Political Science and Politics* 27 (December 1994): 670.

3. David Osborne and Ted Gaebler, *Reinventing Government: How the Entrepreneurial Spirit is Transforming the Public Sector* (Reading, Mass.: Addison Wesley, 1992).

4. Charles Handy, "The New Language of Organizing and Its Implications for Individuals," in *The Leader of the Future,* ed. Hesselbein et al., p. 4.

5. Sally Helgeson, "Leading from the Grass Roots," in *The Leader of the Future,* ed. Hesselbein et. al., p. 22.

6. Rosabeth Moss Kanter, "World-Class Leaders: The Power of Partnering," in *The Leader of the Future,* ed. Hesselbein et. al., pp. 90, 97.

7. For discussion of this subject, and reviews of recent books that relate, see George M. Fredrickson, "America's Caste System: Will It Change?" *New York Review of Books,* 23 October 1997, pp. 68–75.

8. Jennifer Hochschild, *Land of Opportunity* (Princeton: Princeton University Press, 1995). Also see Tamar Jacoby, *Someone Else's House: America's Unfinished Struggle for Integration* (New York: Free Press, 1998).

9. Henry Louis Gates Jr., "The Charmer," *New Yorker,* 29 April and 6 May 1996, p. 128.

10. Juan Williams, "For Powell, It's Now or Never," *Washington Post National Weekly Edition,* 11–17 April 1996, p. 23.

11. Both Cleaver and Gates are in Gates, "The Charmer," p. 128.

12. George Fredrickson, "Far from the Promised Land," *New York Review of Books,* 18 April 1996, p. 16.

13. "Gaps and Barriers, Women and Careers," *New York Times,* 28 February 1996, p. D2.

14. Robert Samuelson, "Fashionable Statement," *Washington Post National Weekly Edition,* 18–24 March 1996, p. 5. Also see H. Erich Heinemann, "The Downsizing Myth," *New York Times,* 25 March 1996, p. A15.

15. *New York Times,* 3 March 1996, p. A1.

16. Simon Head, "The New Ruthless Economy," *New York Review of Books,* 29 February 1996, pp. 47–52.

17. John Cassidy, "Who Killed the Middle Class," *New Yorker,* 16 October 1995, pp. 113.

18. Lester Thurow, "Why Their World Might Crumble," *New York Times,* 19 November 1995, pp. 78–79.

19. Quoted in Bob Herbert, "Why Does America's Brilliant Run Seem Over?" *International Herald Tribune,* 28 January 1997, p. 8.

20. Bill Bradley, *Time Present, Time Past: A Memoir* (New York: Knopf, 1996), p. 374.

21. "Leaving the Suburbs for Rural Areas," *New York Times,* 19 October 1997, p. A34.

22. Joel Kotkin, "Beyond White Flight," *Washington Post National Weeekly Edition,* 18–24 March 1996, p. 26.

23. The phrase is Benjamin Barber's. See *Jihad v. McWorld* (New York: Times, 1995).

24. Louis Begley, "Time is Everything," *New Yorker,* 16 October, 1995, p. 158.

25. "The Great Unplugged Masses Confront the Future," *New York Times,* 21 April 1996, p. E6.

26. For Gates's version of what the future holds, see Bill Gates, *The Road Ahead* (New York: Viking, 1996).

27. Clifford Stoll, "The Internet? Bah!" *Newsweek,* 27 February 1995. Also see his book *Silicon Snake Oil: Second Thoughts on the Information Superhighway* (New York: Doubleday, 1995).

28. Kirkpatrick Sale, *Rebels Against the Future: Lessons for the Computer Age* (Reading, Mass.: Addison-Wesley, 1995).

29. Gregorian wrote in the *Bulletin of the American Academy of Arts and Sciences.* He is quoted in ibid., p. 18.

30. Joseph Nye Jr. and William Owen, "America's Information Edge," *Foreign Affairs* 75 (March/April 1996): 20.

31. Bradley, *Time Present,* pp. 4, 5.

32. Ibid., p. xiii.

33. See, for example, Robert Putnam, "The Strange Disappearance of Civic America," *The American Prospect,* no. 24 (Winter, 1996).

34. Michael Sandel, *Democracy's Discontent: America In Search of a Public Philosophy* (Cambridge: Harvard University Press, 1996). The quotes are from Sandel, "America's Search for a Public Philosophy," *Atlantic Monthly,* March 1996, pp. 57–59.

35. Mark Gerzon, *A House Divided: Six Belief Systems Struggling for America's Soul* (New York: Putnam, 1996).

36. "For the Record," *Washington Post,* 4 December 1996, p. A24.

37. Robert Michels, *Political Parties* (New York: Free Press, 1962), p. 15.

38. "For the Record," *Washington Post,* 4 December 1996, p. A24.

Chapter 9. Ties that Bind

1. Peter Drucker, *The Age of Discontinuity: Guidelines to our Changing Society* (New York: Harper & Row, 1969).

2. Henry Mintzberg, "Managing Government: Governing Management," *Harvard Business Review,* May–June 1996, p. 77.

3. Light, *Thickening Government,* p. 1.

4. Ibid., p. 61.

5. Neal Peirce, "Britain and New Zealand Are Showing the Way," *International Herald Tribune,* 19 February 1997, p. 8

6. Peter Passell, "Economic Scene," *New York Times,* 14 December 1995, p. D2.

7. "Ambitious Update of American Navigation Becomes a Fiasco," *New York Times,* 29 January 1996, p. 1.

8. "IRS Admits Lag in Modernization," *New York Times,* 31 January 1997, p. 1.

9. James O'Toole, *Leading Change: Overcoming the Ideology of Comfort and the Tyranny of Custom* (San Francisco: Jossey-Bass, 1995), p. xiii.

10. Gifford Pinchot, "Creating Organizations with Many Leaders," in *The Leader of the Future,* ed. Hesselbein et al., p. 38.

11. Peter Senge, "Leading Learning Organizations: The Bold, the Powerful, and the Invisible," in *The Leader of the Future,* ed. Hesselbein et al., p. 42.

12. Mark Warren, "Deliberative Democracy and Authority," *American Political Science Review* 90 (March 1996): 58.

13. See Walter Ulmer Jr., "Leadership Learnings and Relearnings," Kellogg Leadership Studies Project, unpublished paper, 1996, p. 10.

14. Gary Wills, "The Real Scandal," *New York Review of Books,* 20 February 1997, p. 4.

15. Fred Wertheimer, "The Dirtiest Campaign Ever," *Washington Post National Weekly Edition,* 11–17 November 1996.

16. Henry Mintzberg, "Musings on Management," *Harvard Business Review* 74, (July–August 1996): 62.

17. Thomas Teal, "The Human Side of Management," *Harvard Business Review* 74, (November–December 1996): 37.

18. Bruce Posner and Lawrence Rothstein, "Reinventing the Business of Government: An Interview with Change Catalyst David Osborne," *Harvard Business Review* 72, (May–June 1994): 137.

19. Ibid., p. 135.

20. Mark Schneider and Paul Teske with Michael Mintrom, *Public Entrepreneurs: Agents for Change in American Government* (Princeton: Princeton University Press, 1995), p. 1.

21. Harlan Cleveland, *The Knowledge Executive: Leadership in an Information Society* (New York: Dutton, 1985), p. 88.

22. State of the Union Speech delivered 4 February 1997.

23. Daniel Yergin and Joseph Stanislau, *The Commanding Heights: The Battle between Government and the Marketplace that is Remaking the Modern World* (New York: Simon and Schuster, 1998), pp. 369–91.

24. Harlan Cleveland, *Leadership and the Information Society* (Minneapolis: World Academy of Art and Science, 1997), p. 8.

25. "Cyberpower," *Forbes,* 2 December 1996, p. 146.

26. Cleveland, *Leadership*, p. 21.

27. "Wired World," *Time,* 3 February 1997, p. 37.

28. Cleveland, *Leadership,* pp. 44, 45.

29. Jeffrey Garten, "Business and Foreign Policy," *Foreign Affairs,* May/June 1997, p. 67.

30. Ibid., p. 68.

31. "In Manila, Asians Pore Over Washington's Inner Truths," *New York Times,* 24 November 1996, p. A1

32. Thomas Friedman, "Fed Up," *New York Times,* 4 December 1996 p. A21.

33. Jessica Mathews, "Tricky Talks," *Washington Post,* 27 January 1997, p. A19.

34. Robert Lighthizer, "What did Asian Donors Want?" *New York Times,* 25 February 1997, p. A27.

35. Ethan Kapstein, "The Welfare State? An Economic Cornerstone, Not a Luxury," *International Herald Tribune,* 30 January 1997, p. 8.

36. Peter Drucker, "The Global Economy and the Nation-State," *Foreign Affairs,* September/October 1997, p. 160.

37. Haynes Johnson and David Broder, *The System: The American Way of Politics at the Breaking Point* (Boston: Little, Brown, 1996), passim.

38. State of the Union speech delivered February 4, 1997.

39. David Chrislip, "Transforming Politics," unpublished paper, 1995, p. 21.

40 "From Harlem's Worst to City's Star," *New York Times,* 3 August 1997, p. B29.

41. Chrislip, "Transforming Politics," p. 22.

42. Chrislip and Larson, *Collaborative Leadership*, p. 120.

43. David Chrislip, "New Directions: The Challenge of Growth in the West," unpublished paper.

44. Mark Gerzon, *A House Divided: Six Belief Systems Struggling for America's Soul* (New York: Putnam, 1996), p. 265.

45. Unpublished memo received from Bruce Adams, dated 4 February 1997.

46. John W. Gardner quoted in Neal Peirce and Curtis Johnson, *Boundary Crossers: Community Leadership for a Global Age* (College Park, Md.: Academy of Leadership, 1997), p. 1.

47. Ibid., p. 12.

48. Ibid., p. 32.

49. *Life in the City,* Report by the Urban Neighborhoods Task Force, Center for National Policy, Washington, D.C., 1996.

50. Unless otherwise noted, all the quotes in this section are from World Economic Forum documents.

51. "At Davos, Networking for the World's Most Powerful," *International Herald Tribune,* 30 January 1997, p. 2.

52. "One of the Greatest Shows on Earth," *Forbes,* 2 December 1996, p. 72.

53. Hedrick Smith, *Rethinking America: A New Game Plan from the American Innovator: Schools, Business, People, Work* (New York: Random House, 1995), pp. xx, xxii.

INDEX

DATE DUE

~~JAN 0 6 2000~~			
~~MAY 0 1 2000~~			
~~SEP 1 8 2000~~			
~~NOV 0 3 2001~~			
			Printed In USA

HIGHSMITH #45230